BASIC
MACRO-
ECONOMICS

L.J. Fourie · F. van den Bogaerde

Department of Economics, University of South Africa

J.L. VAN SCHAIK

Published by J.L. van Schaik (Pty) Ltd,
1064 Arcadia Street, Hatfield, Pretoria

First edition 1982
Second impression 1983
Third impression 1985
Second edition 1986
Second impression 1987
Third impression 1988
Third edition (in soft cover) 1989
Second impression 1990
Third impression 1991
Fourth edition 1992
Fourth edition, second impression 1993

ISBN 0 627 01829 7

Typeset in $^{10}/_{12}$ pt Palatino by ORBiT CC, Pretoria
Printed and bound by National Book Printers, Goodwood, Cape

Hierdie boek is ook in Afrikaans beskikbaar as *Basiese Makro-ekonomie*

PREFACE

More than ten years have elapsed since the publication of the first edition of this book. Most of the economic problems that faced South Africa at the beginning of the decade are still not resolved today. Unemployment has probably retained its position as our major economic problem, while we have not moved any closer to a solution to the problems of inflation, the balance of payments constraint or the lack of economic growth. In spite of dramatic political developments, uncertainty regarding the future still dominates the economic climate, with little hope of a solution to the above-mentioned problems.

The aim of the book has therefore remained the same, namely to explain the above topics and problems in the most simple and understandable way possible. In the first place the book is written for students following a beginner's course in Economics and secondly for the casual observer who wishes to gain a better understanding of economic concepts as they are discussed daily in newspapers and on television.

From the title it is clear that the book deals with **basic** concepts of **macro**-economics. As will be explained more fully in chapter one, macro-economics is concerned with economic aggregates, that is to say with totals, applying to the economy as a whole. The study of these aggregates is called macro-economics to distinguish it from **micro**-economics which concentrates on prices in separate markets. The development of macro-economics as a subject took place during the nineteen forties and originally was only offered in advanced courses of Economics. Today the subject of macro-economics has trickled down to the elementary levels of economic teaching. Whereas macro-economics was seldom taught at first year level a decade or two ago, this is no longer the case. All well-known introductory textbooks today are divided between micro- and macro-economics. Many lecturers even prefer to introduce their students to economics by way of macro- rather than the more traditional micro-economics.

This text fits into the framework whereby economic theory is divided between micro- and macro-economics in order to offer both at an elementary level. Such a text – especially if it also addresses a wider public – must always be clear and intelligible. Although we attempt to maintain strict economic logic and rigorous argument, we prefer clarity of exposition to the completeness of the subject matter. No apology is therefore made for omitting some well-known subjects in macro-economics, especially if they are so subtle that they contribute little or hardly at all to the understanding of practical or contemporary economic problems.

Various reasons necessitated an update of the book during the last number of years. The **second edition** (1986), was mainly concerned with a revision of outdated statistical data which appeared in most of the chapters of the first edition. The rapid changes with regard to national accounting magnitudes, exchange rates, interest rates and other economic data compelled such a revision. In addition to this, innovations in the field of monetary policy also required revision of certain sections of chapter 7. Despite these revisions the basic structure of the individual chapters remained intact.

The **third edition** entailed a more drastic revision. Over and above the normal updating of statistical data many of the chapters were totally reconstructed with new sections being added or existing sections being omitted. These changes were mainly the result of teaching experience gained from the course at Unisa's Department of Economics during the last number of years. In this regard a significant contribution was made by Professor Philip Mohr and the first year team under the guidance of Professor Cilliers Swart.

The need to update obsolete statistical data in practically every chapter and to rectify certain omissions and errors in the previous edition necessitated this **fourth edition**. In this regard we wish to thank Elna Krause of the Department of Economics at Unisa who revised the statistical data for the entire book. Throughout the period of revision she was also involved in proof-reading. She was ably assisted by Carel Grové, Liza Niedermeier and Geoff Parr. It is with gratitude that we acknowledge the contribution made by these colleagues of the Department of Economics. We also wish to express our gratitude to Elna van Rensburg who undertook the task of wordprocessing under a great deal of pressure. Her efficiency and perception certainly made our task so much easier.

Lastly we wish to express the hope that this book will contribute not only to a better understanding of basic economic problems, but also to an increase in interest and a wish on the part of readers to pursue their studies in Economics.

Louis Fourie
Frans van den Bogaerde

Pretoria 1992

CONTENTS

1 Introduction

1.1 Micro as against macro-economics

The field of Economics is not entirely new to us. In our daily lives we continuously deal with the problems studied in Economics. To spend money, look for work, have a job, pay taxes, etc. are only a few of the everyday actions which form a part of the problems studied in Economics. Traditionally, the subject is subdivided into two main fields of study, viz. micro-economics and macro-economics.

> In **micro-economics** the prices and quantities of specific goods and services are studied on individual markets and an attempt is made to explain the changes on these markets.

The study of micro-economics is therefore aimed at explaining, *inter alia*, why the prices of certain products are at a certain level, why so many people are active in a particular industry, why the production of certain commodities is localized in a specific area and how changes in the price of one product (for example coffee) will affect the price of another product (for example tea or sugar). Because the emphasis in micro-economics is mainly on the **prices** of goods and services, it is frequently also referred to as **price theory**.

A part of this chapter is devoted to the basic principles involved in micro-economics, while the rest of the chapter and the other chapters in the book deal exclusively with the other aspect of economics, viz. macro-economics.

> In **macro-economics** we look at the economy as a whole. The causes and effects of the determination of aggregate or global economic quantities such as gross domestic product, total employment, the general level of prices in the country, etc. are analysed.

In micro-economics it would therefore be possible to look at events on a

1

specific market in isolation, without taking into account the possible effect thereof on the rest of the economy. For example, the effect of a sudden decline in the supply of xyz's on the price of xyz's could be analysed without considering its influence on total employment in the economy or the production of the xyz industry. In macro-economics, where by definition we look at the economy as a whole, such an individual (or partial) analysis cannot be undertaken.

Although micro and macro-economics are regarded as two almost completely separate branches of the economy, it is undeniable that one should at least know something about micro-economics and its **basic instruments of analysis** before macro-economics can be properly understood. The following two sections are intended to give a brief review of those concepts in price theory that are indispensable to macro-economics. If you are already familiar with the basics of supply and demand analysis and price formation, you can ignore these sections.

1.2   Micro-economics: supply and demand curves

The average person's first introduction to economics is normally related to prices and the reasons behind them. Everyone is concerned with prices; not only the price you have to pay for the goods and services needed to satisfy your daily requirements, but also because income is the product of the price of the services rendered, whether by teachers, mechanics or opera singers.

Are prices determined by the government?

So the next question is, how do prices come into existence? The answer of the uninitiated would perhaps be something along the lines of "someone, most probably the government, sets the price". There is no lack of examples where this idea would be quite correct. There are goods such as mineral water, cement, coal, dairy products and other foodstuffs (via agricultural control boards) where the prices are controlled directly by the government; there are also prices and tariffs set and administered by the government itself. The general public is frequently convinced that the government is involved in the process of price formation to the extent that many are surprised when they find that the government can often do little about prices, nor has any desire to.

The question is then, of course, how do prices come about if they are not in some way controlled and administered by a central authority? This is precisely what price theory is about, i.e. the determination of prices, without any deliberate intervention on the part of the government, through the working of the supply and demand mechanism.

The supply curve

The first important instrument we have to understand in an explanation of prices, is called the **supply curve**.

> The **supply curve** shows in diagrammatic form the quantities of a particular commodity that will be offered for sale at various prices.

An example of a supply curve is given in figure 1.1. In this diagram quantities are measured along the horizontal axis and prices are measured vertically. The supply curve shows that a greater quantity, such as Q_2, compared with Q_1, will generally be offered for sale at a higher price of P_2 in comparison with P_1.

In other words:

> The supply curve is generally taken to run **upwards from left to right**, showing greater quantities being offered for sale at higher prices.

The reason for the supply curve running upwards from left to right can in the first place be found in the **profit motive**. The higher the price offered for a product, the more profitable it will be to produce and sell more of it. Apart from this natural tendency to wish to sell more at a rising price, another explanation for the upward slope of the supply curve is to be found in the **law of returns**, also called the **law of diminishing returns**. This "law" is based on the observation that at some stage it becomes progressively more difficult for a firm to increase the amount it produces. In terms of costs, this means that additional output can only be produced at a higher cost. In other words, for a greater quantity, the price to be paid becomes higher, hence the upward slope of the supply curve.

Looking at an industry as a whole this tendency is reinforced by the fact that raw materials of the right type, suitable labour and other services become more difficult to obtain; they therefore become more costly, so that the cost at higher levels of production will also be higher.

How supply can change

Fundamentally the supply curve – and this applies equally to the total supply curve that we are going to discuss in chapter 4 – is a (collective) cost curve and it is this tendency for products to cost more when more is

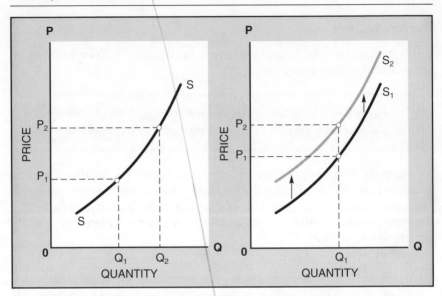

Fig. 1.1 Example of a supply curve

The supply curve normally runs upward from left to right. This means that at higher prices more is offered for sale.

Fig. 1.2 The effect of an increase in cost on supply

An increase in costs (of raw materials, labour, etc.) causes an upward shift in the supply curve. This means that each quantity is only supplied at a higher price.

produced that determines the shape of the curve. At the same time this means that when an across-the-board increase occurs in the prices of raw materials, labour and other production factors, there will be an upward shift in the supply curve as indicated in figure 1.2.

Figure 1.3 shows in greater detail what the effect could be. According to S_1 the quantity Q_1 would be offered for sale at a price of P_1. After the increase in cost this same quantity would be offered for sale at the higher price of P_2. Alternatively, the quantity offered at the original price of P_1 would be much smaller, viz Q_2. For this reason an upward shift in the supply curve can also be regarded as a **decrease in supply**.

A last important point to be made in regard to the supply curve is illustrated in figure 1.4. An industry can grow in two ways. The firms in the industry may grow in size; and it can also happen that the number of firms in the industry increases. In such a case the supply curve will move to the right as from S_1 to S_2, which means that at the same price, e.g. P_1, the amount Q_2 will now be produced, rather than Q_1. Alternatively Q_1 could now be supplied at the considerably lower price P_2 and, as we shall see later, this can lead to a drop in price. But, before we can explain that, we need to have a look at demand.

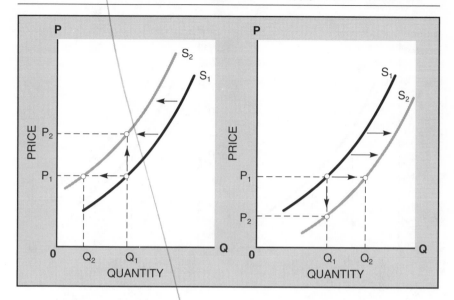

Fig. 1.3 A decrease in supply

The upward shift in the supply curve caused by the increase in cost is the equivalent of a decrease in supply (a shift to the left). This is because at each price less will be offered for sale.

Fig. 1.4 An increase in supply

Supply increases when the supply curve moves to the right or downward, so that more is offered at each price. This may be caused inter alia by an increase in the number of firms, an increase in their size or a decrease in costs.

The demand curve

The demand curve is the counterpart of the supply curve.

> The **demand curve** shows in diagrammatic form the quantities of a particular commodity that will be bought at different prices for this particular commodity.

An example of the demand curve is given in figure 1.5, which is a diagram with the same P and Q axes we have been using for the supply curve. As shown in figure 1.5:

> The demand curve is generally taken to run **downwards from left to right** showing that more will only be purchased at a lower price.

Own experience is probably all that is needed to understand that figure 1.5

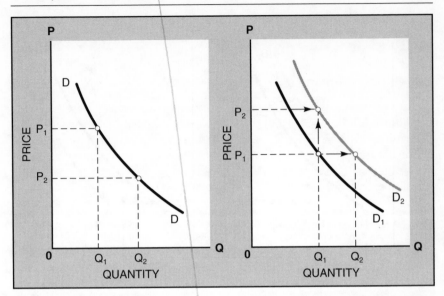

Fig 1.5. Example of a demand curve

The demand curve normally runs downward from left to right. This is basically because the buyer can only be persuaded to buy more at a lower price.

Fig. 1.6 An increase in demand

This is represented by a shift to the right of the demand curve. It may be caused by an increase in the number of buyers or an increase in their income; at similar prices more will now be bought.

does in fact show the general shape and nature of the demand curve. One point is especially important: the lower the price of a commodity, the more of it can be **afforded**. Of course, this also means that the more one earns, the more one will probably buy at a given price.

A change in demand

Just as in the case of supply, there is a possibility of an increase in demand, which in figure 1.6 is illustrated as a shift to the right of the demand curve.

In the present context there are two causes for a shift in demand which we wish to single out for special mention (there are other causes which do not concern us now). The first is the same as that mentioned in the case of supply: the increase in the number of consumers. At each price, quite obviously, more will now be bought, because there are more people to buy the product.

The second cause we have alluded to already: a general increase in income means that consumers in general can afford to buy more consumer goods or, alternatively, can pay more for these goods than before. As in figure 1.6, at P_1 the greater quantity Q_2 would be bought *or* (if no more than Q_1 were available), consumers would be willing to pay P_2 for this quantity.

1.3 Supply, demand and price

We are now in a position to understand what it means when it is said, sometimes a little glibly, that it is the forces of supply and demand that determine price. In figure 1.7 supply and demand curves are represented in one diagram. These two curves intersect at M and this point of intersection indicates that at price P_0 the quantities supplied and demanded are equal to each other.

f 1.7.

Market forces and equilibrium

Market forces will generally move the system towards the equilibrium as indicated by M; for instance, if price is at P_1 as in figure 1.8 the amount supplied would be Q_2 and the amount demanded would be Q_1. AB therefore represents a quantity of goods that has been or is being produced, but not bought. This is called **excess supply** and one can suppose that competition between sellers will point price in the direction of P_0 because the price is too high. In much the same way the price P_1 in figure 1.9 would lead to an **excess demand** of EF, and by way of competition between buyers, price will tend to be forced *up* to P_0.

f 1.8.

It is justified to say that these market forces exist and that there will be such tendencies towards the equilibrium price. However, it cannot be said

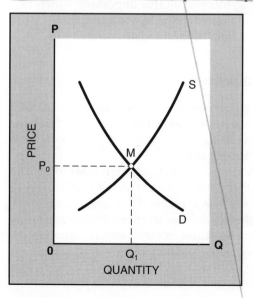

Fig. 1.7 The supply and demand system

Price is determined at the intersection of the supply and demand curves because at that point price is such that the quantity for sale equals the quantity demanded.

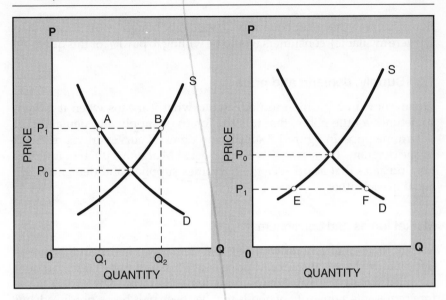

Fig. 1.8 The case of excess supply

If the price is higher than the equilibrium price, excess supply AB will tend to drive the prices down to P_0.

Fig. 1.9 The case of excess demand

At a price P_1 there will be excess demand of EF; this will tend to force the price up to P_0.

that in practice an equilibrium position will be reached quickly or easily. In reality conditions may change significantly and rapidly, so that a move towards a quite different price may follow. Another important point is that all of this may happen without any intervention by the authorities.

Two important questions arise from the above discussion:

Changed conditions change the solution

The **first** question is, what will happen when the producers of a particular commodity experience an increase in the cost of their raw materials? The answer is found in figure 1.10. As explained (cf. fig. 1.2), a rise in costs leads to an upward movement in the supply curve.

The point of intersection between S and D changes from M_1 to M_2 and price will therefore show a tendency towards P_2, which is higher than P_1 **but not by the full amount of the cost increase**. Of course, this is small comfort to the consumer, who achieves this less-than-full-cost increase only by buying less (cf. Q_2 with Q_1 in fig. 1.10). In other words, although the consumer pays more than before, he gets less in exchange. (If consumers still wished to buy the quantity Q_1, then the full cost increase would be for their account.) This, incidentally, is one possible reason for the phenome-

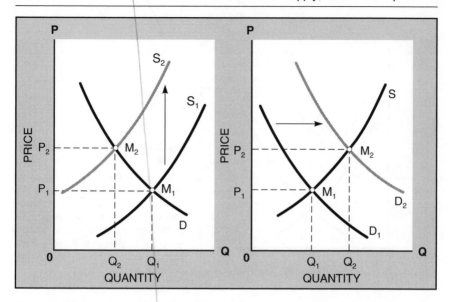

Fig. 1.10 Result of a decrease in supply

The effect of an increase in costs is an upward move in supply from S_1 to S_2 this causes a rise in price which is smaller than the increase in costs.

Fig. 1.11 Result of an increase in demand

An increase in demand from D_1 to D_2 causes a rise in price from P_1 to P_2; the quantity bought is also increased.

non that a general sales tax or an excise duty does not necessarily raise price by the full amount of the tax.

The **second** question we wish to answer is, what would happen when an increase in demand occurs, especially as a result of an increase in incomes. The answer is provided in figure 1.11, which shows that the point of intersection of supply and demand moves from M_1 to M_2. This raises price as well as the quantity produced and purchased.

An example of an inflationary spiral

We are now in a position to determine what would happen when a shift in supply (as in fig. 1.10) occurs simultaneously with a shift in demand (as in fig. 1.11). This leads to the explanation of an important phenomenon, known as the **inflationary spiral** (or the **wage-price spiral**). Such a situation is depicted in figure 1.12.

The question actually is, what would happen if the majority of residents in a country experience an increase in income? Such a rise in income will on most markets cause an increase in demand. In figure 1.12 this is repre-

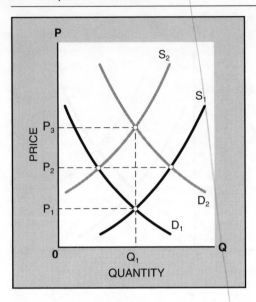

Fig. 1.12 Example of a wage-price spiral

A general rise in income can cause demand on different markets to rise from D_1 to D_2. Such a rise in income may be caused by a rise in wages, i.e. costs, thus causing supply to fall from S_1 to S_2. This leads to a rise in price, raising income more and thus raising prices again.

sented by the shift in the demand curve from D_1 to D_2. By itself this would raise price to P_2.

However, if a majority of citizens experience an increase in income as a result of an increase in salaries (and if there is no simultaneous and significant increase in productivity) then an increase in **cost** is also likely to occur (as a result of the higher salaries and wages paid), as indicated in figure 1.12 by the upward shift in the supply curve from S_1 to S_2. Thus it can be seen that, were an **increase** in demand and a **decrease** in supply to occur at the same time, the rise in prices would be more pronounced (cf. P_3) but the level of output would remain virtually the same. This is an example of a wage-price spiral. It is also an example of the way in which **inflation** can come about. That is to say, how the general level of prices may rise, as has happened since the beginning of the seventies.

The role of relative prices

The different prices which come into being on these markets play an extremely important part in the smooth functioning of the production system. For example, an urgent need for additional resources is indicated by a rise in a specific price. The price system therefore determines how productive resources are chanelled to the most effective use. From this vantage point, micro-economics is therefore also concerned with relative prices, that is, how much one commodity is worth in terms of another commodity. As the economy changes and develops, all these prices may also change and develop, which means that certain commodities may disappear while others appear on the market.

1.4 The basic methods of macro-economics

Aggregation

Now that we have some idea of how prices come into being on individual markets, we can return to the subject of this book, which is macro-economics. As you will realise, it can become extremely difficult to trace in detail the influence of events on one single market as it affects the rest of the economy. To trace the diverse influences on prices and quantities of all the various goods and services is virtually impossible. The only solution, and this is the solution espoused by macro-economics, is to simplify the economic system by means of **aggregation**. Aggregation, which means "to combine", enables us to combine separate markets and then to deal with the whole as a single market or system. In this way various facets of the economy can more easily be identified. The extent of the aggregation will normally depend upon the specific macro-economic problem we want to investigate. It has for example become customary to subdivide the total production of the country into the contributions made by certain sectors such as agriculture, mining and the manufacturing industry, to name only a few of the more important constituents. In the same way, it is important to group the market participants according to their activities in the macro-economic process, e.g. households or consumers, businesses, government institutions, etc. so that each group's actions or behaviour can be observed separately. By making use of compound markets such as the market for consumer goods, the market for factors of production (e.g. the labour market or the market for capital goods) and the financial market, the number of markets and their interdependencies which the macro-economist has to bear in mind, is restricted to a manageable size.

The circular flow diagram

In a market-orientated economy, as in South Africa, goods and services will only be produced if there is a sufficient demand or market for them. If business ventures produce more than the demand requires, stocks will begin to accumulate, prices will fall, production will be curtailed and labourers will be dismissed. Such a condition may be described as one of excess supply. In a similar way, a condition of excess demand may be created if customers want to purchase more products than have been produced. Stocks will begin to fall, prices will rise, production will be expanded and employment will increase.

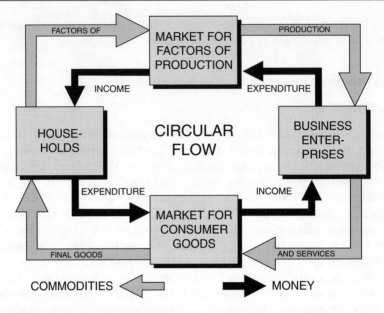

Fig 1.13 A simple circular flow diagram

Only two market participants (households and businesses) are distinguished. These market participants meet each other on the market for factors of production and the market for consumer goods. In the diagram there are also two flows (the commodities flow and the money flow), moving in opposite directions.

In micro-economics, where we are looking at a single business, it is fairly easy to determine whether a balance exists between the money flowing to the business to purchase goods and services, and the money flowing out to pay for the cost of production. In other words, to determine whether the business can be run profitably. In macro-economics it is far more difficult to establish whether the total flow of money is sufficient to ensure adequate employment and production in the economy as a whole. The best way to visualize the problem is by means of a simple macro-economic circular flow diagram. In figure 1.13 we see a graphic representation of such a macro-economic flow diagram. The extent of aggregation (and hence of simplification) underlying the flow diagram can be seen from the fact that only two types of **markets** and two types of **market participants** have been distinguished. We saw above that in fact a much larger number of entities exist. They are ignored in this flow diagram.

In the circular flow diagram we only distinguish between **business enterprises** (the manufacturers of goods and services) and **households** (the consumers of goods and services). These two groups of market participants meet each other on two markets, viz **the market for consumer goods** and the **market for factors of production**.

Business enterprises, which act as entrepreneurs, make use of natural resources, labour and capital which they buy on the market for factors of production in order to produce final goods and services. The final products are then offered on the market for consumer goods.

Households, as the owners of factors of production, offer their labour, resources and capital on the market for factors of production. With the income derived in this way, householders can then make purchases on the market for consumer goods to satisfy their own requirements.

In the diagram we therefore find a money flow (in the inner circle running anti-clockwise) and a commodity flow (in the outer circle running clockwise) moving through the economy. Note that the expenditure (or costs) of one market participant simultaneously represents the income of the other market participants. The analysis of these flows and how they affect total production, employment and the general level of prices, are the subjects of the rest of this book. In the next chapter, for example, we shall concentrate on the **measurement** of the magnitude of these flows. By means of the circular flow we have been able to give more meaningful content to the tentative definition of macro-economics formulated at the beginning of this chapter.

The macro-economic model

The size or value of the flows in the diagram in themselves throw little light on the questions that really interest the macro-economist. The circular flow presentation is simply a way in which the main variables in the economy can be arranged. The scope of total production which can be measured, *inter alia*, on the market for consumer goods, merely serves as an indication of what has happened over a certain period of time (for example the previous year). This does not tell us **why** production was at a certain level during that year or **why** it has changed at a certain rate relative to a previous period. If the total expenditure on the market for factors of production has not resulted in full employment of the labour force available in the economy (in other words has given rise to unemployment) the macro-economist wants to know **why** it was inadequate. What can be done to change expenditure in such a way that full employment can be attained?

To obtain answers to this kind of question it is necessary to employ a macro-economic theory which regards the functioning of the economy in a specific light. Such a theory is normally expressed in the form of a macro-economic model. The model prescribes certain relations between economic variables which enable us to analyse the economy as a whole in

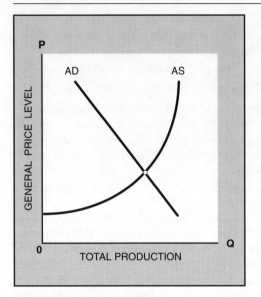

Fig 1.14 Aggregate demand and supply

The aggregate demand and supply curves constitute the basic model used by us in this book to analyse the macro-economy. In chapter 4 this model will be discussed in greater detail.

a systematic manner. Although there are various views on the functioning of the economy, a single general macro-economic model can normally be used to illustrate the various approaches. Often two approaches differ only as regards the emphasis placed on certain variables without actually questioning the way in which the economy functions. The basic model used in this book to answer questions on macro-economics is, in graphic terms, very similar to the basic demand and supply mechanism used in micro-economics. However, as we shall see in the rest of the book, there is a world of difference between the underlying factors determining the aggregate demand and supply of the economy as a whole, and those applicable in micro-economics. In figure 1.14, which gives an example of such an aggregate demand and supply system, the major differences can be seen at a glance. On the P axis the **general level of prices** in the economy is measured, while the Q axis indicates the **total output** or gross domestic product. Furthermore, the shape of the aggregate supply curve is different from the way in which it is normally represented in micro-economics. In later chapters the derivation of these aggregate demand and supply curves will be dealt with in greater detail.

1.5 The main macro-economic theories

The classical model

If one considers that macro-economics, in contrast to micro-economics, only became an issue after the Great Depression of the thirties, the past 50 years may be seen as a period of rapid change. Before the depression economists' view of the economy was based on the **classical model**, which accepts the infallibility of the market mechanism. According to this point of view, the economy would always tend towards a condition of full employment. Any deviation from this optimal condition would merely be of a temporary nature. If the market was left to operate freely and without interference all goods produced would be sold, since the price mechanism would ensure that no excess demand or supply was created. The origin of this school of thought can be traced to Adam Smith, who wrote during the eighteenth century and influenced such subsequent writers as David Ricardo, J.S. Mill, Alfred Marshall and A.C. Pigou. The essence of the classical model is probably best summarised in the words of J.B. Say when he formulated his famous law as follows: "Supply creates its own demand".

The Keynesian model

The reality of the Depression and the fact that no natural tendency back to full employment was forthcoming, forced economists to question the validity of the classical model afresh. In his famous book *The General Theory of Employment, Interest and Money* John Maynard Keynes, a British economist, showed that one couldn't depend solely on market forces to carry the economy back to full employment. According to him, active steps by the government were necessary to bring total **expenditure** (which he identified as the crux of the problem) to more adequate levels. The precepts deriving from the Keynesian model for the first time focussed the attention on the government's budget. Fiscal policy, which is concerned with the scope and interrelationship of the government's expenditure programme and the taxes levied, had now become an integral part of economic policy and had to be employed to cancel out any unfavourable deviations in the level of private expenditure.

At the same time the Depression placed a serious question mark over the usefulness of monetary policy (i.e. action by a central bank to influence interest rates, the money supply and credit availability) in stabilizing the economy. When economic conditions were bad, the availability of credit at favourable rates of interest did not give rise to increased expenditure. For this reason the Keynesian era, which followed on the appearance of *The General Theory*, is associated with a particular preference for fiscal policy and a strong distrust of monetary policy.

The Monetarists

Keynes's policy directives were eminently suited to combat the condition of depression prevailing in the period preceding the Second World War.

After the War, when insufficient demand (or expenditure) was supplanted by the evil of inflation as the most pressing economic problem, fiscal policy alone was not sufficient to bring about the necessary correction. Gradually a spirit of skepticism was built up against Keynes's views. Under the leadership of the American economist, Milton Friedman of Chicago, the neglect of monetary policy was condemned. This school of thought, known as that of the monetarists, argued that the Depression was actually caused by the wrong monetary policy and that it was the responsibility of any government to ensure that inflation was controlled by following a strict monetary policy which would restrict the supply of money to an acceptable rate of growth.

Together with the plea for a more effective use of monetary policy, the monetarists were also extremely critical towards the exaggerated use of fiscal policy to keep total expenditure at an acceptable level. As a result of this, the monetarists also received support from the conservative element in society who were concerned about the increasing involvement of government in the economy. For this reason monetarists are today also seen as proponents of the free-market economy with a minimum interference by the State, while Keynesians are associated with state intervention which stems from a distrust of the functioning of the market mechanism.

Contemporary schools of thought

Since the original debate between the Keynesians and the monetarists in the sixties, several variations of both schools of thought have developed. These variations certainly also contributed towards a blurring of the original distinctions between the two schools of thought. The issues which gave rise to the two schools are no longer as prominent as they once were. The Keynesian theory resulted from the Depression when unemployment was the major consideration. The monetarists, on the other hand, came to the fore after a long period of almost full employment in the world when the evil of inflation had to be combated.

In spite of these divergent origins, both the Keynesian and the monetarist models were largely concerned with the demand side of the economy. The issue was how to control total expenditure in the economy. When the world was confronted in the seventies with the fact that problems could also arise on the supply side, macro-economics underwent a similar change of emphasis. The early eighties were characterised by so-called **supply-side economics**, whereby the most important problems had to be solved by means of shifts in the aggregate supply curve. Furthermore, the decisive influence the **expected** inflation rate began to exercise on important macro-economic variables was largely responsible for the formation of a whole new school of thought, based exclusively on rational expectations.

In an elementary macro-economics textbook it is impossible to deal with all the different schools of thought. Neither is it the intention to keep weighing up the two main approaches (Keynesian and monetarist) against each other in this book. The terms "Keynesians" and "monetarists" will simply occur from time to time, for example in referring to a particular type of approach. The aim of this book is in the first place to make you familiar with the basic macro-economic model according to which the abovementioned schools can be interpreted.

1.6 The challenges to macro-economic policy

Macro-economics, as a science, is in the first place geared towards policy. The priority given to policy in macro-economics is much greater than that in micro-economics and its success depends in the final analysis on the results achieved by the application of the policy directives derived from it. The task of the macro-economist, who is orientated towards policy, is therefore to indicate how the various instruments of policy, such as fiscal and monetary policy, may be employed to achieve certain objectives.

As shown above, the focus during the Depression was on increased production and employment. That is to say, unemployment had to be reduced at all costs, without much thought being given to inflation. After World War II, the emphasis was placed on the combating of inflation. And since the world experienced a remarkable boom during the two decades following the War, little attention was paid to economic growth or unemployment. The problems that had to be faced by the policy-makers therefore arose one by one or separately. To tell the truth, for a long time it was believed that these two evils of unemployment and inflation could not occur simultaneously. During the fifties a British economist, A.W.Phillips, stated on the basis of empirical analysis that a high rate of unemployment is usually accompanied by a low rate of inflation, and vice versa. The implications for policy deriving from this approach were that unemployment could be combated by accepting a higher rate of inflation, or that the rate of inflation could only be reduced at the cost of more unemployment (and therefore lower production).

Events during the past decade or more have made room for a far more complex set of problems. The two evils referred to above no longer took turns in plaguing the economy, but now occurred together. The idea that there was a trade-off between them was largely eliminated by events. In South Africa, as elsewhere, a high rate of inflation was accompanied by a great deal of unemployment and low economic growth. No wonder people began to talk about **the twin evils of inflation and unemployment**. The marked structural change undergone by the South African economy over the past few decades can be clearly seen in table 1.1, where the inflation rate is shown against the growth in production. Note that the marked increase in the inflation rate is accompanied by a significant decrease in the economy's productivity.

Table 1.1

Economic growth and the inflation rate in South Africa

Period	Economic growth	Inflation
	Percentage per year	Percentage per year
1946-50	4,42	4,42
1950-60	4,44	3,50
1960-70	5,90	2,76
1970-80	3,37	10,73
1980-90	1,32	14,65

Sources: Central Statistical Services: *South African Statistics 1986* for 1946–1980
South African Reserve Bank: *Quarterly Bulletin* December 1991 for 1980–1990.

Table 1.1   *An analysis of economic growth and the rate of inflation in South Africa shows that policy-makers are confronted by two major problems. The slow rate of economic growth is now coupled with double-digit inflation.*

Although this table does not show the twin evils of inflation and unemployment contrasted with each other, the **decrease** in the growth rate of production is a reasonable indication of the **increase** in unemployment which must in fact have occurred. Statistics on unemployment for all population groups are unfortunately not reliable in South Africa.

From the table it can clearly be seen that the policy-makers are confronted by more than one problem. It is therefore obvious that more than one policy objective needs to be pursued. The task becomes even more complicated if we bear in mind that the objectives cannot always be reconciled with each other. The South African conditions outlined above clearly require a fuller employment of the available factors of production, but at the same time it is necessary to ensure that such measures do not fan the fires of inflation. In the same way policy measures taken to control inflation should not further inhibit the already inadequate growth in production.

This unenviable task is further complicated by the fact that there are still other policy objectives to be pursued in a market-orientated economy. The following four objectives should form a part of any balanced policy framework:

1. **Full employment**. It is extremely important to ensure that the available

factors of production in the economy are fully employed to avoid losing potential production for good. In addition to the material poverty endured by those without work, there is also the moral degradation of those who were formerly employed and now can no longer support their families. In South Africa unemployment also constitutes a serious threat to social and political stability. Full employment can rightly be regarded as South Africa's most important economic objective and in most of the chapters that follow it will also be recognised as a central theme.

2. **Stability of prices**. Although the desirability of a low inflation rate is less pressing than the objective of full employment, it is generally acknowledged today as one of the policy-makers' chief objectives. Rising prices as such are not a problem, but the unfortunate effects of inflation on certain sectors and groups of the economy are regarded as undesirable. The most important negative effects are related to: the redistribution of income; the country's balance of payments; and the possibility of a misallocation of factors of production. In chapter 9 we shall take another look at the cost of inflation.

3. **External stability**. All countries with a reasonable level of development trade with other countries to increase their general welfare. One of the main features of the South African economy is, in fact, its dependence on the foreign sector (with regard to imports as well as exports) in order to maintain a sound economic growth rate. It is therefore essential that a balance should exist between the value of exports and imports in order to ensure that the country will be able to pay for its essential imports. Policy must ensure that the balance of payments (a statement of all transactions with foreign countries) is stable and that the rate of exchange (the value of the monetary unit in terms of foreign monetary units) consequently remains relatively stable. In chapter 8 more attention is given to this aspect.

4. **Economic growth**. Since a positive ratio exists between economic growth and employment, this objective is often set as a goal together with full employment. The objective of economic growth is probably regarded as a separate policy goal because it relates to longer-term problems. We are therefore here concerned with the creation of an economic climate that will promote growth, rather than with measures intended to stabilize total demand over shorter periods and thus maintain employment at a satisfactory level. In contrast to the foregoing two objectives (price stability and external stability), which can sometimes be irreconcilable with the achievement of full employment, economic growth is largely complementary to greater employment and should always be a priority in South Africa. In chapter 10 economic growth is analysed in greater detail.

In addition to the traditional objectives which we have defined above, each country obviously has certain peculiar characteristics which present a special challenge to its policy-makers. South Africa is certainly not lacking in such unique circumstances. We are thinking here of only a few of the most important problem areas, each of which has to be borne in mind when policy is formulated: the gold mining industry and the unique role of the gold price in the South African economy; the agricultural sector which has, owing to climatic conditions, always necessitated special attention; and finally, the different facets of South Africa's political and social problems which require special policy measures inside as well as outside the country.

We shall not be able to deal with all these questions in this introductory volume, but it is to be hoped that you will gain an idea of the complexity of the subject studied and also emphasise why the study of macro-economics is so important.

1.7 Conclusion

Much has been said in this introductory chapter. The main objective of the chapter was to present the field of study of macro-economics to you. We now conclude the chapter with a brief review of the approach to be followed in the rest of the book.

Because empirical data are so important in macro-economics, the next chapter explains the main methods used to calculate various macro-economic magnitudes.

In chapter 3 the most important components of total spending (demand factors) and their influence on income determination are discussed. This chapter does not, however, make provision for any price changes.

The relationship between aggregate demand, aggregate supply and the general price level is analysed in chapter 4. The aggregate supply and demand model developed in this chapter is used in the rest of the book to analyze various aspects of macro-economics.

In chapter 5 we discuss the role of fiscal policy. We look at the economic consequences of state spending and also point out the effect that taxes may have on total spending. This chapter therefore examines the role of the government in the economy.

The role of money is analyzed in the following two chapters (chapters 6 and 7). Chapter 6 discusses the factors that influence the demand for and supply of money. In the next chapter the different views (Keynesian versus monetarist) on the influence of money on the real economy are considered. The chapter concludes with a short explanation of the main instruments of monetary policy in South Africa.

In chapter 8 we examine South Africa's economic relations with the rest of the world. Topics such as imports and exports, the balance of payments and exchange rates are discussed. The importance of the external sector for South Africa's economic growth is clearly indicated.

Chapter 9 analyzes various aspects of inflation. We look at how inflation is measured and also at the effects and causes of this economic evil.

The final chapter examines the major problem of economic growth and development in the world. In this chapter we review the broad arguments on world development issues.

Selected references:

Baumol, WJ & Blinder, AS. 1985. *Economics – Principles and Policy*. 3rd edition. New York: Harcourt Brace Jovanovich Inc. Chapter 4, 5.

Dernburg, TF. 1985. *Macroeconomics: Concepts, theories and policies*. 7th edition. New York: McGraw-Hill. Student edition. Chapter 1.

Dornbuch, R & Fischer, S (Adapted for South Africa by Mohr, P & Rogers,C). 1987. *Macroeconomics*. Johannesburg: Lexicon Publishers. Chapter 1.

Evans-Pritchard, J. 1985. *Macroeconomics. An introductory text*. London: MacMillan Education Ltd. Chapter 1.

Froyen, RT. 1983. *Macroeconomics: Theories and Policies*. New York: MacMillan Publishing Co. Inc. Chapter 1.

Gordon, RJ. 1984. *Macroeconomics*. 3rd edition, Boston: Little, Brown and Company, Chapter 1.

Morley, SA. 1984. *Macroeconomics*. Hinsdale, Ill.:The Dryden Press. Chapter 1, 2.

Shapiro, Edward. 1982. *Macroeconomics analysis*. Fifth edition. New York: Harcourt Brace Jovanovich. Chapter 1.

2 The measurement of macro-economic quantities

Following on the introductory remarks in chapter 1, we can now begin with the study of macro-economics. Macro-economics is today largely an empirical science in which it is necessary to quantify the totals used in the macro-economic model. As indicated in the previous chapter, we are here concerned with total markets which relate to aggregated quantities. We are therefore interested in concepts such as total production, the general price level and the level of employment in the economy. In order to understand the meaning of these aggregated totals properly, we must know how they are measured.

In this chapter we focus on the problems of measuring the most important macro-economic variables.

2.1 The gross domestic product (GDP)

The most important need of the macro-economist is to have some measure of the total economic activity in the country. This can be achieved by the combination (aggregation) of separate goods and services into one measure of total production or output. The question is, which measure should be used to determine the volume of all goods and services collectively, so that we can work with such a global market. Thanks to developments in the area of **national accounting**, certain measures are available today which can serve as an indication of macro-economic activity. The national accounts, which are the responsibility of the South African Reserve Bank (SARB) and the Central Statistical Services (CSS), are published every three months in the quarterly bulletin of the SARB and the Bulletin of Statistics. These authorities may, in other words, be regarded as the "book-keepers" of the economy, since the accounts provide a comprehensive record of total production, income and expenditure in the country.

The most comprehensive macro-economic measure resulting from these

22

accounts is called the **gross domestic product** (GDP). The GDP may be defined as:

> The **market value** of all final goods and services produced within the boundaries of a country during a certain period (usually one year).

The definition given above at first looks quite clear and simple. Yet it holds a number of problems and ambiguities peculiar to the measurement of any macro-economic total. The first concept in the definition which requires more detailed discussion is the word **value**.

What does the concept of the "value" of all goods and services mean? How is it possible to combine the endless variety of goods and services into a unitary measure named "value"? Is it possible to add together products such as shoes, clothing, medical services, bread and meat to make a meaningful whole?

The obvious solution to the above problem is to use **prices** as the link to combine goods and services in a measure of total output or production. The justification for the use of prices as "weights" to measure the relative importance of goods and services, arises from micro-economic principles. The price consumers are prepared to pay for a commodity or service is a reflection of the value they attach to it. This principle leads logically to the conclusion that a motorcar, for example, will count for more than a loaf of bread in such a global measure.

To calculate the GDP, all the goods and services produced and rendered in a final form during the period concerned are multiplied by their prices and then added together to yield the total **market value** of the GDP. The prices used for this purpose will be the **market prices** paid for the various goods and services during the year.

Double counting and how to avoid it

The next concept in the definition of the GDP to be discussed, is the meaning of **final** goods and services. Final goods and services are to be distinguished from **intermediate** goods and services on the basis that they are bought by consumers for final use. Any commodity or service purchased for reselling or processing (i.e. using it in another production process), is regarded as an **intermediate** commodity or service and does not form part of the GDP. The difference between final and intermediate goods may be explained on the basis of a simple example:

(i)   Suppose a farmer produces 1 000 bags of wheat which he sells to a miller at R10 per bag.
(ii) The miller processes the wheat into flour, which he then sells to a baker for R12 500.
(iii) After baking bread with the flour, the baker sells it to a shop for R18 000.
(iv) The shop subsequently sells the bread to final consumers for R21 000.

These transactions may be summarised as follows:

	Value of sales	*Value added*
Farmer	R10 000	R10 000
Miller	12 500	2 500
Baker	18 000	5 500
Shopkeeper	21 000	3 000
	R61 500	R21 000

The total value of all the transactions (R61 500) cannot, as a whole, be regarded as part of the GDP. Although the miller, for instance, sold goods for R12 500, he did not **produce** goods to the value of R12 500. The farmer has already contributed R10 000 to the production of the flour. This means that the amount of R61 500 includes **double counting** to a considerable extent.

Two methods can be used to calculate the GDP (without double counting):

(i)   By only counting the value of those transactions where a commodity reaches its final destination. As a result only those transactions between the shop and its customers, to a total of R21 000, are taken into account, since only the bread has actually been produced in this process. This method of accounting is also known as the **expenditure approach**. If we go back to the circuit in the previous chapter, we can see that the value of the GDP could in principle be calculated according to the expenditure method on the market for consumer goods. The market for consumer goods is by implication the market where **final** goods and services are sold.
(ii) By counting, in each transaction, only the **value added** (i.e. the addition to the value of the output). This is shown in the second column above and yields the same result as in (i), viz. R21 000.

It may be noted in this connection that it is the ultimate use of a product which determines whether it is a final or intermediate product. The flour in the above example could be a consumer commodity (final destination) if it were bought as such by a consumer. If it is held over to a subsequent period, it becomes part of **stock formation**, which in turn is part of capital formation (see chapter 3); and then the flour could also be an intermediate commodity if, as in the above example, it was to be used in another production process. In addition to this, intermediate goods are also known as **secondary inputs** to distinguish them from **primary inputs**, that is the factors of production themselves.

Three methods of calculating GDP

It is quite instructive to refer briefly to the three methods of calculating GDP. Of particular importance, is the **equality** of the totals reached. Two of these methods have already been mentioned, viz. the **expenditure method** and the **value added** or **production** approach. The composition of expenditure (and hence of demand) will be discussed in more detail in the next chapter. From the example of the bread it has, however, already become evident that with the expenditure method (adding up the market values of all final goods) the same result is achieved as with the value added approach (the adding together of the values added at each stage of the production process). And this must be so, since the value of final goods must necessarily be made up of the successive values added to the raw materials in the different stages of production.

The third method is the **factor income method**, which is also known as the **income approach**. In order to calculate the GDP according to this method, it is necessary to add up all incomes deriving from the production process. In other words, all payments made in respect of the four factors of production (i.e. labour, capital, land – or natural resources – and entrepreneurship) over the year, will together represent the value of the GDP. This implies that the total of all **wages and salaries, interest, rent and profits** is conceptually equal to the GDP as calculated according to the production method.

If we now look back to the circular flow in chapter 1, we see that the GDP, according to the factor income method, will in principle be derived from the market for factors of production. The fact that the expenditure approach and the income approach can both be associated with the two markets in the flow diagram, is a further indication that the two methods of calculation will yield the same result. Both form part of the same flow of money in the flow diagram.

The equality of total income and the value of production

The principle that total production and total income have the same value, is very important and can be illustrated on the basis of our example of the production of bread.

The total income referred to, is of course the same as the total payment for factors of production or total factor payment. The only way in which

income can therefore be earned, is in the form of wages and salaries, interest, rentals and profits.

Before we come to the economy as a whole, the position of the baker in the above example may be taken as a point of departure. The value the baker has added to the final product, bread, amounted to R5 500 (R18 000 − R12 500 = R5 500). In order to be able to produce this added value, the baker had to employ certain factors of production (primary inputs). The value of these inputs could have been as follows:

Wages and salaries	R2 500
Rentals (buildings)	1 000
Interest on loans	500
Total	R4 000

This means that the baker's entrepreneurial profit had to be R1 500. Remember that profit is always calculated as a residual and that it includes the compensation for the baker's own labour. The selling price of the baker (R18 000) is therefore apportioned as follows:

Primary inputs	
Wages and salaries	R2 500
Rental	1 000
Interest	500
Profit	1 500
Secondary inputs	
Intermediate goods and services	12 500
Total	R18 000

Note that the value of the baker's intermediate goods and services is the same as the miller's selling price. This amount of R12 500 can therefore, as in the case of the R18 000 above, be apportioned between primary and secondary inputs. In this way all sales (R61 500) in the economy can be apportioned to the payment for factors of production (primary inputs) on the one hand and intermediate goods and services (secondary inputs) on the other hand. In the following statement it is assumed, somewhat unrealistically, that the farmer has bought no intermediate goods or services. Note also that the entrepreneurial profit has been treated as a balancing amount (residual item) throughout.

	Value of sales	Payment for factors of producton	Value of inter- mediate goods and services
Farmer	R10 000	R10 000	–
Miller	12 500	2 500	R10 000
Baker	18 000	5 500	R12 500
Shopkeeper	21 000	3 000	R18 000
Total	R61 500	R21 000	R40 500

In view of the above, the following identity may be derived for the economy as a whole:[§]

Value of total sales	=	total factor payments (wages and salaries, rent, interest and profit)	+	total intermediate goods and services
(R61 500)	=	(R21 000)	+	(R40 500)

The following will also apply:

Value of total sales	–	Value of inter- mediate goods and services	=	Total factor payments

Since the left-hand side of this equation is also equal to the value of all **final** goods and **services**, the following will also be true:

The value of final goods and services = Total income

In principle it is therefore clear – and this should be remembered – that **output expressed in monetary terms** must be equal to the **total monetary income** deriving from it. We have already seen that the value of output is

§   Cf. J.J. Stadler, *Die Nasionale Rekeninge van Suid-Afrika*, P.37.

equal to the total value of expenditure; consequently the latter must also be equal to total income.

BUT REMEMBER: Although the above identity must always apply in principle, certain complicating factors such as **indirect taxation** and **subsidies** can cause a concept such as GDP and the gross domestic **income**, which is a measure of total income, to differ from each other. Where the former measure is estimated on the basis of **market prices** and the latter is evaluated in terms of **factor income**, items such as sales tax or value-added tax (examples of indirect taxation) would form part of the GDP but would not be taken into account in the case of gross domestic income. This will be explained in section 2.2.

It should also be noted that only goods and services produced during a certain period are included in the GDP.

The GDP therefore concerns the **production** of new products taking place during a specific period and not the **sales** during a specific period. For example, the re-sale of any second-hand article (say a house or a motor-car) would not form part of the GDP. Nor do activities on the stock market affect the GDP in any way.

2.2   Other measures of income and output

The national income total you were introduced to in the previous section, is known as the gross domestic product. Although reference has been made to market prices, the qualification "at market prices" should actually still be added to it, in other words we have up to now been discussing the GDP at market prices. In this section we are going to look at the meaning of the expressions "domestic", "gross" and "at market prices", as well as the other important income totals.

Domestic income versus national income

The reference to "domestic" has a literal meaning and indicates that all production which occurs within the geographic area of a country forms part of the GDP. This can be explained by contrasting the GDP with a similar macro-economic total, viz. the gross **national** product (GNP). In the case of the gross **domestic** product it is not asked who produced the goods (or who are the owners of the factors of production concerned) but rather whether production took place within the borders of the country. Goods manufactured by a German firm, and therefore with foreign capital, in South Africa are therefore regarded as part of its GDP.

However, in the case of the **gross national product** (GNP) the emphasis is on the **national** character of the output. Only that part of production which results from the employment of factors of production (labour, capital, land, etc.) that are in the possession of permanent residents of the country concerned, is regarded as part of the GNP. Whether the production takes place inside or outside the boundaries of the country is of no importance in this case.

To derive the GNP from the GDP, the following must therefore be done:

SUBTRACT (from GDP):

(i) Profits, interest and other income from domestic investments which accrue to non-residents.

(ii) Wages accruing to guest workers, foreign sportsmen, etc.

ADD (to GDP):

Profits, etc. accruing from abroad to permanent residents.

Wages and salaries earned by permanent residents outside South Africa.

South Africa's GDP and GNP will only be equal provided South African interests abroad are precisely the same as the extent of foreign interests in South Africa. In developing countries like South Africa the foreign factors, labour, capital and managerial expertise, employed for local production are normally more extensive than the South African factors of production used in other countries. Consequently the GDP is larger and more comprehensive in South Africa than the GNP.

Table 2.1

Gross domestic product versus gross national product in South Africa (1984–1991)

Year	GDP at current prices	GNP at current prices	GNP as percentage of GDP
	R miljoen million	R miljoen million	%
1984	107 221	102 365	95,5
1985	123 126	116 608	94,7
1986	142 135	134 309	94,5
1987	164 521	157 038	95,4
1988	197 910	190 174	96,1
1989	233 134	223 655	95,9
1990	263 812	253 792	96,2
1991	296 667	288 485	97,2

Source: South African Reserve Bank: *Quarterly Bulletin*, March 1992.

Table 2.1 *In South Africa the GDP is a more comprehensive measure of economic activity than the GNP. From the last column it can be seen that the relation between the two is fairly stable.*

The data in table 2.1 give an indication of the extent of the difference over the past few years. (This difference can also be called net payments for foreign factors of production or net factor payments to foreign countries; see chapter 8). As can be seen from the last column, the relation between the two totals is fairly stable. The difference amounts to approximately 5 per cent, which decreased to 3 per cent during the recent years. Probably an indication of the influence of sanctions. This income accruing to foreigners as owners of factors of production gives an indication of the importance of South Africa to the economies of other countries.

As GDP is the more comprehensive measure, it is to be expected that changes in GDP will be more accurate indications of, for instance, new job opportunities in South Africa. In chapter 1 we indicated that the creation of new employment in South Africa, with its fast growing population, is one of the major policy objectives; for this reason GDP is preferred to GNP as a measure of general economic activity. On the other hand, in the USA, which has extensive interests (mainly investments) in the rest of the world, the GNP is considered more meaningful. Strangely enough, the same applies to less developed countries, that depend to a large degree on the export of labour (guest workers).

The concept of depreciation

The description of the total output of a country as **gross** domestic product means that we use a measure which does not provide for that part of a country's capital equipment (buildings, machinery, tools, etc.) which is "used up" in the production process. During the period for which GDP is calculated, obsolescence and wear and tear cause capital equipment to **depreciate**, which should actually be subtracted from the value of output. If depreciation is not subtracted, double counting occurs, with secondary inputs (intermediate goods and services). Subtracting the provision for depreciation changes the **gross** total to a **net** total. Such a net amount will be a more correct measure of economic performance since it adjusts gross output to include the decrease in the value of capital goods. However, the gross measure is often regarded as sufficient because the calculation of depreciation is not always accurate. For instance, it is not so easy to determine by how much assets such as the Union Buildings, a tractor or a computer have depreciated in a particular year.

The fact that depreciation is a relatively inaccurate concept and is, therefore, often left out of account, does not mean that it is an unimportant or small item in the national accounts. It is important, because it shows which proportion of the total output should actually be saved in order to maintain the economy's production capacity at the same level. From the centre columns of table 2.2 it can be seen that the adjustment for depreciation has constituted more than 15 per cent of the GDP every year. In fact, during 1986 and 1987 it has amounted to about 17 per cent.

Table 2.2

Depreciation, Gross and Net Product Totals in South Africa, 1984–1991

Year	GDP @ market prices	GNP @ market prices	Depreciation		NDP	NNP
	R million	R million	R million	% of GDP	R million	R million
1984	107 221	102 365	16 121	15,0	91 100	86 244
1985	123 126	116 608	19 645	16,0	103 481	96 963
1986	142 135	134 309	24 697	17,4	117 438	109 612
1987	164 524	157 038	27 998	17,0	136 526	129 040
1988	197 910	190 174	32 442	16,4	165 468	157 732
1989	233 134	223 655	38 402	16,5	194 732	185 253
1990	263 812	253 792	43 058	16,3	220 754	210 734
1991	96 667	288 485	47 007	15,8	249 660	241 478

Source: South African Reserve Bank: *Quarterly Bulletin,* March 1992.

Table 2.2 *By subtracting the allowance for depreciation from the GDP and the GNP we arrive at the net values for the respective production totals. Note that depreciation has varied between 15 and 17,4 per cent of GDP.*

If the allowance for depreciation is subtracted from the **GDP**, we arrive at the **net domestic product**, for example R249 660 million in 1991; if, on the other hand, the allowance for depreciation is subtracted from the **gross national product**, we arrive at the **net national product**, for example R241 478 million in 1991. In other words, all the totals can be evaluated in either gross or net terms.

Market prices versus factor cost

The third qualification of national income totals mentioned at the beginning of this section was that GDP was valued **"at market prices"**. It is interesting to note that, if one were to calculate the GDP on the basis of the income method, the result would not be exactly the same as if one had used the expenditure or value added method. This actually contradicts what we said above, viz. that the three approaches would in principle yield the same result.

In principle, this is still the case, but in practice there are two factors which affect the outcome, viz. **subsidies** and **indirect taxes**, so that the **market value** of final goods is not equal to the **income** received by the owners of the factors of production. The above two concepts are explained in more detail below:

(i)   Market prices include all **indirect taxes** such as GST, excise and value-added tax. Indirect taxation is not, however, part of the price paid for factors of production and hence does not form a part of factor income. In order to estimate factor income it is therefore necessary to **subtract** indirect tax from the market price, since the market price exceeds factor income by this amount.

(ii) A much smaller item is that of **subsidies**; subsidies are paid on, for example, bread to keep the market price lower than would otherwise have been profitable. Subsidies are paid to the producer and therefore form a part of factor income but not of the market price; for this reason subsidies are **added** to the market price to arrive at factor income.

Once these calculations have been made, the product totals are valued **at factor cost** rather than market prices. Often, but not invariably, the totals are then no longer referred to as gross domestic or national **product**, but as gross domestic or national **income**; of special importance here is **net national income** (NNI), which is valued "at factor cost".

The derivation of the NNI from the GDP can now be explained in three steps, as follows; this will serve at the same time as a summary of what has been said in this section. The figures used are those for 1991.

Step 1

	R million
Gross domestic product at market prices	296 667
Minus: Net factor payments to the foreign sector[§]	8 182
Gross national product at market prices	288 485

This is therefore how the **domestic** product is changed into a **national** product. In the next step the allowance for depreciation is taken into account and we change the qualification from **gross** to **net**.

Step 2

	R million
Gross national product at market prices	288 485
Minus: provision for depreciation	47 007
Net national product at market prices	241 478

§ I.e. *minus* factor income earned by foreigners locally *plus* factor income earned abroad by permanent residents.

The third step is as follows:

Step 3

	R million
Net national product at market prices	241 478
Minus indirect taxes	35 120
Plus subsidies	5 830
Net national income (at factor cost)	212 188

As indicated in Step 3, it is clear that subsidies represent considerably less than indirect taxes, but that they nevertheless amount to R5 830 million, which is quite substantial.

Other income totals

Another important total which is no longer published in the **Quarterly Bulletin** of the South African Reserve Bank is the **net national disposable income** at factor cost. This total is derived from the NNI by adding foreign transfers (gifts, inheritances and also foreign aid) to it. In 1991 this type of transfer in South Africa represented a relatively small amount (R195 million); the net national disposable income therefore stood at R212 383 million as against the NNI of R212 188 million. For small, underdeveloped countries this total can however be significant, since foreign aid plays a major role in their economies.

The various steps are illustrated more clearly in figure 2.1. The length of the columns is proportional to the amounts represented. In addition to the derivation of NNI at factor cost from GDP at market prices, the diagram gives further interesting deductions viz. that of **personal income** and **personal disposable income**.

In contrast to the wider concept of NNI, personal income concerns only the income of households. To derive personal income from the NNI, the income from incorporated companies (savings, taxes and transfers) as well as the income (from property) of the authorities must be subtracted, while all transfer payments by the State (e.g. pensions) and from abroad to individuals must be added. In addition, the interest due on public debt paid to the private sector must also be added.

In other words, all amounts not paid out to households are subtracted, and, conversely, non-income (i.e. transfer payments) are added to the NNI. In South Africa this type of income is known as **current income**, but the expression **personal income** is actually closer to the mark.

Lastly, in order to obtain an indication of the discretionary income of

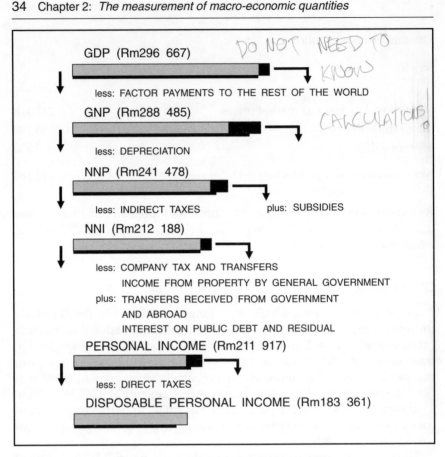

Source: South African Reserve Bank: *Quarterly Bulletin,* March 1992.

Fig. 2.1 The magnitude of various macro-economic measures in South Africa (1991).
The diagram shows clearly how various macro-economic measures can be derived from GDP.

households, personal taxes may be subtracted from personal income. This amount of R183 361 million, which is known as the **disposable personal income**, gives an indication of the income the ordinary man has at his disposal. On the basis of this income concept, private consumers decide on their expenditure pattern. This total is therefore of great importance in determining consumer expenditure.

2.3 The general level of prices

Before we consider the applications and deficiencies of the macro-economic totals we have discussed so far, we first have to see how variations in prices affect these totals.

Inflation and the purchasing power of money

In chapter 1 we saw how prices come into being on individual markets. We saw that micro-economics is *inter alia* also concerned with relative prices, that is the price of one commodity in terms of another commodity. Such arbitrary variations in relative prices do not however affect the general purchasing power of money – i.e. the actual number of goods and services that can be bought with a certain amount of money – in any particular way. But, as we have seen in chapter 1, it can sometimes happen that all or most of the prices show a consistent upward trend; this we called **inflation** and we must now determine how this can be measured and how purchasing power is affected by such variations in the general level of prices.

Table 2.3

Some examples of changes in consumer prices in South Africa, 1980–1992

Consumer item	Weights in CPI	1980 c	1985 c	1988 c	1992 c	Percentage increase		
						1980–1985	1985–1988	1988–1992
Bread: Brown	0,39	21	50	69	149	138	38	116
White	0,68	31	70	85	179	126	21	111
Milk: 1 litre	0,96	48	79	120	190	65	52	58
White sugar: 2,5 kg	0,44	118	199	299	489	69	50	63
Mealie meal: 5 kg	0,37	134	269	389	649	101	45	66
Eggs X large: 1 doz	0,36	74	150	265	345	103	37	30
Petrol: 1 litre	3,21	54	98	95	150	81	–3	58

Source: *Rand Daily Mail*, 30 May 1980 for information up to 1980. The other prices were gathered at random from retailers during the year concerned.

Table 2.3 *The past decade was characterised by general price rises (inflation). However, as this table shows, there are considerable differences between the price increases for different goods. The weights in the Consumer Price Index (CPI) measure the relative importance of the goods in the average consumer's budget. This information is used in calculating the CPI itself (cf. table 2.4).*

To gain an impression of what happens during a rise in the general level of prices we can refer to table 2.3, which gives the prices of a number of products over the period 1980 to 1992. In the last three columns, the per centage increases in the prices of the products are indicated over different periods. Two things are immediately obvious. Firstly, the prices of all the products increased considerably over the full period. Secondly, increases differed considerably between the various products, as well as between different periods, for the same product. For example, the increases for the 1980-1985 period varied between 65 per cent in the case of milk and 138 per cent in the case of brown bread. The exceptional cases were clearly the rise in the price of bread during the period 1980–1985 and 1988–1992 and the slight decrease in the petrol price during 1985–1988. It is clear that in the midst of general price increases, variations in relative prices also occurred.

Although the information we have supplied with these figures already gives an indication that a fall in the purchasing power of money or income has occurred as a result of the rise in the general level of prices, we still cannot predict whether its extent will be in the region of 130 per cent or whether it will be closer to 60 per cent. This is, of course, because the list of items given in table 2.3 is not comprehensive. The items in the table represent only a little more than 8 per cent of the average consumer's total consumer expenditure (this can be calculated by adding up the weights in the first column). It would therefore be presumptuous to **generalise** about the level of prices on this basis. The precise meaning of the weights, (cf. column 2 in table 2.3) will be explained in the next section, where we are going to look at three important price indices in macro-economics.

The calculation of the consumer price index (CPI) (i)

To solve these problems an in-depth study of the composition (weights) and scope (basket) of consumer expenditure in South Africa is carried out by the Central Statistical Services (CSS). On this basis a total consumer price index (CPI) is compiled, which is representative of an average basket of consumer goods and services. The **basket** of goods and services and the **weights** allocated to them are based on family budget surveys done by the CSS and the Bureau for Market Research of UNISA. The aim is to undertake such surveys every five years in future, which means that the next survey will take place in 1995. In addition to this total CPI, a further CPI is published every month for three different income brackets (lower, middle and higher) and for 12 of the main urban areas in South Africa. With the aid of these subindices a more accurate indication can be obtained of consumer prices in particular areas or for people in a specific income bracket.

The weights used in the present CPI are based on a survey done in 1990. The basket at present consists of 600 different goods and services (six of them, together with their weights, are given in table 2.3) which are divided into 17 main groups and 40 subgroups. The weight allocated to each subgroup is based on the relative share (importance) of the item in the representative basket (or the average consumer's budget). It is clear that the greater the weight of a particular commodity or service, the greater the effect of a price rise in that commodity or service will be on the total CPI. The prices of the 600 items are determined every month by means of questionnaires sent to approximately 3 600 retailers.

In table 2.4 the consumer price index is given for a number of the most important goods and services. At the top of the table **two** sets of weights are given namely for 1985 and 1990. Until July 1991 the weights are based on expenditure patterns of households in the different income categories in 1985. The new weights based on the expenditure patterns in 1990 are applied to data as from August 1991. Although the data for 1991 is not strictly comparable with those for the previous years, it should be borne in mind that even considerable changes in weight do not bring about a significant change in the ultimate total indices. You will notice, however, that the relative share of expenditure on services other than housing and transport has risen from 11,1 to 17,3 per cent over the five year period.

Table 2.4

Consumer Price Index (CPI): Seasonally adjusted, 1984–1991.
Index: 1990=100

Period	Services				Goods							Grand total
	Hou-sing	Trans-port	Other	Total	Food	Furniture & equip-ment	Clothing & foot-wear	Vehi-cles	Other trans-port goods	Bever-ages and tobacco	Total	
Weights 1985)	22,5	5,9	11,1	39,5	23,2	4,7	6,0	5,5	5,9	2,3	60,5	100,0
Weights 1990)	20,5	4,3	17,3	42,1	19,3	5,5	7,0	5,5	4,6	2,2	57,9	100,0
1984	49,5	60,6	39,2	47,7	40,5	46,0	41,6	28,7	44,5	40,6	39,7	42,2
1985	57,9	68,8	44,6	55,2	45,4	51,1	46,9	34,9	60,6	46,5	46,2	49,1
1986	66,7	74,7	53,1	63,6	54,6	60,0	54,6	48,1	64,0	53,5	55,6	58,2
1987	74,1	76,9	63,3	71,3	67,0	70,4	65,2	59,3	64,7	60,0	65,7	67,6
1988	80,5	79,0	74,0	78,4	77,6	79,5	75,0	70,1	69,9	69,9	75,2	76,3
1989	91,6	87,1	85,1	89,1	86,2	88,0	86,8	87,7	87,2	84,6	86,6	87,5
1990	100,0	100,0	100,0	100,0	100,0	100,0	100,0	100,0	100,0	100,0	100,0	100,0
1991	105,6	121,2	120,2	112,6	119,6	109,6	112,5	122,4	110,8	121,8	117,0	115,3

Source: South African Reserve Bank: *Quarterly Bulletin,* March 1992.

Table 2.4 *This table shows (i) the importance (weight) of a number of large categories of consumer goods and services, and (ii) the change in the prices of these categories over the period 1984–1991. Jointly, they determine the change in the (total) CPI, as reflected in the final column.*

About a fifth is spent on food, which implies that a rise in food prices would have a considerable impact on the CPI. The totals for the base year, in this case 1990, are made equivalent to 100 and thereafter the figures for each successive year (average over 12 months) are expressed as a percentage of the 1990 figure. This is how the indices in table 2.4 are calculated.

The last column shows that the general price level derived in this way has changed from 42,2 in 1984 to 115,3 in 1991. Vehicle prices have risen more rapidly than most of the other items to 122,4, which is also the greatest increase. The table shows that the price of vehicles has doubled since 1987! The relatively large increase in the price indices of transport services and other transport goods since 1988 (of 79,0 to 121,2 and 69,9 to 110,8) is probably a reflection of the fact that fuel prices increased during this period, coupled with the increase in the price of vehicles.

As we shall see below, the CPI is not the only available price index. Since it is, however, representative of the greatest single expenditure total (viz. consumer expenditure), and also gives the best indication of changes in the purchasing power of money, it is regarded as extremely important. The CPI is generally used as a measure of inflation in South Africa.

The meaning of a change in purchasing power

A change in real purchasing power may be explained as follows: Suppose the general level of prices as measured by the consumer price index doubles, i.e., increases from 100 to 200. This means that the package of goods and services previously purchased by the average consumer now costs twice as much; or, to put it differently, a given amount of money can now purchase only half ($\frac{100}{200}$) of what could be purchased initially. The last column of table 2.4 therefore shows that the purchasing power of one rand in terms of 1990 prices is equal to 87c (= $\frac{100}{115,3}$) in 1991. During the period 1984 to 1991 the purchasing power fell to as little as 36c ($\frac{42,2}{115,3}$). There are further interesting examples. For instance, the purchasing power of R1,00 in 1988 compared with 1940 is equal to 4c and in comparison with 1970, R1,00 is equal to 12c. Such drastic decreases have not always occurred. For instance, in the decade of 1920–30 prices actually **fell,** which meant that the purchasing power of R1,00 increased by 40 per cent between 1920 and 1930. During the period 1930–40 prices remained practically unchanged.[§] It is only since 1940 that the purchasing power began to decrease regularly and at an increasing rate.

§   R.S.A. – *Statistics in brief,* 1979, Republic of South Africa, Department of Statistics.

The calculation of the production price index (PPI) (ii)

The second important price index that we have to know about is the production price index (PPI). Before 1980 this was known as the wholesale price index. From these names one can deduce that prices are measured at the level of the first significant commercial transaction. In contrast to the CPI, this index includes capital and intermediate goods. The basic method of calculation is similar to that of the CPI, and it is published every month by the CSS. As indicated by a summary of the PPI in table 2.5 however, the **basket** as well as the **weights** differ considerably from those of the CPI. The difference is in (i) the nature of the prices themselves, which are wholesale or producer prices and not retail prices; (ii) the fact that services are not reflected in the PPI, whereas they account for 42,1 per cent of the CPI at present; on the other hand, the items "basic metals and products" and "machinery and equipment" are not included under consumer prices; and (iii) there is in any case a considerable difference in the weights allocated, for example, food counts for 19,3 per cent in the CPI but represents only 15,0 per cent in the PPI.

Table 2.5

Production prices with seasonal effect excluded. Index: 1985=100

Period	Agriculture forestry and fishing	Manufacturing industry						Other	Total	Imported goods	Grand total
		Bever- ages & tobacco	Textiles etc.	Basic metals	Machi- nery	Food	Total				
Weights	11,8	4,2	5,4	14,8	7,5	15,0	72,4	15,6	80,5	19,5	100,0
1984	88,0	91,0	86,2	88,9	84,4	87,5	86,8	87,6	86,9	80,9	85,6
1985	100,0	100,0	100,0	100,0	100,0	100,0	100,0	100,0	100,0	100,0	100,0
1986	114,0	111,6	119,4	119,3	128,2	115,5	118,9	122,0	118,7	122,6	119,6
1987	132,9	128,1	139,7	138,3	147,7	135,3	137,1	135,2	136,7	134,5	136,2
1988	149,3	143,2	161,9	157,7	168,9	153,3	156,5	153,3	155,5	149,3	154,1
1989	156,6	165,8	192,4	187,8	203,0	164,0	182,5	179,2	178,5	173,6	177,6
1990	164,6	190,4	220,8	211,9	229,9	175,0	205,0	212,8	200,8	191,2	198,9
1991	181,0	221,3	244,6	236,1	256,1	195,2	229,7	242,7	225,2	207,0	221,6

Source: South African Reserve Bank: *Quarterly Bulletin,* March 1992.

Table 2.5 *The PPI is subdivided into goods produced in South Africa and imported goods. The table shows (i) the importance (weight) of a number of products, and (ii) the variation in prices of these groups for the period 1984–1991. Jointly they determine the change in the (total) PPI as reflected in the last column.*

It should, however, be remembered that the weights at the top of table 2.5 are still based on 1975 figures. Note also that the base year for the indices is 1985 and not 1990 as for the CPI in table 2.4. The table distinguishes between goods produced in South Africa (weight 80,5) and imported goods (weight 19,5). Locally manufactured goods have undergone a somewhat larger increase in prices (225,2) than imported goods (207,0) since 1985.

Because the PPI is measured on the first commercial transaction level, sudden rises in this index can often be regarded as a warning that consumer prices are to rise in the near future. The time lag between the two indices can be anything from 3 to 6 months. Possible advantages are, however, partially cancelled out by a longer time lag in the compiling and publishing of the PPI than of the CPI.

The calculation of the implicit GDP deflator (iii)

The last important price index we are going to consider, is the implicit GDP deflator. In discussing this index we are returning to the topic of national income totals. In contrast with the foregoing two indices (CPI and PPI), which are explicitly or directly calculable, this index, as its name indicates, is implicitly derived by dividing the GDP at current prices (nominal GDP)

Table 2.6

GDP at current and constant prices, as well as the implicit GDP deflator, South Africa, 1984–1991

Year	GDP at current prices	GDP at constant 1990 prices	Implicit GDP deflator
	R million	R million	1990=100
1984	107 221	246 463	43,5
1985	123 126	243 477	50,6
1986	142 135	243 521	58,4
1987	165 524	248 637	66,2
1988	197 910	259 080	76,4
1989	233 134	265 030	88,0
1990	263 812	263 812	100,0
1991	296 667	262 307	113,1

Source: South African Reserve Bank: *Quarterly Bulletin*, March 1992.

Table 2.6   *The GDP can be valued either at current or at constant prices. By expressing the amounts in the second column (current prices) as a percentage of the corresponding amounts in the third column (constant prices) the implicit GDP deflator is derived in the last column.*

by the corresponding GDP at constant prices (real GDP).[§] The price deflator is therefore shown as a quotient which can be converted to an index by multiplying it by 100. Such an index is very comprehensive, because it takes into account the changes in the prices of all goods and services that form part of the GDP. The trend of this derived index is shown in table 2.6. Note that the values of the GDP at current and constant prices are the same only in 1990. This is because the real series (i.e. the series valued at constant prices) is expressed in 1990 prices.

To understand the derivation of this index, it is necessary to know how the GDP at constant prices is derived. It is not, in fact, done by deflating the values of the GDP as a whole on the basis of some or other index. What does happen, is that each of the components of the GDP is estimated or deflated at constant prices. This automatically leads to a weighting process so that, for example, agricultural prices as a whole count for less than prices in the manufacturing industry, since the latter makes a greater contribution to the GDP. The GDP at constant prices is therefore in principle derived by adding up its constituent parts at constant prices.

The GDP deflator is repeated in table 2.7 and shown together with the CPI and the PPI. The annual per centage variation in the three series is also calculated. Each of the three indices, over the period as a whole, shows a reasonable degree of correspondence. During 1980–1981 a considerable deviation in the GDP deflator occurred. This was mainly due to the unstable trend in the gold price during this period. The fluctuations in the price of gold naturally did not produce the same instability in the CPI and the PPI.

2.4   Some applications of the GDP

Now that we have come to know a number of the domestic product and national income totals and have seen which price indices are important, we can discuss a few of the applications of these data.

Measuring the economy's performance

One of the most important reasons for the existence of national accounts was to document the performance of the economy properly. We have seen that in South Africa the GDP is the most important measure of total output during any one year. A single year's GDP data however provide little information on the extent to which the inhabitants of a country have succeeded in improving their welfare. Obviously the extent of the GDP in

---

§   In order to measure a total at constant prices, it is calculated according to the prices ruling during a particular, base year. Although we are only referring to the implicit GDP deflator, it is obvious that the implicit price deflator of any other national total could be derived.

a particular year needs to be compared with those of previous years to see whether any progress has actually been made.

Table 2.7

Price indices in South Africa, 1984–1991

Year	CPI		PPI		GDP deflator	
	Index 1990=100	Annual change %	Index 1990=100	Annual change %	Index 1990=100	Annual change %
1984	42,2	11,6	43,0	8,3	43,5	11,5
1985	49,1	16,4	50,3	17,0	50,6	16,3
1986	58,2	18,5	60,1	19,5	58,4	15,4
1987	67,6	16,2	68,5	14,0	66,2	13,4
1988	76,3	12,9	77,5	13,1	76,4	15,4
1989	87,5	14,7	89,3	15,2	88,0	15,2
1990	100,0	14,3	100,0	12,0	100,0	13,6
1991	115,3	15,3	111,1	11,1	113,1	13,1

Source: South African Reserve Bank: *Quarterly Bulletin,* March 1992.

Table 2.7   *The more important price indices are the consumer price index, the index of production prices and the GDP deflator. Although there are differences in the annual changes of each index, the general trend revealed over the period is one of increasing inflation.*

If we look again at the second column of table 2.6, where the GDP is shown at current prices (nominal GDP), it appears that the economy shows a significant degree of progress every year. Yet we know, from the insight we gained in the previous section, that this creates a false impression of what actually happened, since the total production of the various years was valued in terms of every year's ruling prices. In the previous section we saw that prices in general rose considerably over the same period. What we therefore actually observe in column two (table 2.6) is the rise in prices, without there necessarily having been an increase in the number of goods and services produced. That our deduction is correct, can be clearly seen from column three, where the influence of price rises on the GDP has been excluded. In this column the volume of production in the various years is valued in terms of the ruling prices in one single year, viz. 1990. We can therefore speak here of a real (or actual) GDP, the values of which have not been affected by a rise in prices. When we talk about a "real" quantity in macro-economics it always means that the influence of prices has been excluded.

The real series occurring in table 2.6 have 1990 as their base year. This means that all the different products or groups of products that the GDP consists of, are valued for every year in terms of the prices paid for these products in 1990. Since the composition of products making up the GDP will necessarily change over time, the same base year cannot be used for ever without resulting in some distortion of the figures. In order to keep the series of the real GDP as reliable as possible, the base year is therefore regularly revised (approximately every fifth year).

That the economy has not been doing too well is evident from the third column, which shows that there was actually a decrease in real production, compared with the previous year, in 1985, 1990 and 1991. If we want to make an economic analysis that will be at all useful, it is extremely important that we should work with real data. The graphic representation of the two measures of the GDP in figure 2.2 shows very clearly how price rises can give a distorted picture of economic growth within a very short period.

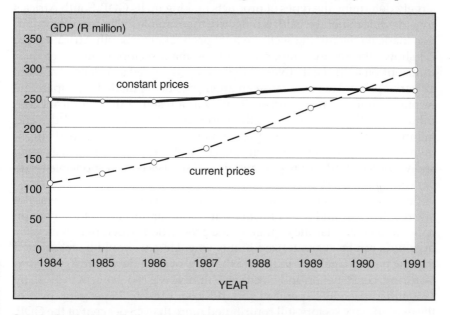

Source: South African Reserve Bank: *Quarterly Bulletin,* March 1992.

Fig. 2.2 The growth in GDP at constant and at current prices (1984–1991)

The GDP can be valued at either constant or current prices. The considerable difference between the two measures reflects the degree of inflation over the period concerned.

To get an even better idea of an increase in economic welfare it is necessary to calculate the growth in the real GDP per capita of the population. An increase of this real GDP per capita (per capita means per head) will of course supply a better measure of progress than a mere growth in real GDP. For example, if the growth in the real GDP is smaller than the growth of the population, it certainly does not indicate a higher standard of living. If we bear in mind that the population of South Africa is at present growing at 2,3 per cent per annum, the real figures in table 2.6 look even worse.

Determining the origin of the GDP

The following application relates to the origin of the GDP. In the calculation of the GDP, whether according to the factor income method or the value-added approach, one almost automatically takes into account the branches of industry or economic sectors where this income or added value originates. On this basis the parts played by the different sectors in the economy can be determined.

The extent to which a country is endowed with natural resources will largely determine the types of products making up its GDP. South Africa's considerable mineral wealth is reflected, for example, in the large contribution made by the mining sector to total production in South Africa. Figure 2.3 shows the relative importance of the main sectors in terms of their contribution to the GDP. (Note that the GDP is valued at *factor cost* and not at *market prices*. This is because an attempt is being made to compare the incomes from different sources.) Mainly as a result of the significant contribution of the mining sector, the two primary sectors (agriculture and mining) were responsible for approximately 14 per cent of the total output of the country. The services sector, which includes activities such as retail and wholesale trade, transport and financial services, is responsible for 38 per cent of the GDP.

Secondary industry accounts for almost a third of the GDP. This was not always the case, and it is a further interesting application of the data on national income that the change in the production structure of a country over time can be characterized in this way. Here it should be mentioned that the per centage contribution to the GDP of secondary industry (manufacturing, construction and electricity supply) was 9,5 per cent in 1920. By 1950 it had risen to 23 per cent and in 1960 it came to 26 per cent. In 1920 the two primary sectors still contributed more than 45 per cent of the GDP, which has declined in favour of secondary activities to approximately 14 per cent in 1991.

The composition of the national income

Apart from the origin of the national product, its composition can also be studied in terms of types of income. Figure 2.4 distinguishes between payment for labour and other kinds of income such as interest, rent and

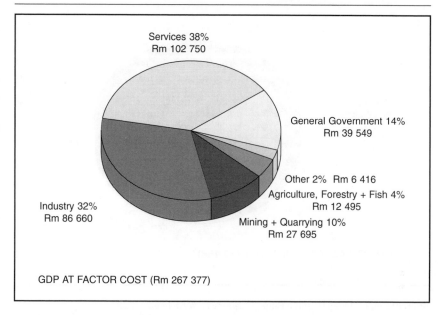

Services 38%
Rm 102 750

General Government 14%
Rm 39 549

Other 2% Rm 6 416
Agriculture, Forestry + Fish 4%
Rm 12 495

Industry 32%
Rm 86 660

Mining + Quarrying 10%
Rm 27 695

GDP AT FACTOR COST (Rm 267 377)

Source: South African Reserve Bank: *Quarterly Bulletin,* March 1992.

Fig. 2.3 The importance of the main sectors in terms of their contribution to the GDP (1991)

Secondary industry accounts for almost a third of GDP while the primary sectors (agriculture and mining) were responsible for 14 per cent of total output in 1991.

profits. This division emphasises the dominant part played by labour in the production process. Payment for wages has been one of the most stable components of the NNI over the years. During the years when the NNI does not undergo abnormal deviations, the share of labour forms approximately three quarters of the total. In exceptional years like 1980 when the national income of the country was particularly high as a result of the high gold price, labour's share represented only 62 per cent of the total. In the years of poor economic performance labour's share is high again. Although the relative share of labour may be subject to fluctuations, the absolute level of payment is particularly stable, which is an indication of the strong negotiating power of this factor of production.

Expenditure on the GDP

The final important application to be discussed is the division of the GDP according to the types of expenditure involved. Even with the simple circular flow diagram appearing in chapter 1, and in the discussion of the GDP, it was clear that the expenditure on the GDP necessarily had to be

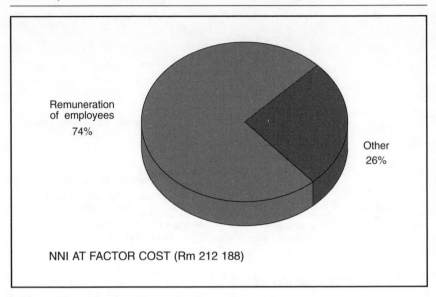

Remuneration
of employees
74%

Other
26%

NNI AT FACTOR COST (Rm 212 188)

Source: South African Reserve Bank: *Quarterly Bulletin*, March 1992.

Fig. 2.4 The composition of the Net National Income at factor cost (1991)

The diagram distinguishes between payment for labour (74%) and other kinds of income such as interest, rent and profits (26%).

equal to the value of the GDP at market prices. In the final analysis a product or service only becomes a part of the GDP when it is bought or sold. Very interesting information on the components of total demand may be obtained by means of these expenditure categories.

		R million
Private consumption expenditure (C)	(60%)	179 000
Capital expenditure (I)	(16%)	48 226
Consumption expenditure by general Government (G)	(21%)	61 856
Residual item		−7 824
Gross domestic expenditure (GDE)		281 258
Exports of goods and non-factor services (X)	(25%)	74 589
less Imports of goods and non-factor services (Z)	(20%)	59 180
Expenditure on GDP (1991)	(100%)	296 667

When the various components of expenditure are classified, it is some-times useful to distinguish between (i) the nature or type of expenditure involved and (ii) the sector of the economy in which it occurs. As regards the former, we distinguish between **consumer expenditure** and **capital expenditure**, and as regards the latter, it is sometimes desirable to deal with the following groupings or sectors individually: the **private**, the **government** and the **external sector**. In the light of this dual distinction the national accounts identify the following components:

The meaning of the different expenditure components will be dealt with in detail in chapter 3 when total demand is discussed. In this section we shall confine ourselves to a few remarks:

It is clear that the GDP, seen from an expenditure point of view, offers a new perspective that we did not have before. Private consumption expen-diture, representing the public's expenditure on goods and services, is the largest single element of expenditure in the economy. Approximately 16 per cent of the GDP is spent on capital goods, which have an influence on the production capacity of the country. This expenditure therefore leads to capital formation, which we call **investment** in economics. Since we are here concerned with the **gross** domestic product, no provision is made for depreciation in this amount of R48 226 million. The next item represents the consumption expenditure of the general government, which constitutes about 21 per cent of the GDP. Remember, however, that this amount does not include the government's capital expenditure. The latter is taken into account in investment above. Together, these three items represent the gross domestic expenditure (GDE). The residual item is ignored since it is purely a balancing item.

The treatment of imports and exports in the above statement requires further explanation. Since the total of the expenditure components must add up to the GDP at market prices, it means that all products produced in the country must be taken into account. Since the domestic expenditure items (C, I and G) do not distinguish between goods and services manufac-tured locally and those manufactured in other countries (such as French wine, Italian shoes and German machinery and equipment), all imports (Z) have to be **subtracted** from the GDE. For exactly the same reason ex-ports (X) such as coal, wool, fruit, etc. which do not form part of the GDE, but which have definitely been produced in this country, have to be **added** to the GDE. The difference between exports and imports (X – Z) is called net exports. The extent of exports and imports, which jointly constitute about 45 per cent of the GDP, are an indication of the importance of the foreign sector for the South African economy. In economic parlance we say that the South African economy is particularly "open".

From this perspective the following extremely important identity in macro-economics can be derived:

$$\text{GDP (or Y)} \equiv C + I + G + (X - Z) \dots\dots\dots\dots\dots\dots\dots\dots \quad 2.1$$

In the chapters that follow, this identity will frequently occur and often form the basis for discussion.

2.5 Some shortcomings of the GDP

So much has been said about what the GDP is supposed to measure and how the GDP itself can be measured and applied, that the impression may have been created that this is an extremely accurate and comprehensive measure of all possible economic activity. From the residual item which occurred in the previous section, it could however have been deduced that the macro-economic totals, seen purely from an accounting point of view, are not accurate. Such deviations are understandable if we look at the extent of the measuring problems involved and are not, in fact, regarded as a major problem. A far more serious criticism that can be made against the GDP and other national accounts totals is related to these estimates being used as a measure of economic welfare. The main objections are the following:

Only goods and services appearing on a market and therefore with a **market price**, are included in the calculations. This principle has for instance resulted in the value of a meal at a restaurant being fully included in the GDP, while a similar meal prepared at home (apart from the purchased ingredients) is excluded. This applies to all work done by housewives. When a motor-car is serviced at a garage, the GDP is increased because of the service rendered, but if it is serviced at home the GDP is not affected.

Closely related to the above problem is the large number of transactions which do go through the market but are never recorded anywhere so that they can be included in the measurement of the GDP. Examples of such transactions are the wages of many gardeners, repairs done at home, lift clubs, as well as all illegal activities such as smuggling. Such activities are known as the **informal sector** or the **unrecorded economy**. This sector is regarded by many economists as extremely important in South Africa's struggle against unemployment. Although by definition no accurate assessment can be made of the scope of these activities, they are thought by some to represent as much as 30–40 per cent of the official GDP. Even if this estimate is grossly exaggerated, it is apparent that the underground economy, as it is sometimes called, can make a significant contribution towards the welfare of South Africa's heterogeneous population. For this reason the government has given official recognition to the possibilities of the informal sector and the authorities are at present more inclined to encourage the development of healthy activities in this sector.

The inclusion of goods and services for which a market price can be determined, has also had the effect that certain negative elements can lead to an increase in the GDP. In South Africa a deterioration of the security situation on the country's borders will lead to increased defence expenditure (and a consequent increase in the GDP), which can hardly be regarded as an increase in welfare. Increased production is often accompanied by increased pollution. But no correction is made in the GDP for this decline in welfare. Finally, it should also be noted that the availability of leisure time (i.e. a shorter working day or week) is not reflected in the GDP measure.

Economists who were concerned about the possible misrepresentations which could result from the above defects, attempted to find a more acceptable measure of economic welfare. They endeavoured to determine the impact of factors such as leisure time, pollution, the inconvenience of overpopulated cities, etc. in terms of money and to add or subtract it from the GDP. Unfortunately the problems involved in establishing such a measure were so complex and extensive that these attempts were largely a failure. The GDP and other similar macro-economic totals remain, in spite of their defects, the best indication of the level of economic activity maintained during a specific period.

Selected references:

Baumol & Blinder: 7 appendix B.
Dernburg: 2, 11.
Dornbusch & Fischer: 2.
Evans-Pritchard: 2, 3, 4.
Froyen: 2, 8.
Gordon: 2, Appendix A.
Mohr, PJ; Van der Merwe, C; Botha, ZC and Inggs, J. 1988. *The Practical Guide to South African Economic Indicators*. Johannesburg: Lexicon Publishers, Various sections.
Morley: 2, 6.
Shapiro: 1, 2, 3.

3 Total spending and income determination

NOT MULTIPLIER   NO MATHEMATICS PROOF

As indicated in chapter 1, we are going to use a basic model to analyse the functioning of the macro-economy. For this purpose we shall employ the aggregate demand and supply model. Before the aggregate demand and supply curves, which constitute the model, are derived in the next chapter, we are going to look in this chapter at the various components of aggregate demand and the influence they exercise on the determination of income. We have seen that macro-economics was, until quite recently, mainly concerned with problems arising on the demand side. Supply, on the other hand, was largely ignored, since the macro-economic problems involved were mainly related to a variable aggregate demand. The simple approach adopted in this chapter can in fact be associated with a Keynesian analysis where inflation plays no part. In the model of income determination developed in this chapter, we concentrate solely on demand-side factors while prices are being ignored completely. The implications of such an approach will only become clear in the next chapter, when we have to deal with the actual aggregate demand curve. Only then will the total demanded be seen in the context of the **general price level**.

3.1 The composition of the demand for GDP

The basic background to this chapter was given in the previous chapter when we identified the expenditure components of the GDP. We intend now to examine in greater detail the components appearing in equation 2.1. The amount spent on output in South Africa (as well as the composition of this expenditure) for the period 1984–1991, is shown in table 3.1. The data are expressed in current prices as well as in constant prices (1985), i.e. in real terms. The first important item requiring our attention is that of **gross domestic expenditure**, i.e. the value of all expenditure on goods and services in South Africa during a specific year. During the period indicated in table 3.1 (1984–1991) gross domestic expenditure increased from R105 021 million to R281 258 million, an increase of 166 per cent. The greater part of this increase can however be attributed to inflation, as in real terms

Table 3.1

Expenditure on Gross Domestic Product, 1984–1991

	1984	1985	1986	1987	1988	1989	1990	1991
At current prices								
Private consumption expenditure	59 705	66 167	77 965	93 353	111 324	131 940	154 675	179 000
Consumption expenditure by general government[1]	17 927	21 297	25 672	30 599	35 276	43 946	51 028	61 856
Gross domestic fixed investment	26 209	28 715	28 707	31 497	39 381	48 575	53 176	53 957
	485	– 3 734	–1 702	355	3 230	961	–2 549	–5 731
Residual item	695	–883	–2 382	–4 798	–1 680	–4 655	–8 021	–7 824
Gross domestic expenditure	105 021	111 562	128 260	151 006	187 531	220 767	248 309	281 258
Exports of goods and non-factor services	28 182	39 973	45 856	48 791	56 923	66 317	69 487	74 589
Less: Imports of goods and non-factor services	25 982	28 409	31 981	35 273	46 544	53 950	53 984	59 180
Expenditure on gross domestic product	107 221	123 126	142 135	164 524	197 910	233 134	263 812	296 667
At constant 1985 prices								
Private consumption expenditure	68 536	66 167	66 272	68 827	72 453	74 478	76 026	76 148
Consumption expenditure by general government[1]	20 589	21 297	21 785	22 600	22 975	23 822	24 223	25 600
Gross domestic fixed investment	30 885	28 715	23 493	22 929	24 977	26 260	25 819	23 646
Change in inventories[2]	421	–3 734	–1 638	291	2 112	519	–2 887	–2 626
Residual item	870	–883	1 717	276	1 952	–1 294	–2 633	–2 699
Gross domestic expenditure	121 301	111 562	111 629	114 923	124 469	123 785	120 548	120 069

	1984	1985	1986	1987	1988	1989	1990	1991
Exports of goods and non-factor services	36 609	39 973	39 288	39 890	41 391	45 254	46 799	47 380
Less: Imports of goods and non-factor services	33 274	28 409	27 769	29 078	34 844	35 014	33 938	34 801
Expenditure on gross domestic product	124 636	123 126	123 148	125 735	131 016	134 025	133 409	132 648

1. Current expenditure on salaries and wages and on goods and other services of a non-capital nature of the general departments, but not the business enterprises, of public authorities. Public authorities include central authorities, provincial administration and local authorities of the defined territory and extra-budgetary funds.

2. After inventory valuation adjustment.

Source: South African Reserve Bank: *Quarterly Bulletin,* March 1992.

Table 3.1 *This table shows how GDP has been applied to the various major expenditure items over the period 1984–1992. Note the significant difference between the data at current prices in one part of the table and the data at constant 1985 prices in the other part. This difference is, of course, the result of inflation.*

there was an actual decrease of 1 per cent from R121 301 million to R120 069 million (compared to a 6,3 per cent increase in real GDP over the same period).

The composition of gross domestic expenditure

Table 3.1 also shows that *gross domestic expenditure is the sum of three expenditure items*:

1. **Private consumption expenditure,** also known as consumption and abbreviated to C;
2. **consumption expenditure by general government,** sometimes referred to as current government expenditure and abbreviated to G;
3. **gross domestic investment,** consisting of **fixed** domestic investment and changes in inventories. This item is often simply referred to as investment and abbreviated to I. An item frequently included in I (but appearing separately in the table) is the **change in inventories**.

The residual item is used to reconcile the expenditure items (demand) with the income/product items (supply). This is merely a correction of the statistical discrepancy (between total expenditure and the GDP) and plays no further part in our analysis.

Although the symbols C, G and I are largely self-explanatory, they will be getting more attention in later sections of this chapter. In table 3.2 these totals are expressed as percentages of the gross domestic product (GDP). The table shows that 53 to 60 per cent of the GDP consists of private consumer spending. The second most important item, which represents about a fifth of the GDP, is investment (I), while G, or current government expenditure, takes the third place. The share of current government expenditure shows a rising trend which, in some years, made it almost equal to investment. In 1991 G even exceeded I. This percentage nevertheless still underestimates the importance of the role of government in the economy, since the government's capital expenditure is not reflected here. As we shall see in table 3.4, the public sector plays a decisive part in domestic investment.

Table 3.2

The components of gross expenditure as a percentage of gross domestic product (GDP), 1984–1991

	1984	1985	1986	1987	1988	1989	1990	1991
Private consumption expenditure (C)	55,7	53,7	54,9	56,7	56,2	56,6	58,6	60,3
Consumption expenditure by general government (G)	16,7	17,3	18,1	18,6	17,8	18,9	19,3	20,9
Gross domestic fixed investment(I)	24,4	23,3	20,2	19,1	19,9	20,8	20,2	18,2
Change in inventories	0,5	−3,0	−1,2	0,2	1,6	0,4	−1,0	−1,9
Gross domestic expenditure	97,9	90,6	90,2	91,8	94,8	94,7	94,1	94,8
Exports (X)	26,3	32,5	32,3	29,7	28,8	28,4	26,3	25,1
Imports (Z)	24,2	23,1	22,5	21,4	23,5	23,1	20,5	19,9

Source: South African Reserve Bank: *Quarterly Bulletin,* March 1992.

Table 3.2 *Here we see the expenditure items of table 3.1 expressed as a percentage of GDP. Consumer spending is clearly the most important item. The part played by the government is actually larger than is indicated here, since a part of the gross domestic investment (cf. table 3.4) is investment by public authorities and public corporations.*

The role of imports and exports

Although gross domestic expenditure (GDE = C + G + I) is a measure of the amount spent by residents on the items concerned, this is not the full story. As we explained in the previous chapter, exports (X) must be added to the GDE in order to obtain a more accurate idea of the total amount required from local manufacturers. Imports (Z), on the other hand, which are included in the domestic expenditure items (C, I and G), cause the GDE to overestimate the aggregate demand for domestic production and must therefore be subtracted from the other items in the table. The reason for including imports with the other components is that some consumer goods (C) are directly imported by the consumers. In fact, as we shall see in chapter 8, a large proportion of imports are capital goods (I) which are used in the production of consumer and other goods.

Table 3.2 also shows quite clearly the importance of imports and exports in the South African economy. With the exception of 1990 and 1991, when the joint share of these two components represented less than 50 per cent of the GDP, this percentage has always been higher than 50 per cent. In 1980 (owing to the rise in the gold price during that year) exports alone contributed almost 36 per cent to the GDP. In our analysis these two foreign items are just as important as the traditional and better known totals, such as C, G and I.

3.2   The nature and composition of consumption

We mentioned earlier on that one of the advantages we have today is the availability of high quality data. We saw this in chapter 2 and it also applies to this section. Table 3.3, for example, gives details on consumption which are broken down into a number of functional categories, and also subdivided according to the durability of the various consumption items (the data are also available in constant prices or real values). Although the information contained in table 3.3 is largely self-explanatory, it will nevertheless be useful to look at a few of the more striking features in greater detail.

The information in table 3.3 gives a good indication of the variety of ways in which consumers can spend their money. At the same time, it shows the complexity of their choices. In the first place, consumer goods can be divided into four broad categories which are distinguished according to their degree of durability.

Durable goods

The first group consists of **durable goods**. This type of commodity can be used repeatedly in the consumption process and has an expected life of one year or more. Examples are on the one hand, furniture and household

Table 3.3

Private consumption expenditure, 1984–1991, at current prices (R million)

	1984	1985	1986	1987	1988	1989	1990	1991
Durable goods	6 490	6 034	6 669	9 054	11 478	13 171	15 641	17 657
Furniture, household appliances etc.	2 156	2 172	2 538	3 248	4 277	4 865	6 039	6 603
Personal transport equipment	2 839	2 404	2 540	4 032	4 860	5 433	5 946	6 911
Recreational and entertainment goods	982	969	1 070	1 263	1 722	2 137	2 680	3 024
Other durable goods[1]	513	489	521	511	619	736	976	1 119
Semi-durable goods	9 384	10 352	12 081	14 594	18 192	22 053	25 895	29 302
Clothing and footwear	4 430	4 641	5 491	6 740	8 189	9 950	11 553	13 095
Household textiles furnishings, glassware etc.	1 268	1 459	1 760	2 219	3 071	3 763	4 250	4 606
Vehicle tyres, parts and accessories	1 502	1 762	2 089	2 594	3 129	3 546	4 063	4 746
Recreational and entertainment goods	1 008	1 147	1 219	1 278	1 620	2 084	2 771	3 110
Miscellaneous goods[2]	1 176	1 343	1 522	1 763	2 183	2 710	3 258	3 745
Non-durable goods	26 836	30 766	37 234	44 453	52 552	62 166	73 620	87 432
Food, beverages and tobacco	19 925	22 528	27 905	34 157	40 489	47 333	56 205	67 547
Household fuel and power	1 556	1 773	2 108	2 449	2 937	3 394	3 989	4 605
Household consumer goods	1 619	1 638	1 950	2 166	2 528	2 878	3 381	3 897
Medical and pharmaceutical products	894	1 047	1 294	1 499	1 802	2 260	2 736	3 224
Pretroleumproducts	2 236	3 088	3 146	3 226	3 667	4 810	5 587	6 228
Recreational and entertainment goods	606	692	831	956	1 129	1 491	1 722	1 931

1. Jewellery, watches, therapeutic appliances, etc.
2. Personal goods and writing and drawing equipment and supplies.

(Table 3.3 continued)

	1984	1985	1986	1987	1988	1989	1990	1991
Services	16 995	19 015	21 981	25 252	29 102	34 550	39 519	44 609
Rent[3]	5 647	6 228	7 068	8 067	9 090	10 637	11 686	12 230
Household services including domestic servants	1 452	1 638	1 874	2 091	2 253	2 419	2 793	3 306
Medical services	1 650	1 898	2 161	2 527	3 115	4 138	5 075	5 990
Transport & communication services	3 204	3 779	4 343	4 922	5 857	6 682	7 710	8 882
Recreational, entertainment and educational services	1 841	2 133	2 485	3 014	3 543	4 618	5 332	6 212
Miscel. services[4]	3 201	3 339	4 050	4 631	5 244	6 056	6 923	7 989
Total private consumption expenditure	59 705	66 167	77 965	93 353	111 324	131 940	154 675	179 000

3. Including imputed rent for owner-occupied dwellings.
4. After adjustment for net expenditure of foreigners in the domestic market.

Source: South African Reserve Bank: *Quarterly Bulletin*, March 1992.

Table 3.3 *This is a more comprehensive listing of all the different items of consumer spending. It gives a good indication of the many decisions consumers have to make regarding their budgets.*

equipment, and, on the other hand, motor vehicles. Table 3.3 shows, *inter alia*, that expenditure on these two items represents approximately 80 per cent of total expenditure on durable goods.

An interesting point in this connection is the fact that the most durable of all goods, viz. housing, does not appear in this grouping. The reason is that expenditure on new houses is regarded as investment.

Semi-durable and non-durable goods

The second category in table 3.3 is called **semi-durable goods**. These goods obviously do not last as long as durable goods and are not as expensive either. In other words, durability is, strictly speaking, not the only criterion used to distinguish one type of commodity from another. In any case, the table shows that considerably more is spent on semi-durable goods than on durable goods. Of this group, clothes and shoes are easily the most important and expenditure on these items has in certain years exceeded joint expenditure on furniture and motor vehicles.

According to the durability criterion, the greatest single category is that of **non-durable goods**. Such goods are either perishable (e.g. fresh vegetables or flowers) or are used only once (food, fuel, etc.). The table shows that almost 50 per cent of consumer spending was on non-durable goods. Of this, the largest amount was spent on food, beverages and tobacco (almost three-quarters of the non-durable goods).

Expenditure on services

Between a quarter and a third of total consumption is spent on **services** such as medical, domestic, transport and recreational services, and on rent. The item "rent" is probably the most interesting since it includes "imputed rent on owner-occupied housing". This agrees with the point we mentioned a moment ago, viz. that spending on the building of houses is regarded as investment. In other words, if a person lives in his own house, an amount equal to the amount he would have paid in rent, is added to his income. Of all consumer goods, services are of course the least durable. They are, you could say, used up as they are produced; take for example the services of a doctor, a taxi driver or the owner of a theatre.

Consumer spending and economic fluctuations

Naturally, the purchasing of semi-durable and even durable goods can be postponed if the consumer does not find himself in a favourable financial position, for example when his income is falling or rising more slowly than before; or if credit is not so freely available. The result is that expenditure on durable and semi-durable goods is usually more erratic than that on non-durables.

For instance, it is interesting to note that expenditure on durable consumer goods (at the top of table 3.3) shows a drop in absolute terms for the years 1985 and 1986 if the figures are expressed in real terms – i.e. in constant prices. An important implication of the variability of this part of consumer spending, is the fact that it can also be the *cause* – rather than the effect, as stated above – of poor (or good) economic conditions.

3.3   Consumer spending and the level of income

In section 3.1 it was stated with reference to table 3.2 that consumption spending (C) is the largest single item of domestic expenditure. It is customary to mention at the same time that consumption comprises a relatively stable percentage of income and that it is subject to fewer fluctuations than investment (I), which we shall discuss in more detail in the next section.

Consumer spending is more stable and predictable than investment in spite of the variability of expenditure on durable and semi-durable goods, as discussed in the previous section. The reason for this is that spending on non-durable goods largely overshadows the other expenditure items.

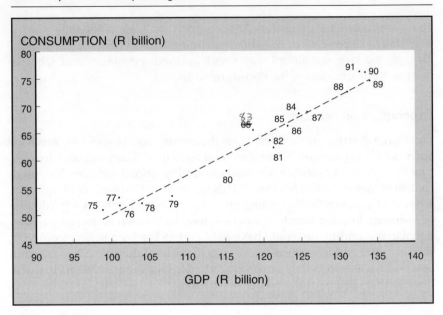

Source: South African Reserve Bank: *Quarterly Bulletin,* March 1992.

Fig. 3.1 Scatter diagram: Consumption and GDP, 1975 to 1991 (constant 1985 prices)

The diagram shows a clear ratio between the level of the GDP and that of private consumer expenditure, both calculated at constant prices.

Consumption and the scatter diagram

The relative stability of consumer spending can be gauged from a comparison of data showing consumer spending at constant prices and GDP figures at constant prices in table 3.1. Taking real consumption as a percentage of the real GDP, percentages of very close to 50 per cent are derived. In other words, in real terms consumption constitutes a relatively stable part of the gross domestic product. This ratio can also be illustrated in a diagram, as in figure 3.1.

Figure 3.1 is a **scatter diagram**. In this case the value of the real GDP (or the GDP at constant 1985 prices) is measured on the horizontal axis. On the vertical axis we measure consumer spending in real terms. Beginning with the final year 1991, we first find the real value of the GDP in table 3.1, viz. R132 648 million. In the same year real consumption expenditure amounted to R76 148 million. These two figures provide us with a point in the diagram which is indicated by the figure 91. In the same way, the other points can be traced backwards in the diagram up to and including 1975. The scatter diagram contains more points than the data appearing in table

3.1. The points for the years 1975 to 1983 are based on similar information to that given in table 3.1.

These points are scattered across the diagram – hence the name "scatter diagram". But the points do not occur at random in the diagram; they are scattered according to a definite pattern. The higher the GDP, the higher the consumer spending normally associated with it. This ratio can be represented by a straight line which, apart from a few years, runs fairly close to the points. The straight line therefore indicates the approximate value of real consumer spending at various levels of real GDP. Since C increases from left to right, this means that, in terms of real figures, it can normally be assumed that consumption will increase if there is a rise in the level of income or production, and that it will fall if the GDP decreases. As can be seen from the points on the scatter diagram in figure 3.1, this general conclusion does not apply to every year. Such exceptions prove once again that Economics is not an exact science.

The consumption function

Figure 3.1 serves as a preparation for figure 3.2, one of the most important types of diagram in macro-economics, viz. the **expenditure diagram**. Actually, the diagram is fairly similar to the scatter diagram in figure 3.1. The most important difference lies in the fact that the vertical axis measures not only consumption (as in figure 3.1), but all expenditure, including consumption expenditure, as we shall see. In the figure we call this TS (total spending).

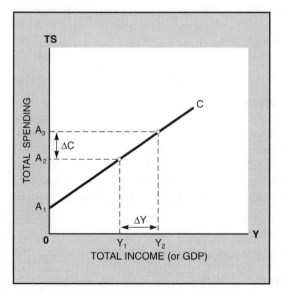

Fig. 3.2 The consumption function

The line C is called the consumption function and is the generalisation of C in figure 3.1. Note that consumption is thought not to fall to zero when Y falls to zero (cf. the distance OA_1).

The horizontal axis measures Y, or the real GDP, as we have called it thus far. But now we want to go one step further than merely defining Y as the gross domestic **product**. It is very important to realise, within the context of the total expenditure diagram, that the horizontal axis also measures **income**. In chapter 2 we explained why, in principle, the value of income and product (i.e. the amount produced) is the same. We shall come back to this, but bear it in mind in the meantime.

The C line in figure 3.2 is called the **consumption function**. This is a generalisation of the trend found in figure 3.1. The first principle with regard to the nature of the consumption function is quite simple. From personal experience and introspection you will no doubt agree with the statement that as income increases, individuals are enabled to spend larger amounts on consumption (especially on the more expensive durables and semi-durables). It is fairly certain that a similar ratio will obtain for the economy as a whole and that hence C will rise as income increases – this is also borne out by practical experience as reflected in table 3.1.

The marginal propensity to consume

A second principle reflected in the consumption function, is that while consumption does in fact increase when there is a rise in income, it increases by a *smaller* amount than the rise in income. In the diagram, for example, income rises by ΔY from the level Y_1 to Y_2, while consumption increases from A_2 to A_3; this amount, ΔC, is however smaller than ΔY. A consumption function with a steeper slope than that in figure 3.2 would imply that a greater proportion of the additional income was spent on consumption. The additional amount consumed can never, of course, exceed the additional income earned. In technical terms, this means that the gradient of the consumption function cannot be greater than *one*. It also implies that the ratio $\frac{\Delta C}{\Delta Y}$, as in figure 3.2, must necessarily be smaller than one ($\frac{\Delta C}{\Delta Y} < 1$). This ratio is called the **marginal propensity to consume**.

A final characteristic of the consumption function that is of importance to us is that consumption cannot fall to zero. People have to live, even if income falls to zero. This is represented by the intersection A_1 of the C line with the vertical axis in figure 3.2. This distance OA_1 can, in a certain sense, be regarded as the minimum consumption necessary to keep a community alive. It is also called autonomous consumption since it is independent of the level of income.

The position of the consumption function

The position of the consumption function in the diagram depends on a

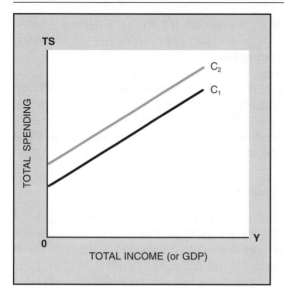

Fig. 3.3 The position of the consumption function

The position of the consumption function depends on a number of non-income factors. The stability of C is taken to mean that a shift, e.g. from C_1 to C_2, will not easily take place.

number of non-income factors. Consumption has its counterpart in saving, since the part of income that is not consumed, is saved. The level of consumption in a community will therefore depend, *inter alia*, on the **attitude of people in respect of economic independence** and the provision made for their old age. The greater the desire to be independent, the more people will save and the lower the position of the consumption function will be. Saving is also related to the **distribution of income**; the assumption here is that the more rich people there are, the more *can* be saved and the lower the level of the consumption function will be. Compare for example C_1 and C_2 in figure 3.3. **Age distribution** also plays an important part here, as the more old people there are in the community, the greater the consumption will be. Finally, consumption expenditure will also be influenced by the **value** of **durable goods** already in the hands of the consumers. The more of these goods they possess, the smaller the need to buy more and consequently the lower the position of the consumption function.

One is justified in assuming that the above-mentioned factors are not subject to sudden change and on this basis the relative stability of the consumption function may be explained, since it means that the consumption function will not easily move up or down. However, there are other factors more immediately affecting the consumption function's position in the diagram.

The first of these is consumers' **holdings of financial assets**. The real value of such assets is affected by the general price level. A rise in the price level lowers the real value of bank balances etc., thus making people poorer in general and possibly forcing them to spend less. This effect may however be cancelled by a second factor, viz. **expectations**. It can for instance happen that a rise in prices leads to the expectation of even higher prices, which then results in **increased consumption**.

As we have seen in the previous section, durable goods constitute an important part of consumption and it is therefore to be expected that **consumer credit** and the conditions laid down by the government in this respect will have a significant influence. A related factor is the **rate** of **interest**. The higher the interest rate, the more expensive a product will be if it is purchased on credit and the less will be spent on such goods.

3.4   Investment and the level of income

We now come to the expenditure item which is generally considered to be the most variable and the least predictable of the three categories of domestic expenditure: **investment**. This item is often regarded as the chief cause of fluctuations in economic activity.

As in the case of consumption, there is more to investment than the mere symbol I or so many millions of rands in a table. Investment is **capital formation**, i.e. the **production** of **goods** which are the **means of production**, such as buildings, machinery, etc.; it is therefore capital which can be distinguished from other factors of production such as natural resources (land) and human resources (labour and entrepreneurship). In this connection, it should be remembered that "investment" in an existing asset, e.g. the buying of a house, is not regarded as investment in the sense of capital formation, since no new asset is created in the present period. Such "investment" constitutes no more than a change in ownership of both money and the asset concerned.

Fixed investment versus changes in inventories

Before continuing, we should first reconsider the fact that a part of investment does not consist of machinery or other durable means of production such as buildings. Some investment goes into inventories, i.e. goods of any kind, including raw materials and consumer goods that have not reached their final destination in the year concerned. If you turn back to table 3.1, you will see that this item is called the **change in inventories**. In other words, **additions** to inventories are included in investment; if inventories have decreased, i.e. if **disinvestment** has occurred, this amount is subtracted from investment.

Judging by table 3.1, there can be little doubt that inventory investment is an extremely volatile component of South Africa's expenditure pattern. During the period 1984–1991 the change in inventories varied from a positive entry of over R3 200 million in 1988 to a negative amount of R5 731 million in 1991. Although these amounts are by no means negligible, the most significant component of total gross investment is **fixed investment**.

By adding gross domestic fixed investment to the change in inventories, we get a total known as "gross domestic investment" (see table 3.4). In 1991, for example, these totals amounted to R53 957 million (gross domestic investment) and –R5 731 million (change in inventories); the total of R48 226 million is shown as **gross domestic investment** in table 3.4.

Gross versus net investment

In the previous chapter we pointed out that the national income totals can be changed from a "gross" to a "net" evaluation basis by subtracting an allowance for depreciation. Depreciation is the amount by which fixed

Table 3.4

Gross and net domestic investment according to type of organization, 1984–1991 at current prices

	1984	1985	1986	1987	1988	1989	1990	1991
Gross domestic investment[1]	26 694	24 981	27 005	31 852	42 611	49 536	50 627	48 226
Public authorities	5 758	6 627	6 706	7 049	8 003	9 053	9 364	10 382
Public corporations	4 711	5 441	5 435	3 950	5 296	8 118	6 376	6 147
Private business enterprises	16 225	12 913	14 864	20 853	29 312	32 365	34 887	31 697
Provision for depreciation[2]	16 121	19 645	24 697	27 998	32 442	38 402	43 058	47 007
Public authorities	2 690	3 010	3 533	4 089	4 895	5 665	6 529	7 083
Public corporations	2 737	3 486	4 580	5 173	5 960	7 078	7 938	8 650
Private business enterprises	10 694	13 149	16 584	18 736	21 587	25 659	28 591	31 274
Net domestic investment	10 573	5 336	2 308	3 854	10 169	11 134	7 569	1 219
Public authorities	3 068	3 617	3 173	2 960	3 108	3 388	2 835	3 299
Public corporations	1 974	1 955	855	–1 223	–664	1 040	–1 562	–2 503
Private business enterprises	5 531	–236	–1 720	2 117	7 725	6 706	6 296	423

1. After inventory valuation adjustment.
2. At replacement value.

Source: South African Reserve Bank: *Quarterly Bulletin*, March 1992.

Table 3.4 *Gross domestic investment is equal to fixed investment plus change in inventories (cf. table 3.1). This table shows the importance of the allowance for depreciation (concentrated in the private sector), so that net investment is dominated by the government and public corporations.*

investments decrease in value as a result of obsolescence and wear and tear. The value of **net investment** can therefore be derived by subtracting such an allowance for depreciation from **gross investment**. The relevant totals are given in table 3.4.

According to the table, the allowance for depreciation constitutes a large section of gross investment. Without exception depreciation amounted to considerably more than 50 per cent of gross investment. The lack of investment which has characterised the South African economy over the past few years can be clearly seen from the tremendously high percentages of gross domestic investment constituted by depreciation. Conditions gradually worsened until percentages of 85 and 97 were reached in 1990 and 1991. The adverse effect this has had on the extent of net domestic investment is obvious from the negligible amounts realised from 1985 to 1987 and since 1990.

Net investment is a very important concept since it gives an indication of the extent to which (if at all) the capital stock of a country has increased over a certain period – especially if the calculation is done at constant prices. Nevertheless, just as in the case of **gross** domestic product, **gross** investment is regarded as the more significant of the two investment totals, since it shows what has **actually** been bought or spent during the period concerned.

Investment by type of organisation

Table 3.4 also shows how domestic investment is distributed between three types of organisations: public authorities (central, provincial and local government), public corporations and private business enterprises. Since a few public corporations are still under the direct control of central government, the importance of the role of the government in South Africa's investment processes is evident.

The allowance for depreciation sometimes plays a somewhat surprising role. During 1985 and 1986 depreciation in respect of private business enterprises exceeded gross investment. This meant that net investment by the private sector was negative for those years. As a result, the share of public authorities in net domestic investment was more than 100 per cent! Proponents of a free-market economy are decidedly concerned about this state of affairs. The year 1988 was of course a more favourable year, as can be seen from the fact that the relevant figures for private net investment were higher.

The formal treatment of investment

In contrast to consumer spending, investment is not regarded as a function of income. In other words, investment is taken to be independent of the level of income. The scatter diagram in figure 3.4, which reflects investment and the GDP for the period 1975–1991, shows that such a statement is not far-fetched. As the points in the diagram clearly indicate, there is no obvious pattern to be discerned from a comparison of investment and the GDP. Investment is clearly too variable a quantity.

In a more theoretical context, e.g. that in figure 3.5, investment is represented as being similar to a straight line A_1I, running parallel to the horizontal axis. This line shows that investment is equal to OA_1, irrespective of the level of income. In contrast to consumption, which consists of two separate components, investment **as a whole** is regarded as being autonomous. As there is no indication of a marginal propensity to invest, the gradient of the investment function will also be equal to zero. If consumption is represented by the consumption function A_2C, investment at various levels of income can be added to it. The result is the line $(C + I)$ which shows the total of consumption and investment at various levels of income. Since C increases together with Y, $(C + I)$ will increase at the same rate and is therefore parallel to A_2C.

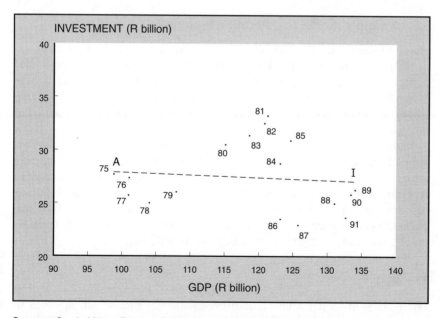

Source: South African Reserve Bank: *Quarterly Bulletin*, March 1992.

Fig. 3.4 Scatter diagram, Investment and the GDP, 1975–1991 (constant 1990 prices)

This scatter diagram shows that there is no apparent connection between investment and the GDP.

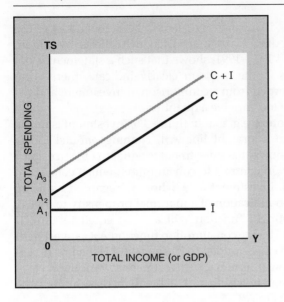

Fig. 3.5 Adding I to C
The line A_1I is similar to AI in figure 3.4. If A_2C represents the consumption function, then $A_3(C+I)$ represents the sum of investment and consumption at various levels of income.

3.5   A simple model to determine income

Having established the theoretical connection between the two main expenditure items and the level of income in the last two sections, we can now proceed to a more formal model of income determination. It should always be remembered that, in spite of our knowledge of the trend of C and I, we still do not know at which level income (or production) will stabilise on the horizontal axis of the expenditure diagram.

In order to keep the discussion as simple as possible, we shall make **two simplified assumptions**. Firstly, we shall assume an imaginary economy with no **government**, and secondly that this economy has no relations with **foreign countries**. These assumptions will enable us to ignore the other components of total expenditure, viz. government spending (G), imports (Z) and exports (X), for the present. Here total expenditure consists only of consumer expenditure and investment (C + I).

The 45° line

The next step in the analysis comprises the 45° line which appears in figure 3.6 as a dotted line. This line shows all the points where expenditure is equal to income; it is therefore the line where TS = Y, and this equivalence can occur nowhere else in the diagram. Since both the axes are on the same scale, the 45° line means that any horizontal distance can be converted to an equal vertical distance. This line is therefore a **line of equilibrium** since

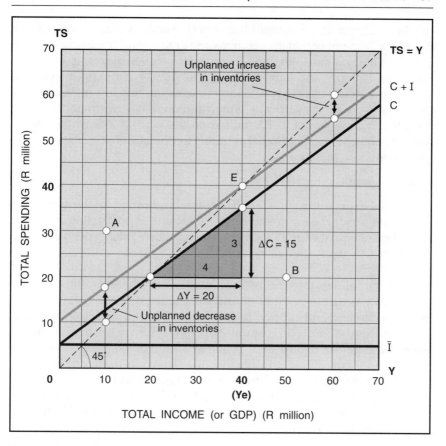

Fig. 3.6 A model for income determination

At the point of equilibrium E the total expenditure is equal to total production (or income). At any other point on the C + I line there would be an unplanned decrease or increase in inventories. The equilibrium level of income will therefore be equal to R40 million (cf. Y_e).

it connects all possible points in the diagram where no excess demand or excess supply is possible. For example, point A in the diagram represents a condition of excess demand (expenditure = 30 and production = 10) and point B represents a condition of excess supply (expenditure = 20 and production = 50). Such points are obviously not points of equilibrium, since they cannot continue to exist for any length of time.

In terms of the national accounts discussed in the previous chapter, the two axes in the figure may be associated with the real expenditure on the GDP (vertical axis) and the real GDP at market prices (horizontal axis). According to our assumptions, we recognise only C and I as possible components of expenditure on the vertical axis.

In addition to the 45° line, the diagram also contains a consumption function (C) and an investment function (I), similar to those occurring in figure 3.5. Remember that the positions and gradients of these functions are based on observations obtained by means of scatter diagrams. The only difference is that C and I are drawn to a fictitious scale in figure 3.6. You will, for example, notice that autonomous consumption (the intersection of the C function with the vertical axis) and autonomous investment are, quite fortuitously, both equal to R5 million on the vertical axis in the figure. Remember that these amounts are entirely fictitious and do not necessarily correspond to actual figures.

In the diagram we therefore have:

(i)   a total expenditure function (C + I line) indicating total expenditure (or demand) at each possible level of income or production.

(ii) a line of equilibrium (TS = Y) indicating where total expenditure will be exactly equivalent to income.

From this it follows that the intersection between these two lines (E) can be the only possible point of equilibrium since it ensures equivalence between demand and supply. In order to reconcile a principle of equilibrium in this diagram with the point of equilibrium in micro-economics, we must therefore regard the 45° line as a kind of "supply curve". It is not a supply curve, but it fulfils a similar function in determining the equilibrium in figure 3.6 (cf. for example figs. 1.8 and 1.9 in chapter 1). According to the above, it is clear that **equilibrium income** must be equal to R40 million. Any other level of income will inevitably lead to excess demand or supply.

The case of excess supply

This logic can be further elucidated. Suppose manufacturers believed they would be able to sell goods to the value of R60 million, which they then produce. Since production and income are identical on the horizontal axis, we know that the level of income will now also have to be R60 million. But according to the consumption function (C) we note that at this level of income people have only planned to consume R50 million and to invest (I) R5 million. Total expenditure (C + I) would therefore be R55 million, which means that the R5 million not sold by the producers would have to be retained as **unplanned** inventories. Since more has been produced than has been sold, a condition of over-supply would exist. In a national accounting table such as table 3.1, this amount is entered as an increase in inventories. Unfortunately the figures as such do not show whether or not it was a planned increase.

Since production is intended to be sold, such an accumulation of **un-**

wanted inventories would be an indication (or a sign) to entrepreneurs that they are overproducing. They would therefore decrease production and since production and income are identical in value, the income level would decrease in the direction of the equilibrium income level. Incidentally, we do not at this stage of the analysis assume that there is any decrease in the level of prices. As we have said, prices are not taken into account in this analysis.

The case of excess demand

Exactly the opposite condition is represented at an income level of e.g. R10 million. Expenditure exceeds the value of production at this level of income by R7,5 million, which means that entrepreneurs now experience an un-planned **decrease in inventories**. They will therefore expand production and this will automatically lead to an increase in income in the direction of Y_e. (Remember that the value of income and production are identical.)

The conclusion from figure 3.6 is that the level of Y will tend to move towards Y_e, determined by intersection E of the C + I line and the 45° line. At Y_e the amount produced is equal to expenditure and no unwanted accumulation or decrease of inventories therefore occurs. For this reason Y_e is called an **equilibrium income.**

The consumption function as an equation

The important part played by the position and gradient of especially the consumption function in the above analysis, makes it essential to consider its characteristics in greater detail. As we have seen, the ratio $\frac{\Delta C}{\Delta Y}$ is called the marginal propensity to consume, since it indicates the extent to which consumption will increase if there is an increase in income. Assuming that $\frac{\Delta C}{\Delta Y} = \frac{3}{4}$, as is the case in figure 3.6, it follows that for every 4 units by which income increases, consumption will increase by 3 units. More generally, we could say that for every R1,00 increase in Y, C would increase by 75c. According to the scale in figure 3.6 $\frac{\Delta C}{\Delta Y} = \frac{15}{20}$, which is also equal to $\frac{3}{4}$.

It is interesting to note that the relationship between C and Y, indicated by means of a straight line and a positive gradient (C line), can also be expressed in the form of an equation:

$$C = \overline{C} + cY \quad \dots\dots\dots\dots\dots\dots\dots\dots\dots\dots\dots\dots\dots\dots\dots\dots\dots\dots \quad 3.1$$

where $\overline{C} > 0$ and $c < 1$ but > 0

For those who do not quite understand the algebraic representation, we can explain this as follows:

(i) $\overline{C}$ in the equation is the autonomous portion of consumption which is independent of the level of income. It is also equal to the intercept on the vertical axis. In the figure $\overline{C}$ = R5 million. Remember, a constant is always indicated by a dash above the symbol.

(ii) c represents the marginal propensity to consume ($\frac{\Delta C}{\Delta Y}$) or the gradient of the consumption function. In the figure it can be seen that the gradient is equal to $\frac{3}{4}$ or 0,75.

(iii) The equation therefore distinguishes clearly between the two components of consumption:
(a) autonomous consumption ($\overline{C}$)
(b) a portion which is dependent on the level of income (cY).

(iv) The conditions to be complied with by $\overline{C}$ and c in order to render the equation a true reflection of the straight line in the diagram, are given at the bottom of the above equation. $\overline{C}$ is always positive while the value of c is greater than 0 but smaller than 1.

(v)   That this is in fact a true reflection of the consumption function may be verified by positing different values of Y in the equation. At an income level of R60 million we know from the diagram that consumption would be equal to R50 million. The algebraic calculation is as follows:

$$C = \overline{C} + cY$$
$$= 5 + (0{,}75 \times 60)$$
$$= 5 + 45$$
$$= \text{R50 million}$$

The answer therefore agrees with the representation in figure 3.6.

A model with three equations

The question now arises whether the derivation of the equilibrium income can be demonstrated by means of equations? It can in fact be done by taking the various functions in the diagram, together with the equilibrium condition (the 45° line) in the form of a set of equations, as a unit or a model of our imaginary economy. We can identify the following three equations:

$$C = \overline{C} + cY \dots\dots\dots\dots\dots\dots\dots\dots\dots\dots\dots\dots\dots 3.1$$
$$TS = C + \overline{I} \dots\dots\dots\dots\dots\dots\dots\dots\dots\dots\dots\dots\dots 3.2$$
$$Y = TS \dots\dots\dots\dots\dots\dots\dots\dots\dots\dots\dots\dots\dots\dots 3.3$$

Equation 3.1 is the consumption function which has already been discussed. Equation 3.2 defines the components constituting total expenditure in our simplified economy, and equation 3.3 describes the equilibrium condition or the 45° line. By means of substitution the following equations can be derived:

$$Y = TS \qquad \text{(equation 3.3)}$$
$$\therefore \quad Y = C + \overline{I} \qquad (TS = C + \overline{I}, \text{according to equation 3.2})$$
$$\text{and hence } Y = \overline{C} + cY + \overline{I} \qquad (C = \overline{C} + cY \text{ according to equation 3.1})$$

Since Y occurs on both sides of the equation, a solution for the equilibrium income, Y, may be found by means of re-arrangement:

$$Y - cY = \overline{C} + \overline{I}$$
$$Y(1 - c) = \overline{C} + \overline{I}$$

Now divide both sides by $(1 - c)$:

$$\therefore \quad Y_e = \frac{1}{1-c} (\overline{C} + \overline{I}) \dots\dots\dots\dots\dots\dots\dots\dots\dots\dots\dots 3.4$$

And if we substitute the values for the symbols we find that:

$$Y = \frac{1}{1 - 0{,}75} (5 + 5)$$
$$= \frac{1}{0{,}25} (5 + 5)$$
$$= 4 \times 10$$
$$= R40 \text{ million}$$

We therefore see that exactly the same result as obtained in the diagram, can be obtained with the model.

The model also enables us to determine what would happen to the equilibrium income should an increase in, for instance, autonomous investment ($\overline{I}$) take place. Let us assume that investment doubles from R5 million to R10 million. By means of equation 3.4 the following solution is obtained:

$$Y = \frac{1}{1-c} (\overline{C} + \overline{I})$$
$$= 4 \times (5 + 10)$$
$$= R60 \text{ million}$$

To ascertain the increase in income (ΔY) the following useful formula or equation may be derived:

$$Y + \Delta Y = \frac{1}{1-c} (\overline{C} + \overline{I} + \Delta I)$$
$$= \frac{1}{1-c} (\overline{C} + \overline{I}) + \frac{1}{1-c} \Delta I$$
$$\therefore \Delta Y = \frac{1}{1-c} \Delta I$$
$$= 4 \times 5$$
$$= R20 \text{ million}$$

This change is represented in graphic terms in figure 3.7. Autonomous investment increases from A_1 to A_2, which causes the equilibrium income to rise from Y_1 to Y_2.

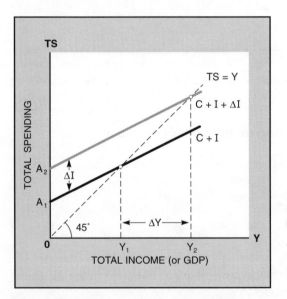

Fig. 3.7 Investment and the level of income

An increase in autonomous investment leads to a rise in the equilibrium income.

3.6   Current government expenditure

Before going into the implications of the model in the previous section, we first have to get rid of the simplified assumptions made earlier on. We need to be more realistic in giving recognition to those expenditure components which were ignored in the previous section.

In section 3.1 we established that current government expenditure in South Africa during the past few years has amounted to almost 20 per cent of the gross domestic product, and that this percentage showed a rising trend over the same period. If a longer period had been analysed, there would be a general tendency for this percentage to rise. The extent to which the present privatisation campaign in South Africa is likely to affect this tendency, is difficult to determine. That the government will continue to be an important factor, cannot be doubted however. The rising trend may be attributed to the fact that people expect the government to assume increasing responsibilities in fields such as **education, health, social services, defence**, etc. In chapter 5 this will be discussed in greater detail.

As indicated in previous sections, to take account only of **current** government expenditure would be to seriously underestimate the government's direct control over aggregate demand in the South African economy. In our discussion of investment, we pointed out that more than half of the gross investment is undertaken by the government and public corporations. If we take 1991 as an example, we shall find that investment to the value of R16 529 million was undertaken on behalf of the government (public authorities and public corporations) (see table 3.4). If this amount is added to the general government consumption expenditure, the total government expenditure amounts to R78 385 million, which constitutes 26,4 per cent of the GDP – considerably more than the 20,9 per cent of the total constituted by current expenditure in table 3.2.

Although a strong case may be made for the fact that government expenditure – whether or not G includes investment – like consumption, exhibits a positive relation to the level of income, we are formally going to deal with it in the same way as investment. In principle the **autonomous nature** of G can be easily understood as the scope of government expenditure is, in the final analysis, determined by government itself. For this reason the government expenditure line A_1G in figure 3.8 is drawn parallel to the horizontal axis. This means that G is regarded as autonomous; in other words, G is not affected by the level of Y, but is affected by other factors.

This fixed amount which constitutes G is added to (C + I), yielding the domestic expenditure line (C + I + G). Since G as well as I are regarded as being autonomous, (C + I + G) is still parallel to the consumption function.

Algebraically the model can therefore be represented as follows:

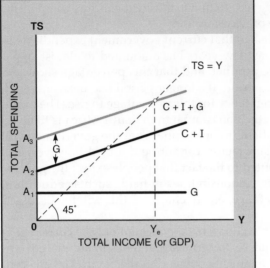

Fig. 3.8 Government expenditure (G)

Like I, G is regarded as being independent of Y. A_1G shows G as an autonomous element of expenditure. It can be added to the line $A_2(C+I)$ to give $A_3(C+I+G)$; this line represents domestic expenditure.

$$C = \overline{C} + cY \dots\dots\dots\dots\dots\dots\dots\dots\dots\dots\dots\dots\dots\dots 3.1$$
$$TS = C + \overline{I} + \overline{G} \dots\dots\dots\dots\dots\dots\dots\dots\dots\dots\dots\dots\dots 3.2a$$
$$Y = TS \dots\dots\dots\dots\dots\dots\dots\dots\dots\dots\dots\dots\dots\dots\dots\dots 3.3$$

The only difference between this model and the previous one is that autonomous government expenditure (G) now also forms a part of total expenditure in the economy. The equilibrium income is derived by means of the following equation:

$$Y_e = \frac{1}{1-c} \ (\overline{C} + \overline{I} + \overline{G}) \dots\dots\dots\dots\dots\dots\dots\dots\dots\dots 3.4a$$

3.7   Exports and imports

The final adjustment we have to make before the model can be regarded as "complete", is to allow for the influence of the foreign sector on the economy. We have already seen that domestic expenditure does not represent all expenditure on the domestic product. The reason is that exports do not constitute a part of domestic expenditure (i.e. expenditure by residents). On the other hand, a proportion of domestic expenditure is not spent locally since a certain proportion is spent on imports. In order to obtain an

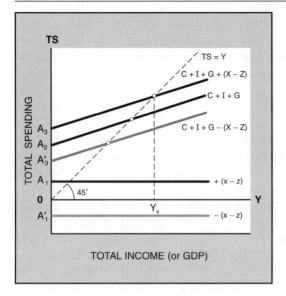

Fig. 3.9 The inclusion of exports (X) and imports (Z)

When exports exceed imports (X – Z) will be positive; total expenditure through A_3 will then exceed domestic expenditure at all values of Y and vice versa (when Z exceeds X).

indication of the **demand for the domestic product**, imports must therefore be subtracted from and exports added to domestic expenditure. Once again we assume that **exports (X)** and **imports (Z)** are autonomous, i.e. their values are not determined by the level of income. In more advanced textbooks the assumption is usually made that imports are in fact affected by the level of income; it stands to reason that people will be more inclined to import goods from overseas if their income is higher. This complication will however not be considered here.

Although a change has been noticeable lately, American textbooks on macro-economics in the seventies largely ignored the existence of X and Z. This is not only because of the relatively small percentages represented by these GNP totals (between 3 and 10 per cent) in the USA, but also because X and Z in reality largely cancelled each other out. In South Africa this was definitely not the case, as can be seen from table 3.1, where X was mostly larger for the period 1984 to 1991. The percentages in table 3.2 further indicate that X and Z constituted between 20 and 33 per cent of the GDP. This means that domestic expenditure could be considerably more than domestic income and product; in other words, a country could spend more than it can earn, and this would be reflected in the balance of payments.

If we assume that X and Z are autonomous, i.e. not related to Y, they can be brought into the graphic analysis as shown in figure 3.9. We begin our analysis with the **domestic expenditure line** (C + I + G) which goes through point A_2. With regard to X and Z there are now three possibilities. The first is represented by the line going through point A_1^*. In this case X is exceeding Z and hence (X – Z) is positive (more than zero). To derive total expenditure, we now *add* (X – Z) to the domestic expenditure line, which gives us the line through point A₃ above (C + I + G). That means that **total expenditure** is here greater than the **domestic expenditure** at every level of income or product. A surplus exists on the trade balance of the balance of payments (cf. chapter 8).

It is however also possible that the current account of the balance of payments will show a deficit, when imports exceed exports. In such a case (X – Z) will be a negative total, i.e. less than zero, and if both X and Z are autonomous, (X – Z) could be represented by the dotted line through point A′₁. In this case (X – Z) would be *subtracted* from domestic expenditure (C + I + G) as represented by the dotted line through point A′₃.

There is of course a third possibility, viz. that X will be exactly equal to Z, i.e. that (X – Z) = 0. In this case the line representing (X – Z) would coincide exactly with the OY axis; the **domestic expenditure curve** (C + I + G) would be identical to the **total expenditure curve** (C + I + G + X – Z). To simplify matters, however, the last two possibilities will be ignored and we shall therefore assume that (X – Z) is more than zero. The equilibrium income in this case is therefore Y$_e$ in figure 3.9.

Finally, we can now see how the addition of (X – Z) to our definition of total expenditure affects the triple-equation model:

$$C = \overline{C} + cY \dotfill 3.1$$
$$TS = C + \overline{I} + \overline{G} + (\overline{X} - \overline{Z}) \dotfill 3.2b$$
$$Y = TS \dotfill 3.3$$

and equilibrium income is calculated as follows:

$$Y_e = \frac{1}{1-c} [\overline{C} + \overline{I} + \overline{G} + (\overline{X} - \overline{Z})] \dotfill 3.4b$$

3.8   The determination of GDP and the multiplier

As most of you have probably realised by now, an important conclusion has been reached by means of equation 3.4(b) above. As can be seen from equation 3.2(b), the definition of total expenditure is now complete for the first time. We have dispensed with the initial simplifying assumptions that no government or foreign sector exists.

It is also interesting to note that the equilibrium level of income in each of the above models has yielded a certain formula for calculation. To summarise, we can briefly list the various equations once more:

$$Y = \frac{1}{1-c}\,(\overline{C}+\overline{I}) \quad\dots\dots\dots\dots\dots\dots\dots\dots\dots\dots\dots\dots\dots \quad 3.4$$

$$Y = \frac{1}{1-c}\,(\overline{C}+\overline{I}+\overline{G}) \quad\dots\dots\dots\dots\dots\dots\dots\dots\dots\dots\dots \quad 3.4a$$

$$Y = \frac{1}{1-c}\,[\overline{C}+\overline{I}+\overline{G}+(\overline{X}-\overline{Z})] \quad\dots\dots\dots\dots\dots\dots\dots\dots \quad 3.4b$$

It can now be seen that the equilibrium income level is derived in each case by multiplying the term $\frac{1}{(1-c)}$ by the value of the **intercept** of the relevant expenditure line. The other symbols on the right-hand side of the equations are all autonomous components which determine the value of the intercept on the vertical axis. In more general terms the equation could be as follows:

$$Y = \frac{1}{1-c}\,\overline{A} \quad\dots\dots\dots\dots\dots\dots\dots\dots\dots\dots\dots\dots\dots\dots \quad 3.5$$

Where $\overline{A}$ = level of autonomous expenditure
= intercept on vertical axis of the expenditure line.

Let us see, without taking price variations into account, what would happen if total expenditure (TS) were to move up or down and **why** this could happen. We can perform the analysis on the basis of figure 3.10. As we have seen, the equilibrium income is determined by the intersection of the total expenditure line and the 45° line. If total expenditure $(C+I+G+X-Z)$ is represented by TS_1, the intersection would be E_1 and the level of income would be equal to Y_1.

What happens if there is a shift of TS from for instance TS_1 to TS_2? The answer is simple, since the new intersection E_2 causes income to *rise* from Y_1 to Y_2. Similarly, Y will fall if total expenditure shifts *downward*, for instance from TS_2 to TS_1.

Why is this so? In other words, why would a shift in total expenditure occur? We have explained that consumption is a stable function which will not easily move up or down. But the other components are autonomous and may be affected by a variety of factors such as interest rates, credit conditions and, in regard to $(X-Z)$, rates of exchange. Any increase in G, I and X will move TS upwards and therefore cause Y to **increase**; by the

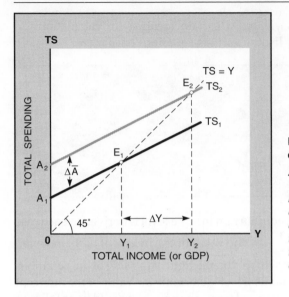

Fig. 3.10 A shift in total expenditure

A shift in total expenditure from TS_1 to TS_2 will cause the GDP to increase from Y_1 to Y_2; on the other hand, a decrease in expenditure from TS_2 to TS_1 will cause the GDP to fall from Y_2 to Y_1. This forms the background to macro-economic policy.

same token, a decrease in these components will cause Y to **fall.** With imports (Z) the effect will be exactly the opposite. Less imports will cause Y to rise (less being subtracted from domestic expenditure) while an increase in imports will cause Y to fall since **more** will be subtracted from domestic expenditure.

The multiplier

As we have seen, this change in the value of the equilibrium income (ΔY in figure 3.10) can also be derived by means of an equation:

$$\Delta Y = \frac{1}{1-c} \, \Delta \overline{A} \quad\dots\dots\dots\dots\dots\dots\dots\dots\dots\dots\dots\dots\dots\dots\dots\quad 3.6$$

According to this equation any increase in autonomous expenditure would cause income to rise by a multiple of the original increase in A. It is clear that we here have to do with a multiplier effect. The value of the multiplier is equal to $\frac{1}{1-c}$.

This conclusion is an important component of income determination and is known as the theory of the multiplier. According to this theory, a change in any component of total expenditure (I, G, X or Z) has an influence on the level of income which is equal to a multiple of the original change in expenditure. Assuming that autonomous expenditure increases by R10 million and that the marginal propensity to consume (c) is equal to 0,5 (= ½), the increase in Y can be derived as follows:

$$\Delta Y = \frac{1}{1 - 0,5} \times 10$$
$$= 2 \times 10$$
$$= R20 \text{ million}$$

The nature of the multiplier

Although the principle of a multiplier effect can easily be illustrated with the aid of an equation (cf.3.6) and also graphically (cf. fig. 3.10), a thorough grasp of the working of the multiplier is not so simple. How is it in fact possible for an expenditure of R10 million to lead all of a sudden to an increase of R20 million (or more if the marginal propensity to consume is higher than 0,5) in the level of income? The answer to this is simply that it does **not** happen "all of a sudden" and that the change should be regarded as a **process** taking place over time. Although the process can be described by means of mathematical formulae, we shall here try to give you an actual "feel" for it. Our explanation will therefore be mainly descriptive with reference to figure 3.11.

In figure 3.11 an initial equilibrium condition is assumed at E_1. This lies on the intersection between the total expenditure line TS_1 and the 45° line. As a result of an autonomous increase in investment, an upward shift takes place from TS_1 to TS_2. In other words, an increase in autonomous expenditure of R15 million. As can be seen from the gradient of the TS_1 line, a marginal propensity to consume of ½ (or 0,5) is assumed which, according to the term $\frac{1}{1-c}$, can be converted to a multiplier effect of 2.

According to our theory, the new equilibrium income should rise by R30 million (2 × R15 million) to R40 million, i.e. a movement towards the intersection E_2 in figure 3.11. Let us see what actually happens in order to bring about this shift from E_1 to E_2:

(i) The increased expenditure immediately causes a shift from E_1 to point z. At this point total expenditure is equal to R25 million while production still temporarily stands at a level of R10 million.

(ii) Over the next period (approximately as long as it takes to produce the goods) production will also expand to the level of R25 million in order to meet the increased demand. We are therefore moving towards point y in the figure.

(iii) At point y income has however also increased by R15 million, which means that consumption expenditure will, as a result of the marginal

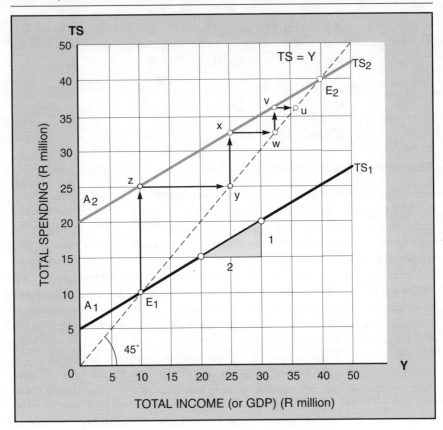

Fig. 3.11 The multiplier process

The working of the multiplier should be seen as a process taking place over several periods. An initial increase in autonomous expenditure from A_1 to A_2 will therefore lead step by step to a change of the original equilibrium point E_1 to the new equilibrium point E_2.

propensity to consume, also increase by R7,5 million ($c\Delta Y = 0,5 \times 15 = 7,5$) and we move to point x.

(iv) The increased demand (from y to x) encourages manufacturers to once again increase production by the same amount (R7,5 million) to point w.

(v) The process repeats itself with diminishing increments of expenditure and income until the new equilibrium point E_2 is reached. At point E_2 the gap between expenditure and the level of income is completely eliminated and there is no reason to increase or reduce production.[§]

§   The process can also be analysed with the aid of actual amounts. The change in the equilibrium income (ΔY) can be calculated by adding up the changes in the level of income

One last point to remember in connection with the nature of the multiplier is the fact that the above analysis will only apply if the increase in autonomous expenditure is of a permanent nature. If the rise of R15 million in autonomous expenditure is an isolated phenomenon and investment then returns to its previous level, the position of E₂ will not be maintained.

The size of the multiplier

At this stage it is probably unnecessary to say any more about the factors determining the size of the multiplier. In the graphic representations you all probably "sensed" that the gradient of the total expenditure line (which is determined by the marginal propensity to consume) had something to do with the size of the multiplier. In figure 3.12, where we postulate two sets of expenditure lines with different gradients, this intuition is confirmed.

TS₁ and TS$_a$ are two expenditure lines, both intersecting the equilibrium

---

which occurred in each period of the process. As can be seen, income increases in the initial period by the full amount of the rise in autonomous expenditure (R15 million, a movement from z to y). In the second period the rise in income is only half of this, since the marginal propensity to consume is equal to 0,5. It is the rise from x to w which is equal to $(0,5 \times 15)$ = R7,5m. In the third period, i.e. during the increase from v to u, the rise in income is once again only half of the previous rise $(0,5 \times (0,5 \times 15)) = R3,75$ million. The equation is therefore as follows:

$$\Delta Y = 15 + 0,5 \times 15 + 0,5 \times (0,5 \times 15) + \ldots\ldots\ldots + \ldots\ldots\ldots$$
$$= 15 + 7,5 + 3,75 + \ldots\ldots\ldots + \ldots\ldots\ldots + \ldots\ldots\ldots$$

More generally, the equation could be expressed as follows if we assume that $\Delta\overline{A} = 15$ and $c = 0,5$:

$$\Delta Y = \Delta\overline{A} + c\Delta\overline{A} + c^2 \Delta\overline{A} + \ldots\ldots\ldots + c^n\Delta\overline{A}$$
i.e. $\Delta Y = \Delta\overline{A}(1 + c + c^2 \quad + \ldots\ldots\ldots + c^n)$ ....(i)

Multiply both sides by c:

$$c\Delta Y = \Delta\overline{A}(c + c^2 + c^3 + \ldots\ldots\ldots + c^{n+1})..(ii)$$

Now, subtract equation (ii) from equation (i) to obtain the following result:
$\Delta Y - c\Delta Y = \Delta\overline{A}$ (note that all the terms between brackets cancel each other, with the exception of the 1. Since "n" is infinite, the last terms in both equations also cancel each other).

$$\therefore \Delta Y(1 - c) = \Delta\overline{A}$$
$$\therefore \Delta Y = \frac{1}{(1 - c)} \Delta\overline{A}$$

which gives exactly the same result as equation 3.6.

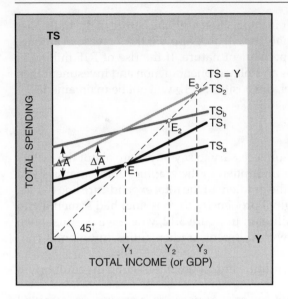

Fig. 3.12 The size of the multiplier

The greater the gradient (and hence the marginal propensity to consume) the greater the multiplier effect. The same increase in autonomous expenditure (A) leads to different increases in the equilibrium income level (Y_2 and Y_3) if the gradient of TS is different.

line at E_1. In spite of their differing gradients, the lines are drawn in such a way that both go through point E_1. An autonomous increase of $\Delta\overline{A}$ will move both these lines up by $\Delta\overline{A}$, but since the gradients and hence the multipliers are different, this will lead to different increases in Y. The shift from TS_1 to $TS_2 (= \Delta\overline{A})$ leads to a new equilibrium income of Y_3 ($\Delta Y = Y_1Y_3$) while the same rise from TS_a to TS_b ($= \Delta\overline{A}$), increases income to only Y_2 ($\Delta Y = Y_1Y_2$).

We also know that the multiplier in our model may be defined as follows:

$$\text{Multiplier} = \frac{1}{1-c}$$

This means that the greater the marginal propensity to consume, the greater the multiplier will be. On the basis of the definition above, it can be verified that: if $c = \frac{1}{2}$, the multiplier is equal to 2; if $c = \frac{3}{4}$, the multiplier is equal to 4; and if $c = \frac{7}{8}$ the multiplier is equal to 8.

In following chapters we shall always use the multiplier effect to determine the influence of changes in autonomous expenditure on the economy. This technique is especially useful in establishing the effect of an increase in government spending (ΔG) on the equilibrium income level. It should nevertheless be remembered that the multiplier we have derived in this chapter was regarded in isolation and based on certain simplified assumptions.

Selected references:

Baumol & Blinder: 7 appendix A.
Dernburg: 4, 6.
Dornbusch & Fischer: 3.
Evans-Pritchard: 5, 6.
Froyen: 13.
Gordon: 3, 13, 14.
Morley: 3, 11.
Shapiro: 4, 5.

4 Aggregate demand and supply analysis

We have a threefold task in this chapter. In the first place we have to combine what we have learned about total spending in the previous chapter, with the general price level; we must in other words try to determine an aggregate demand curve. Secondly, we have to derive an aggregate supply curve which will indicate the quantity of products that manufacturers will be prepared to produce at different price levels. Thirdly, we have to combine the aggregate demand and supply curves in order to identify some of the main economic problems of today and yesterday and to see how they are reflected in the system (model) we have constructed.

4.1 Total spending and the general price level

Up to now we have completely ignored two factors in our analysis. In the first place, the **supply** of the GDP has been dealt with in a totally passive manner. Whenever the TS line moved up or down, it was simply assumed that production would adapt to this new demand. Supply factors (for instance the availability of labour or other factors of production) were therefore not allowed to influence the eventual equilibrium income level. Secondly, and this is related to the first point, **prices** (or the general price level) were ignored throughout or, by implication, assumed to be constant.

This unrealistic state of affairs can be seen in figure 4.1 where the general price level is fixed at $\overline{P}$ and the aggregate supply curve of the economy (AS) is completely elastic. This completely elastic supply curve at the price level $\overline{P}$ therefore implies that supply can adjust to changes in demand (from Y_1 to Y_2) without any change in the price level. The diagram does not contain an aggregate demand curve because the analysis in the previous chapter did not include prices. There can obviously be no demand curve if prices do not constitute a known variable. The **aggregate demand curve** in fact indicates the levels of total expenditure that can be associated with different price levels.

In chapter 1 we looked, amongst other things, at the micro-demand

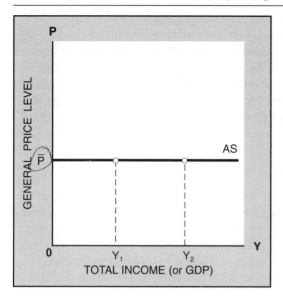

Fig. 4.1 Passive treatment of aggregate supply and the price level

In the previous chapter the influence of aggregate supply or prices on the equilibrium income was not recognised. The diagram shows that the equilibrium income (Y_1 and Y_2) is only determined by demand at a constant price level (P).

curve. It was explained that, generally speaking, a drop in prices would result in an increase in the quantity demanded (the **opposite** also applies: a rise in prices leads to a decrease in the quantity demanded – this is the **law of demand**). The reason for this is, *inter alia*, that at a lower price consumers can **afford** more of the goods concerned. Consumers will also use less expensive goods as **substitutes** for others where prices have not fallen.

One of the characteristics of macro-economics, as against the separate markets studied in **micro**-economics, is that what is true for the parts (micro) is not necessarily true for the whole (macro). To assume that this is so, is called the **fallacy of composition**.

It would for instance be wrong to conclude that the aggregate demand curve (in a PQ diagram) runs downwards from left to right simply because most micro-demand curves behave in this way. The reason is that two of the main factors which determine the direction of the demand curve in micro-economics do not necessarily apply in macro-economics, particularly in the case of consumption expenditure.

> *Firstly*: with all prices falling at the same rate, there is no sense in the consumer substituting one good for another; after all, relatively speaking – i.e. if the price of one good is measured in terms of another – there has been no change.

> *Secondly*: we must remember that income is based on a price – i.e. the price of productive services rendered – and if all prices come down, then income must likewise come down, which means that consumers are not necessarily able to afford more. The main micro-economic reasons for a negative slope of the aggregate demand curve therefore do not apply.

The slope of the aggregate demand curve

In spite of the abovementioned valid objections to simply assuming that the aggregate demand curve (AD) will, like many individual demand curves, run down from top left to bottom right, there are enough other considerations to indicate that the AD curve does in fact have a normal slope. And these considerations do not relate to consumer spending only, but include the other components of domestic expenditure as well as exports and imports.

With reference to figure 4.2, we can assume that an equilibrium condition arose at income level Y_3 at a price level of P_1. Let us now try to find out what will happen to the level of total expenditure if there is a rise in the general price level from P_1 to P_2.

We have already seen that a change in the price level does not necessarily have a *direct* impact on consumer expenditure. There are however *indirect* influences which may affect total expenditure. The best known is the so-called **wealth effect**.

Where the wealth effect probably exerts the most decisive influence on total expenditure, is in the impact of a price rise (cf. once again our example in fig. 4.2) on the **real value of the quantity of money** in the country. As we shall see in chapter 6, a certain amount of money is in circulation in the economy at any given moment and a price rise leads inevitably to a fall in the real value of this money stock. (Cf. also the purchasing power of money in chapter 2.) There are now two possibilities, both of which confirm our presumption regarding a falling aggregate demand curve.

(i) Owing to the fall in the value of the quantity of money, owners of money will want to hold more money in order to be able to carry out the same number of real transactions. In order to increase their money holdings, they will be obliged to either borrow money or sell assets (particularly financial assets such as securities). Both these actions will give rise to an increase in interest rates, which in turn will lead to a drop in investment (I). It is obvious that the more an investor has to pay for his capital, the fewer projects can be gainfully undertaken. The outcome of all this is that total expenditure (of which I forms a part)

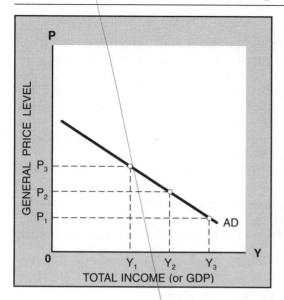

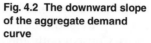

Fig. 4.2 The downward slope of the aggregate demand curve

There are various indirect effects which will ensure that the aggregate demand curve (AD) will run downward in the normal way from top left to bottom right.

will fall to Y2 as a result of the price rise to P2; which serves to confirm a downward aggregate demand curve such as AD in figure 4.2.

This so-called **interest rate-investment effect**[§] is probably the single most important reason for the normal slope of the aggregate demand curve. But there could also be other reasons why the AD curve should have a negative slope.

(ii) In the above example it could also happen that the money holders, as a result of the increase in prices and the fall in the value of their cash balances (one of the various assets in which wealth is held), would now regard themselves as being poorer and would therefore **consume** less. This effect is known as the **real cash balance effect.**[§§] The fall in consumption once again agrees with the slope of the AD curve in figure 4.2.

Another influence on consumption occurs via the tax system and is called the **tax effect.** Personal income tax is progressive (cf. chapter 5), which means that a person will pay a greater percentage of his income in taxes at a higher income and *vice versa*. If income rises with prices, the percentage paid in taxes will also increase. The tax payer's disposable income will be proportionally lower, so that C will once again be decreased.

The final indirect reason for the falling aggregate demand curve that we

§ Also known as the Keynes effect.
§§ Also called the Pigou effect.

wish to bring to your notice is the **foreign trade effect.** A rise in the price level of all goods means that exports become more expensive (X will therefore tend to fall) while imports, relative to local goods, become less expensive (Z therefore increases), with the result that (X – Z) becomes smaller – which again leads, just as before, to a fall in total expenditure. The foreign trade effect can be of particular importance in South Africa where imports and exports form a relatively large percentage of total expenditure. As we shall see in chapter 8, timeous adjustments to the exchange rate can however neutralise this effect to a large extent.

All these arguments lead us to the conclusion that most total expenditure items – provided nothing else changes – will decrease if there is a rise in prices. Consequently the **aggregate demand curve** will in all probability **run in the normal way from top left to bottom right.** This is an important conclusion and determines the way in which we shall present the aggregate demand curve from now on.

The position of the aggregate demand curve

In addition to the slope of the aggregate demand curve, it is also necessary to know which factors determine the **position** of the curve. To be able to do this, we must go back to the analysis of the total expenditure diagram and the multiplier in the previous chapter. We must, in other words, find out what relationship exists between the aggregate demand curve (AD) and the total expenditure line (TS).

On the basis of the total expenditure diagram we found that the equilibrium income level reacted via the multiplier to any change in autonomous expenditure. Algebraically, the change in the income level could be calculated as follows:

$$\Delta Y = \frac{1}{1-c} \, \Delta \overline{A}$$

In figure 4.3 we see how the AD curve would react to a shift in the TS line. Assume that there is an increase in autonomous expenditure of $\Delta \overline{A}$ which shifts the total expenditure line from TS_1 to TS_2. With our knowledge of the multiplier we are aware that this will also cause income to rise from Y_1 to Y_2. As may be expected, this increase in total expenditure will shift the aggregate demand curve to the right. Unfortunately we do not have sufficient information to determine by exactly how much the AD curve will shift to the right. In other words, we cannot determine exactly how great the **horizontal** shift (A_1A_2) in figure 4.3 will be. In more advanced macro-eco-

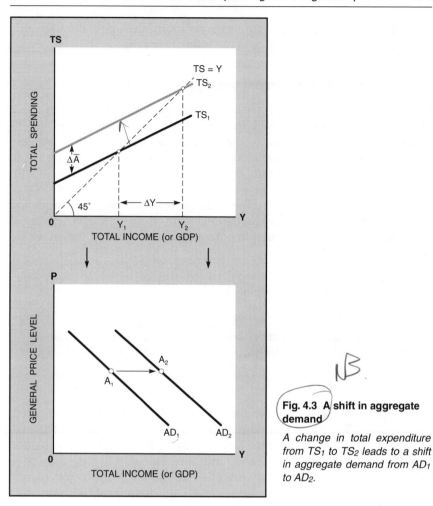

Fig. 4.3 A shift in aggregate demand

A change in total expenditure from TS_1 to TS_2 leads to a shift in aggregate demand from AD_1 to AD_2.

nomic textbooks, where they deal with the derivation of the aggregate demand curve more formally and technically, it is in fact possible to determine this distance. With the knowledge we do have, we can however assume that the horizontal shift of the AD curve will in all probability be **greater** than the vertical shift of the TS line (i.e. $\Delta \overline{A}$) but **smaller** than the horizontal increase in the income level ($\Delta Y = Y_1 Y_2$). The shift from AD_1 to AD_2 therefore does not occur with the full multiplier effect experienced in the upper part of the diagram. For our purposes all we need to know is that **an increase in total expenditure (TS) shifts the aggregate demand curve (AD) to the right.**

The important question now is, what would happen to the equilibrium income and the general price level when such a shift occurs in AD? To answer this, we must first determine the position and slope of the aggregate supply curve. This will be done in the following sections.

4.2   The level of employment and aggregate supply

You may think it strange that we have taken so long to get to the other leg of the macro-economic model we wish to develop. The erroneous impression may have been created that the aggregate supply curve was less important, as a separate chapter has not, as in the case of aggregate demand, been devoted to the background of the curve. Chapter 3, which dealt with **total expenditure**, prepared us for the analysis of the position and slope of the aggregate demand curve. The "background" or preparation for the derivation of the supply curve (in the next section) is to be found in the level of **employment or the production potential** of the economy, which we are now going to discuss.

Meaning of the aggregate supply curve

The **aggregate supply curve** of an economy describes the value of the real GDP which manufacturers will be prepared to produce at different price levels.

If we ignore the price level for the moment, the question may be asked: What is a country's absolute production potential? It is clear that the level of technological development, together with the availability of production factors such as labour, capital and natural resources, will have a decisive influence on the maximum capacity of the economy. These factors place a theoretical ceiling on the magnitude of the value of the real GDP and must therefore exercise an influence on the aggregate supply curve.

If we were to measure real GDP on the horizontal axis of figure 4.4, a point on this axis could in principle be found which would be representative of a level of production which could only be attained if all production factors were **fully utilised**. Such a point is called the full employment level of production (Y_f). The vertical supply curve (AS) which runs through this point is therefore totally insensitive to any price changes that may occur on the vertical P axis. Before pursuing the argument further, we have to explain what exactly is meant here by the "full employment level" of production.

Different kinds of unemployment

From a macro-economic point of view no literal meaning is attached to the term "full employment". The production level Y_f therefore does not imply that every labourer is using every bit of capital equipment in the economy 24 hours a day. The full employment referred to here, is a more realistic employment level which can be attained in normal but favourable conditions. Such an interpretation of full employment takes into account the fact that, even under favourable conditions, a certain percentage of production factors will not be utilised. This ever-present underutilisation of certain production factors is called **frictional unemployment** or **natural unemployment**.

Frictional unemployment includes the position of those labourers who find themselves temporarily between jobs. In a free-market economy there will constantly be a number of labourers who will be without work for certain periods because they are busy moving from one job to another. Unemployment of this kind is regarded as being *unavoidable* and is not related to unemployment arising from

(i) a slump in the economy as a result of a temporary lack of demand – i.e. **cyclical unemployment**; or

(ii) changes in the nature and location of employment opportunities – i.e. **structural unemployment**.

As the name indicates, the latter arises as a result of structural changes, usually accompanied by economic growth and development. When the motorcar replaced the horse as a means of transport, great numbers of farriers and harness makers were left unemployed. More recently there have been developments in the field of computers which have had an adverse impact on certain professions. Attempts to counter this type of

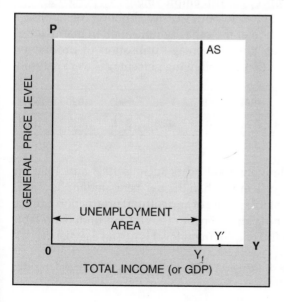

Fig. 4.4 The classical aggregate supply curve and the unemployment area

The full employment level of production (Y_f) can be represented by a vertical aggregate supply curve (AS). Any point to the left of Y_f implies that production factors are not being fully utilised.

unemployment by means of broadly stimulatory economic policy measures will be unsuccessful. Normally more specific measures, such as training programmes to equip people in the use of the new technology, are needed.

Of the three kinds of unemployment referred to, only *cyclical* and *frictional unemployment* are of any particular importance to the derivation of the aggregate supply curve. The presence of frictional unemployment means that full employment and the associated level of production Y_f in figure 4.4 are indicated at a lower, more realistic level than the literal meaning of the term **full employment** would imply. If frictional unemployment were not accepted as unavoidable, Y_f would be further to the right on the horizontal axis, i.e. it would be shifted to Y'.

Full employment

In the USA, where data with regard to unemployment are fairly reliable, full employment is at present set at 96 per cent of the total labour force. This implies that the economic policy-makers in the USA accept that 4 per cent of the labour force will always be unemployed due to frictional unemployment. In South Africa no such traditional measure exists of what full employment actually means. This is mainly due to the deficiency of data with regard to Black unemployment. In South Africa we have information only on registered Whites, Coloureds and Indians who are unemployed.[§] The information with regard to Blacks is extremely doubtful and inaccurate. It is therefore not feasible to express the proportion of the labour force which corresponds to the concept of **full employment** as a percentage.

The Central Statistical Services in South Africa do however publish a series which gives an indication of the capacity utilisation in manufacturing. This series is known as the "Percentage utilisation of production capacity". Over the past few years the following percentages were realised:

Year	1984	1985	1986	1987	1988	1989	1990	1991
% utilisation	82,8	80,8	78,4	80,3	83,6	84,5	82,2	81,1

It appears that even in relatively good years such as 1988 and 1989 the estimated utilisation was still more than 15 per cent under the "full" employment level. If the unstable nature of agricultural production and the special circumstances of mining are taken into account, it is understandable that the quantification of a full employment level is not an easy task.

§   This information is probably also incomplete, since not all the unemployed people register, and highly paid categories are not included.

If the economy were always able to maintain production at a point such as Y_f, i.e. the full employment level, the policy-makers would have far fewer problems. As we saw in chapter 1, it was believed for many years, up to the publication of Keynes's book *The General Theory of Employment, Interest and Money* in 1936, that the economy would move towards the full employment level automatically and rapidly. Any deviations from this ideal condition were regarded as purely temporary since natural and strong forces were believed to exist, which would impel the economy back towards full employment. This confidence of the classical economists, who did not regard **underemployment** or unemployment as one of the central problems of the economy, received a serious set-back in the thirties when for nearly a decade mass unemployment reigned in large parts of the world. A new theory to account for the possibility of unemployment was urgently needed. The answer came from Keynes, and his ideas will largely determine the rest of this book.

Keynes's main conclusions

Although we have already referred to Keynes's contribution in the first chapter of this book, it may be helpful to give a brief summary of his main conclusions:

- In contrast to the classical economists, Keynes was not of the opinion that natural market factors existed which would impel the economy back to full employment **in the short term**. According to him, the economy could remain in a state of equilibrium at a level of production which was associated with **large-scale unemployment.**

- The large-scale unemployment was caused, according to Keynes, by an insufficient demand for goods and services. The reason for unemployment was therefore attributed to the fact that the level of **expenditure** in the economy was insufficient.

- As a solution to the problem, Keynes proposed that aggregate demand be stimulated. The most effective way of doing this, was by increasing **government expenditure.**

We can now return to the aggregate supply curve AS in figure 4.4. Keynes's most important contribution in this respect was that he showed the vertical AS curve might not provide a realistic picture of what could happen in practice. The real output of the economy could well be at a level to the left of Y_f, an area associated with cyclical unemployment.

In contrast to the classical economists, who acknowledged only the vertical AS curve (at full employment), we have to be thoroughly aware of what happens to aggregate supply in this **unemployment area.**

4.3   Aggregate supply, real GDP and the price level

The extreme Keynesian case

In the previous section we saw the classical opinion was that the price level had no influence on the equilibrium level of the GDP, since this equilibrium would always be found at Y_f. In other words, as in figure 4.4, the AS curve was parallel to the vertical axis. Keynes, on the other hand, felt that equilibrium *could* in fact occur where N (employment) was lower than N_f (full employment) and Y therefore smaller than Y_f.

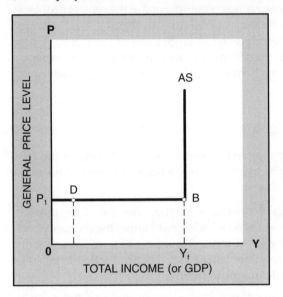

Fig. 4.5 The extreme Keynesian aggregate supply curve

The Keynesian aggregate supply curve has an inverted L shape. In the horizontal part prices are constant. At point B full employment is attained.

In our further study of the aggregate supply curve, and particularly of the relationship between the GDP and the general price level, we can take point D in figure 4.5 as our point of reference. This point presupposes a certain real GDP which is accompanied by a general price level P_1. This is obviously a condition of considerable underemployment (full employment being at Y_f). Because there are unemployed production factors, production can be expanded without any significant pressure being exerted on the existing capacity of the economy. Consequently there will be little or no pressure on prices and we can expect that the original price level will be maintained even with an increase in production. In these conditions the AS curve is therefore horizontal or perfectly elastic and prices are constant. This, then, was the assumption Keynes was working on when he formulated his theory. This assumption is not unrealistic if the conditions of **depression** for which the theory was formulated, are taken into account.

Prices and the accompanying wages were regarded as being institutionally fixed over the short term. If an increase in aggregate demand occurred, it was reflected in an increase in production and employment while prices remained constant. On the other hand, it was argued that a decrease in demand would lead to a decrease in production and job opportunities. Prices and wages therefore do not vary at all to accommodate the change in demand.

Once the full employment level is reached, further increases in demand merely give rise to price increases without any associated increase in real production. The horizontal part (DB) together with the vertical full employment level of production at Y_f form an inverted L-shaped AS curve (fig. 4.5) which may be called the **extreme Keynesian aggregate supply curve.**

A more realistic view

Why do we describe this AS curve as an "extreme" representation of the situation? Is it realistic to expect that the economy will react as predictably as implied by the L-shaped curve? In other words: Can we expect prices to remain absolutely constant when production is expanded to the full employment level? Is there really such a watershed between full and underemployment as indicated by point B on the AS curve? These problems must now be studied in greater detail.

Even in the conditions for which the AS curve was actually "designed", i.e. the Depression of the thirties, second thoughts about its validity could arise. Prices, and to a lesser extent wages, fell sharply when the aggregate demand began to decrease from 1929 onwards. This fall in prices was accompanied by a decrease in real production. This contradicted the horizontal as well as the vertical parts of the AS curve in figure 4.5. When an increase in demand was eventually experienced after the Depression, prices as well as wages began to rise long before full employment was reached.

The realities of the Depression, as well as own intuition, result in the idea that pressure on prices will come into being before full employment is achieved. This possibility implies that the AS curve will show a rising trend in the unemployment area. Such an AS curve can be seen in figure 4.6.

In the final analysis, the price of final products is strongly influenced, and even determined, by the price of the factors of production used in the production process. Any rise in the price of one of the inputs will, if it is not accompanied by a corresponding increase in productivity, normally lead to a rise in the price of the final product, since the supply curve moves to the left or upwards. The opposite is of course also true, viz. that decreases in costs will in normal conditions lead to a fall in the price of final products (cf. the discussion on demand and supply in chapter 1). Let us analyse the situations that will occur when an economy moves from a position of significant underemployment to a position of full employment:

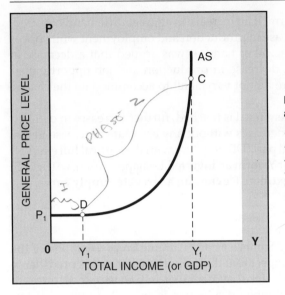

Fig. 4.6 The "three-phase" aggregate supply curve

In contrast to figures.4.4 and 4.5, it is more realistic to assume an AS curve consisting of three phases: (a) The area P₁D where prices remain constant while the GDP increases; (b) the intermediate area (DC) where prices as well as production increase; and (c) the vertical area where Yf is attained and only inflation can still occur.

(i)   We begin with the case of **large-scale unemployment**. This means that all factors of production, including capital equipment, are underutilised. In reaction to an initial increase in demand, producers will probably prefer to expand production rather than increase prices. Increased production will immediately result in fuller utilisation of the existing capital equipment and give rise to an increase in profits. Since most producers are underutilised, preference will be given to increased production rather than endangering their market share as a result of price increases. The above arguments agree with the extreme Keynesian point of view and make it acceptable that a part of the AS curve (P₁D) in figure 4.6 does have a completely elastic trend.

(ii) In **the second phase** the profit position improves together with the general economic climate and the expectations with regard to a further increase in demand become stronger and stronger. To be able to meet the expected demand, an increase in the demand for labour takes place. Although the initial influence of this development may be negligible, the increased demand for labour indicates the possibility of cost increases in the form of higher wages. The expansion of production continues and the utilisation of capital equipment likewise continues to increase. Surplus capacity consequently shrinks and the possibilities of expanding production and therefore profits with the existing capital equipment become smaller and smaller. These conditions on the labour market are further accentuated as unemployment decreases and business enterprises find it increasingly difficult to obtain certain kinds of labour or even to keep labourers at the current wage. All these factors together tend to cause production costs to rise. Increased wages, together with costs related to capacity expansion, make it increasingly attractive for businessmen to think of price increases as a solution. This tendency to increase prices is reinforced as the fear abates that price increases will allow competitors to take over a share of the market.

The conditions sketched above can in other words be associated with the DC phase of the AS curve in figure 4.6. In this area production can only be increased if a degree of inflation, or general increases in prices, is accepted.

(iii) We now come to the **third part of the supply curve.** Full employment is associated with an "acceptable" degree of underemployment. The level of unemployment that should be regarded as acceptable, is largely a matter for the economic policy-makers to decide. In the USA we saw that a certain percentage of unemployment would not be regarded as unacceptable. In South Africa this percentage would probably, owing to various structural characteristics, be considerably higher. It is clear that in deciding on an acceptable level of unemployment, the economic policy-makers will also pay due attention to its implications for general price stability. Full employment is therefore associated with an acceptable combination of underemployment and price stability. The result is that the output Y_f is not quite as clearly fixed as is implied by the diagram.

Nevertheless, even before Y_f is attained, all the arguments used to explain the pressure on prices in the initially increasing (second) phase of the supply curve, become increasingly persuasive. Where labourers in the initial stages of the rising phase were still worried about keeping their jobs, in this overheated stage their main concern is for higher wages. Businesses begin to experience *bottlenecks*, which leads to aggressive competition on the labour market and the market for other essential inputs. Production costs and prices rise out of proportion to the slight increase in real production. When Y_f is reached, the slope becomes vertical and the positive effect of increased production can no longer compensate for the negative results of inflation. In other words, when point C is reached, the economy has apparently reached its absolute maximum production level and no further stimulation of demand can lead to an increase in real production.

To summarise, the aggregate supply curve can be divided into the following three phases:

- **The Keynesian area** where prices remain constant while the GDP is expanded (P_1D).

- **The intermediate area** where the slope of the curve continues to change. Initially production can still be expanded without any significant increase in prices. As production gets closer to the full employment level, the slope becomes steeper, which implies that the change in prices is beginning to dominate the increase in production. The dilemma of economic policy is located in this area.

- **The vertical** or **classical area** of the supply curve where the maximum level of production is reached. Policy-makers will naturally endeavour to prevent the economy from moving into this area, since price increases are the sole result of an increase in demand.

It is important that you should realise that the supply curve described above is only a reflection of an intuitive perception about the way the economy works. The three phases identified are only one interpretation of the possible connection between prices and aggregate supply and should not be elevated to the status of a final answer to the problem. In more advanced macro-economic textbooks the aggregate supply curve is more **formally derived** and a distinction is normally made between long and short-term aggregate supply curves. For the purposes of this book we shall however be satisfied with this general interpretation of aggregate supply.

4.4   The interaction between aggregate demand and aggregate supply

We are now at last in a position to analyse the interaction of demand and supply in a macro-economic context. The model referred to in chapter 1 can now be discussed with reference to figure 4.7 where the two curves occur simultaneously.

In the diagram there is an aggregate demand curve (AD) which shows that the higher the price level the smaller the total expenditure, and an aggregate supply curve (AS) which shows that manufacturers will be prepared to produce more goods and services (up to a maximum of Y_f) as the price level rises.

From this it is clear that there is only one equilibrium point (E) where the quantity demanded is exactly the same as the quantity that will be supplied. Since the analysis applies to macro-economics, we must be sure that we understand clearly why the price level and the equilibrium income level will tend towards P_1 and Y_2 respectively.

Let us try and determine whether a price level of P_2 which would be

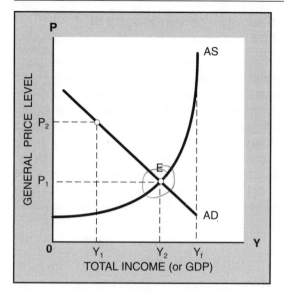

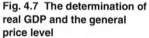

Fig. 4.7 The determination of real GDP and the general price level

The intersection of AS and AD simultaneously determines the equilibrium income level (Y2) and the equilibrium price level (P1).

accompanied by an income level of Y_1 can continue to exist. The meaning of the AS curve was dealt with in detail in the previous section. One of the points mentioned was that AS shows how much manufacturers would be **prepared** to offer at a specific price, but not necessarily what will be offered. This means that at a price level of P_2 we do not actually have to do with the concept of **oversupply** which occurs in the derivation of the equilibrium price in micro-economics. At price level P_2 producers will be inclined to restrict production to the amount demanded (Y_1).

What the AS curve does show, however, is that the potential GDP at this price level is much greater than Y_1. On the various micro-markets this means that there will be surplus capacity and unemployment, which will prompt producers to lower their prices in the hope of selling more. Via the **indirect** effects (wealth effect, foreign trade effect, etc.) which are responsible for the downward sloping aggregate demand curve, total expenditure (demand) will begin to increase and a shift will take place along the demand curve until equilibrium is reached at point E. It is clear that any price which is lower than this equilibrium price will give rise to **excess demand**, which will result in inflation and cause a movement back towards the equilibrium level. Beneath this equilibrium level the AS curve therefore does represent the quantity that will be supplied at different prices.

By the above analysis of equilibrium we demonstrated how the level of real income **and** the general price level come into being. We must now endeavour to ascertain how shifts in the curves can come about and what the effects of such changes will be.

4.5 Shifts in demand and supply – certain aspects of macro-economic policy

The different threads of our model can now be combined to further illustrate some of the basic policy problems referred to in chapter 1. As we have said, the shape and position of the aggregate supply curve is of decisive importance in analysing the influence of shifts in demand. It is interesting to note that the three aggregate supply curves discussed in section 4.3 give a clear indication of the evolutionary process undergone by policy problems. But we have not yet explained what is meant by economic policy. Such an explanation is not difficult to give, since **economic policy** is the process whereby the government attempts to attain a condition better than the existing one. The rest of this book will be mainly concerned with macro-economic policy.

The classical case

As we have already explained, the classical economists basically believed that, in the long run, equilibrium in an economy could only occur at a condition of full employment. According to our analysis in section 4.3, this means that the aggregate supply curve is completely inelastic as indicated in figure 4.4. Such an inelastic aggregate supply curve (AS_1) is also shown in figure 4.8, and our aim is to see how this relates to the problem of macro-economic policy.

As was indicated with reference to figure 4.7, the equilibrium values of

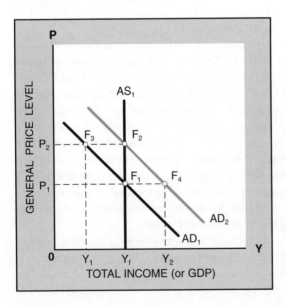

Fig. 4.8 Change in demand in the classical case

A rise in total expenditure increases the demand from AD_1 to AD_2. In the classical case, with aggregate supply at AS_1, this will not cause the GDP to increase but will merely raise the price level (from P_1 to P_2).

GDP and the general price level are found at the intersection of the demand and supply curves. If the aggregate supply in figure 4.8 is represented by AS_1 and the aggregate demand by AD_1, then equilibrium is situated at F_1, which means that GDP is equal to Y_f and that the general price level is P_1.

Now suppose that, as a result of an increase in investment, there is a rise in total expenditure which causes aggregate demand to move towards the right, e.g. to AD_2. If the economy were not already at the full employment level, the GDP would probably have risen to Y_2. But, as we know, production cannot be raised above the Y_f level, and the rise in aggregate demand causes an excess demand of F_1F_4. We have already seen that excess demand leads to a rise in prices; the rise can in this case be called **inflation** since it involves the general price level. But what has happened to (real) GDP? The change in demand via the change in the level of total expenditure has not changed the level of real income. The only change is that prices have risen from P_1 to P_2. The new equilibrium point is now F_2 where aggregate demand (AD_2) and aggregate supply (AS_1) are equal to each other.

This is an important conclusion and helps one to understand why the classical economists were not particularly concerned about unemployment; on the contrary, they actually believed that aggregate demand had no influence on the real income level and hence on employment. If a fall in demand (e.g. from AD_2 to AD_1) causes income to fall to Y_1 (at the price level P_2) and thus brings about unemployment, there is an automatic movement back in the direction of Y_f by means of excess capacity, a drop in the price level and a consequent increase in expenditure.

The Keynesian case

In most macro-economic textbooks – at an elementary as well as an advanced level – you will find that the most important diagrams are similar to those at the end of chapter 3 and in the upper part of figure 4.3. We called such diagrams **total expenditure diagrams**, but they are also known as **Keynesian cross diagrams**, and their main aim is to determine the income level. One could well ask how the price level could be completely ignored. The answer may be found in the **extreme Keynesian** case of the supply curve, as originally explained with reference to figure 4.5 in section 4.3.

This kind of supply curve is repeated in figure 4.9 and, as you will recall, the supply curve in the Keynesian case is completely elastic (parallel to the horizontal axis) until the full employment level (Y_f) is reached; after this the supply curve becomes completely inelastic (i.e. vertical) as indicated by AS_2.

In contrast to the classical case, a definite policy problem now arises which may be explained as follows: In the first place, it should be remembered that an income level that is lower than Y_f falls within the **unemploy-**

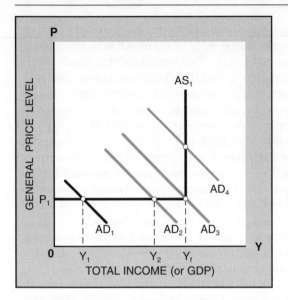

Fig. 4.9 A change in demand in the Keynesian case

A rise in the demand from AD_1 to AD_2 to AD_3 leads to a rise in GDP and full employment at Y_f without an increase in the price level. If there is a further increase in demand, e.g. to AD_4, it gives rise to inflation.

ment area – cf. section 4.2 – of the curve. Now suppose that expenditure is such that the aggregate demand curve is represented by AD_1. The level of income is therefore equal to Y_1, which is considerably lower than the income level at full employment Y_f.

However, since the aggregate supply is completely elastic in this instance, there will be no automatic mechanism, as in the classical case, to drive the economy back to full employment. And this is precisely the policy problem: in the absence of any **automatic mechanism**, the authorities should act in such a way, by means of policy measures, that the income level moves to Y_f. This can be achieved by increasing total expenditure and causing the aggregate demand curve to move to the right. If total expenditure is increased, the aggregate demand curve shifts, e.g. from AD_1 to AD_2. This raises income (or GDP) from Y_1 to Y_2, thus improving the employment position. Full employment can be achieved by increasing expenditure still further so that demand increases to AD_3.

The important point is that the increase from Y_1 to Y_f by manipulation of the demand – this policy is also known as **demand management** – occurs without a rise in the price level. In a purely Keynesian analysis, the price level, and hence the aggregate supply and demand curves, can be ignored as in figure 4.9. In such a case the Keynesian cross diagram suffices. Only if expenditure is further increased (cf. shift from AD_3 to AD_4 in fig. 4.9), will the price level again come to the fore.

This simplifies the policy problem considerably, viz. there is only one specific value (Y_f) where the GDP is at the full employment level. Furthermore, up to Y_f there is **unemployment**, while at values higher than Y_f there is **inflation**. From a policy point of view, this means that until Y_f is reached, total expenditure must be increased by means of demand management (e.g. an increase in G or I); as soon as inflation sets in, demand must be decreased by means of a **drop** in expenditure and the consequent shift of AD to the left.

The trade-off condition

The above argument means that there is no problem in the classical case (fig. 4.8) since the economy looks after itself; in the Keynesian case the policy problems are easily defined. But in today's world things are no longer quite so clear and simple. The reason is that the form of the supply curve as we know it today could in all probability be represented by AS_3 in figure 4.10.

As we explained in section 4.3, this supply curve can be divided into three parts. The first part, which we have called the Keynesian range, extends up to the production level Y_2; up to this point production can be increased with little or no rise in prices. From Y_2 to Y_f it is only possible to increase Y at the cost of a rise in prices. At Y_f, which can also be called the **potential** or **maximum GDP,** no further expansion of Y is possible. When the price level is high, it can also be interpreted as a high rate of inflation.

The problems of the policy-makers are relatively simple in the two extreme situations. If aggregate demand is indicated by AD_5, nothing will be lost by reducing demand from AD_5 to AD_4 – income remains at Y_f while employment of factors of production is also maintained at the maximum

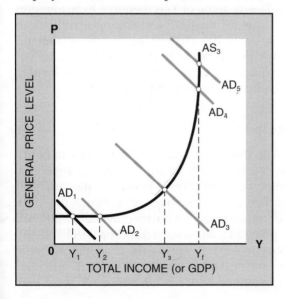

Fig. 4.10 The trade-off-situation

The rising part of the aggregate supply curve holds a clear possibility of a trade-off between unemployment and inflation (the price level).

level. Much is however gained by the fall in the price level (or the inflation rate). From this point onward things become more complicated, however, since a shift from AD$_4$ to AD$_3$ also decreases the level of employment.

The same situation arises, on the other hand, where demand is represented by AD$_1$. The policy-makers will endeavour to shift demand to AD$_2$; this will have a favourable effect on income and employment without affecting the price level. However, the problem again occurs in the rising part of the AS curve where an increase in employment can only be achieved if it is traded off against a rise in the price level – i.e. an increase in the inflation rate.

What then should the government do if the GDP is situated at a level between Y$_2$ and Y$_f$? You will remember that we explained that full employment does not necessarily mean the employment of 100 per cent of the available labour, but that allowances should be made for **frictional unemployment**. This means that a certain unemployment rate, e.g. between 4 and 8 per cent, may be regarded as normal. The GDP that can be produced at this level of unemployment would be called full employment GDP.

The discussion would be simplified by interpreting P on the vertical axis in figure 4.10 as the increase in the general price level, or the inflation rate. We would then have two factors: on the one hand the inflation rate and on the other hand employment (unemployment). Between Y$_2$ and Y$_f$ it is clear that the one changes with the other. The closer we get to Y$_f$, the higher the inflation becomes, and the closer we get to Y$_2$, the greater unemployment becomes. This means that the authorities may, on the basis of a certain level of unemployment plus an acceptable inflation rate, somewhat arbitrarily determine the position of Y$_f$. The meaning of Y$_f$ is therefore to be found in the fact that it becomes the target for the GDP and since it is difficult to manipulate AS, the target can only be achieved by means of **demand management**, i.e. by shifts in AD via total expenditure and the multiplier. In figure 4.10 this means that if Y$_f$ is the target or full employment level of income, the authorities will endeavour to shift demand to AD$_4$.

Demand-pull versus cost-push inflation

To concentrate for a moment on the phenomenon of inflation itself, figure 4.10 shows that inflation is caused by a shift to the right in aggregate demand. For this reason this type of inflation is known as demand-pull inflation. Cutbacks in demand, or demand management, should therefore be able to combat this type of inflation. This is however rendered difficult by the rigidity of wages and prices in a downward direction (cf. chapter 9).

To the dismay of the policy-makers as well as the economists, a new problem made its appearance during the seventies, viz. a rise in the inflation rate without any increase in aggregate demand. What made it worse, was the fact that it was accompanied by a drop in employment. This contrasted sharply and ominously with the analysis based on figure 4.10. Moreover, this version of the diagram offers no explanation of such a phenomenon.

Warnings that this sort of thing could happen had been sounded in the past. In particular, it had been said that inflation would become like a drug, in that more and more of it would be needed; it had also been said that inflation would acquire a life of its own and begin to feed upon itself. This meant that rising prices would result in increased costs, which in turn would give rise to a new round of price increases.

This phenomenon was described as the price-cost spiral in chapter 1. Another example of this involves the wage level. What actually happens nowadays, and has also happened in the past, is that labourers and other employees are compensated for a rise in the cost of living (as measured by the CPI). But this raises wage costs (unless a simultaneous rise in productivity is realized), which can lead to a new round of price increases and consequently further wage increases. This is known as the wage-price spiral. What happens here is not that demand **pulls** prices **up** (demand-pull inflation), but rather that costs exert **pressure** on prices. This is known as **cost-push inflation.**

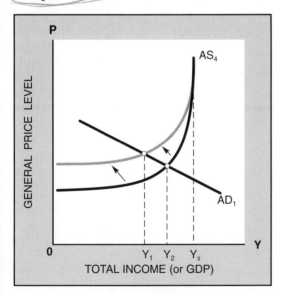

Fig. 4.11 The twin evils of inflation and unemployment

Rising costs push a part of the aggregate supply curve AS₄ upwards. This lowers the GDP, e.g. from Y₂ to Y₁, which entails an increase in unemployment; but at the same time it raises the price level (inflation). These are the twin evils.

This means that aggregate supply is no longer fixed at a certain level, but that it can move upwards and to the left, as shown in figure 4.11. This shift indicates that the same output (Y_1, Y_2, etc.) can only be maintained at higher price levels. The diagram clearly illustrates the extremely undesirable results of the shift, viz. a **drop** in employment (via a drop in GDP, from for example Y_2 to Y_1). This time, however, the drop in employment receives no compensation or trade-off against the inflation rate. On the contrary, an **increase** in the inflation rate accompanies the rise in unemployment. The worst of it all is that there is no obvious solution to the **twin evils of inflation and unemployment**. It is such an important problem that we shall devote chapter 9 exclusively to the problems of present-day inflation. But before we come to this, we are going to turn our attention to specific aspects of aggregate demand in the next four chapters.

Selected references:

Baumol & Blinder: 8, 9, 10.
Dornbusch & Fischer: 6.
Evans-Pritchard: 7.
Froyen: 5, 6.
Gordon: 7.
Shapiro: 4, 5.

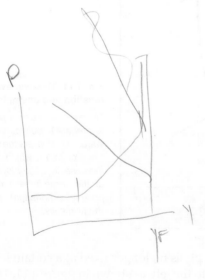

5 Fiscal policy – the role of the government

No mathematical Proof

The government plays a decisive part in the economy by means of its **expenditure programme**, the **taxes** it imposes and general **regulations** concerning various aspects of the economy. Although these regulations (e.g. safety measures prescribed for factories, anti-pollution measures, etc.) can also have an effect on total output, we concentrate in this chapter on aspects of **fiscal policy** which are related exclusively to the revenue and spending of the government.

5.1 The budget

The main instrument for the government's fiscal policy, is the **annual budget** submitted by the Minister of Finance to Parliament. When the budget proposals are approved, the government is empowered to raise certain amounts by way of taxes and to allocate its expenditure for the year in a certain way.

The extent of state expenditure, as well as enormous increases in these expenses over the past decades, necessitates close control and scrutiny. The Treasury draws up the budget in consultation with other state departments and under the direct supervision of the Minister of Finance and the Cabinet. In the final instance the budget is a set of political decisions.

After the budget has been piloted through its various stages in Parliament, the Treasury has to ensure the necessary control so that the budgeted money is spent prudently and for the approved purposes.

The bodies wholly or partly dependent on government funds for their finances are mainly **government departments, statutory bodies** (e.g. SABC, universities, etc.) **provincial administrations, the TBVC states** and **public corporations** (for their share capital).

Although budget procedure and the concomitant control are of primary importance from a parliamentary point of view, in this chapter we are more concerned with the budget's secondary effects on the economy. In other words, we are mainly interested in the way the budget will affect macroeconomic variables such as employment, and the price level. And although we call the influence on these variables **"secondary"** **effects**, there is no doubt that when he presents his budget, the Minister of Finance will thoroughly consider these effects.

What is decisive in this connection, is often the extent of the **aggregates** in the budget such as total spending on the one hand, total taxes on the other hand, and how these two magnitudes compare. That is to say, whether the budget would have a **surplus** or a **deficit**. Traditionally, governments have tried to balance their budgets. In other words, spending had to be equal to income (or revenue) in order to ensure that the budget's effect on the economy would be as neutral as possible.

With the recognition of fiscal policy as a policy instrument in the post-depression years, governments have attempted to draw up their budgets so that their macro-economic effect would be to stabilise the economy. In times of recession (or depression) the budget has to serve as an economic stimulus, but when there is full employment with threatening inflation and/or any balance-of-payments problems, it would be advisable to use the budget to slow down the economy. The primary objective of fiscal policy, therefore, is to stabilise total expenditure (or demand) to such an extent that the most important macro-economic policy objectives (such as full employment, price stability, external equilibrium, etc.) can be achieved.

Fiscal versus monetary policy

We have mentioned that the budget is the government's chief instrument of **fiscal policy**. Apart from fiscal measures, the government can also use **monetary policy** to steer the economy in a chosen direction. These two policy measures are the basis of any government's macro-economic policy. In order to avoid confusion, it is necessary to draw a clear distinction between **fiscal policy** (discussed in the present chapter) and **monetary policy**, which will be explained in the next two chapters.

> **Fiscal policy** is any attempt on the part of the government to influence the economy by means of changes in expenditure and/or taxes in such a way as to minimise unemployment or inflation and encourage economic growth.
> **Monetary policy** is action by the monetary authorities aimed at influencing the quantity of money and/or the rate of interest in order to achieve stable prices and sufficient employment and economic growth.

Although the aims of both sets of measures are essentially the same, there is, in the case of the former, no change in the **quantity of money**; whereas monetary policy can be identified when there *is* such a change in the quantity of money and in the availability of credit. The Reserve Bank and the Treasury together are called the "**monetary authorities**" and are mainly responsible for monetary policy. On the other hand, fiscal policy has its origin in Parliament and reveals itself in the budgetary process.

It is evident that these two policy approaches have to be applied in harmony. For instance, monetary policy may be completely ineffective if not supported by the appropriate fiscal policy. To find the correct "**policy mix**" of the two instruments is one of the more difficult problems facing economic policy-makers (more will be said about this in chapter 7).

Precisely to what extent the government should intervene in the working of the market mechanism is a question economists have been debating since Adam Smith in 1776. The nature and extent of government expenditure differ from country to country and it is not our task at this stage and in our present context to attempt to find the answers to questions such as: What **should** the extent of government spending be and what percentage should it be of domestic expenditure? These are problems that should rather be studied in the framework of another course, **public economics**. It could also be argued that such **normative** problems have no place in the study of economics.

The ever increasing significance of government actions can be observed in all Western countries and in this chapter we merely attempt to determine how this intervention will affect the economy. We can do this by taking a step-by-step look at the nature and extent of both government expenditure and revenue – as well as how each will affect aggregate demand and income. Subsequently we shall examine the combined effect of expenditure and taxation on macro-economic variables.

5.2 Public expenditure

The above reference to the possible effect of public expenditure on macro-economic variables could only be justified if the expenditure was of such an extent that changes in it would significantly affect aggregate demand.

During the nineteenth and early twentieth centuries government spending was largely confined to the most essential services such as the maintenance of law and order, defence of the country's borders and the creation of basic infrastructure. The situation changed radically when the world depression of the thirties showed that the market system did not always lead to the best solution. Influential economists such as Keynes advocated the necessity of government action to lift the economy out of the Depression. An expanded role for the government was also necessary to relieve the misery of the unemployed. Western governments, urged on by their citizens, proceeded to take on more and more responsibilities. Expenditure on social security and welfare services increased enormously while military expenditure and the cost of maintaining the power balance between East and West after the war, reached unprecedented levels.

South Africa was no exception. As a developing country, priority spending went on providing an infrastructure, e.g. roads, electricity, etc. Government expenditure in South Africa has in the past two decades also been characterised by increasing military spending. Tables 5.1 and 5.2 give an impression of the nature and relative extent of public expenditure in South Africa.

Table 5.1 groups the total expenditure for the 1991/92 financial year in five functional categories. It is clear that social services (36,6%) remain the government's first priority, with education (R14 946 million) and health (R8 175 million) the most important subdivisions in this category. The heavy burden placed on the country by protection services (20%) is also clear from the table. The joint expenditure of the police and defence force in the budget, almost equals the amount spent on education. Another item that must be mentioned, is the expenditure on TBVC states (R4 308 million). This amount is related to the development of the so-called homeland policy in South Africa.

The items that fall under economic services underline the importance of the government's involvement in transport, agriculture and the provision of energy, power and water. It is clear that the possibilities of **privatisation** (at present being debated in South Africa) lie in precisely this functional category, representing 11,8 per cent of the total expenditure in 1991/92.

The significance of the public sector as an employer in South Africa, is reflected in table 5.2. If the activities of public corporations and public enterprises (over which the government has effective control) are added to those of general government, it appears that the government is responsible for 34 per cent of all remuneration to employees in this country. The relatively small gross operating surplus of general government activities (compared to labour incomes) is a clear indication of the service character of this sector.[§]

The importance of the government in the South African economy is clearly demonstrated by the fact that almost 30 per cent (last column of table 5.2) of the GDP falls under the direct control of the state.

§   The remuneration of employees plus the gross operating surplus together represent the gross value added of the sector, cf. Chapter 2.

Table 5.1

Important government expenditure items in South Africa. [*] *1991/92 financial year*

Functional classification		R million	%
A PUBLIC SERVICES			
1	Public services	10 440 415	12,3
	Public administration	4 994 569	
	Foreign affairs:		
	TBVC states	4 307 995	
	Other	736 640	
	Public research	401 211	
2	Protection services	16 954 305	20,0
	Defence	9 756 633	
	Police	5 101 656	
	Custody and admin. of justice	2 096 016	
3	Social services	31 078 036	36,6
	Education	14 946 230	
	Health	8 175 228	
	Social security & welfare services	5 477 323	
	Housing	1 086 615	
	Other	1 392 640	
4	Economic services	10 062 356	11,8
	Transport and communication	3 413 985	
	Agriculture	1 521 679	
	Mining	357 788	
	Fuel and energy	139 262	
	Export trade promotion	1 411 542	
	Other	3 218 100	
5	Unallocated	16 350 802	19,2
	State debt cost	12 902 902	
	Other	3 447 900	
Total public services		84 885 914	
B. PUBLIC ENTERPRISE		113 580	0,1
TOTAL		84 999 494	100

[*] Includes current expenditure, capital expenditure and transfer payments.

Source: *Budget review,* March 1991, RSA, Finance Department.

Table 5.1 *An analysis of the more important expenditure items shows that social services and protection services together make up almost 60 per cent of the total budget.*

Table 5.2

Gross domestic product by type of organization (at factor cost), 1991

Type of organisation	Remuneration of employees		Gross operating surplus		Gross domestic product	
	R million	%	R million	%	R million	%
Private business enterprises	88 830	63	76 224	79	165 052	70
Public corporations*	10 578		13 708		24 286	
Government business enterprises**	3 738	33	4 607	21	8 345	28
General government	31 558		1 584		33 142	
Other***	5 494	4	139	–	5 633	2
Total	140 198		96 262		236 460	

*   Includes Transnet
**   Includes Telcom
***   Non-profit institutions and domestic servants

Source: Information supplied by Central Statistical Services.

Table 5.2   *The distribution of GDP generated by various types of organisations between remuneration of employees and the gross operating surplus, shows that organisations under the direct influence of the government are responsible for about 28 per cent of the GDP (last column). Further-more, these organisations pay out 33 per cent of all salaries and wages in South Africa.*

Government expenditure and the level of income

In previous discussions we have repeatedly referred to the effect of govern-ment spending on other macro-economic magnitudes. We saw in chapter 3 (fig. 3.8) how government spending together with other components of **domestic expenditure** could be represented graphically. In this way the $(C + I + G)$ line was constructed. In the subsequent figure 3.9 **total spend-ing** was represented graphically with the addition (or subtraction) of exports and imports $(X - Z)$. We also found that the equilibrium level of income was determined where this total spending line (TS in fig. 3.10) intersected the 45° line. In other words, point E_1 in figure 5.1 is an equili-brium point similar to point E_1 in figure 3.10. Now, if the government were to decide to raise government expenditure by an amount equal to ΔG, the level of income rises from Y_1 to Y_2. Note that the increase in Y (ΔY) is greater than the change in government spending (ΔG).

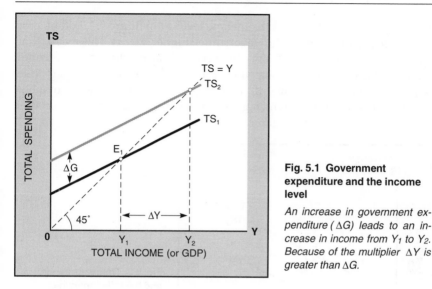

Fig. 5.1 Government expenditure and the income level

An increase in government expenditure (ΔG) leads to an increase in income from Y₁ to Y₂. Because of the multiplier ΔY is greater than ΔG.

So, as could be expected, the **multiplier effect** (which has already been referred to) is operative when G changes. By means of the equation (3.6) which we formulated in chapter 3, the increase in the equilibrium level of income can be calculated as follows:

$$\Delta Y = \frac{1}{1-c} \Delta G \dots\dots\dots\dots\dots\dots\dots\dots\dots\dots\dots\dots\dots\dots \quad 5.1$$

If the marginal propensity to consume is equal to 0,75 (= ¾), an increase of R10 million in government spending (ΔG) will lead to the following increase in the level of income:

$$\Delta Y = \frac{1}{1-c} \Delta G$$

$$= \frac{1}{1-0,75} \times 10$$

$$= 4 \times 10$$

$$= \text{R40 million}$$

The recessionary and the inflationary gap

In spite of active participation by the government it may happen, as was the case during the depression years in the thirties, that total expenditure in the economy is still insufficient to ensure full employment. Suppose the economy is in equilibrium at the income level Y_1 in figure 5.2. Potential or full employment income is, however, much higher, viz. Y_f. This means that there is an **income gap** of Y_1Y_f between actual product and potential product. It is not only desirable, it is even the duty of government to take steps to eliminate this below full capacity product and the unemployment it causes. The amount by which government spending has to be raised is known as the **recessionary gap**.

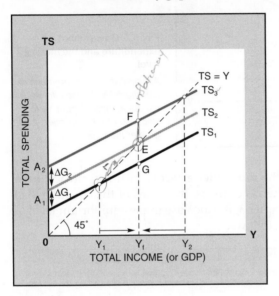

Fig. 5.2 The recessionary and the inflationary gap

The recessionary gap is indicated by the distance between the TS line and the 45° line at the full employment level of income (EG). The inflationary gap is measured in a similar fashion, except that the TS line will lie above the 45° line (EF above).

The recessionary gap in figure 5.2 is equal to EG. An increase of EG in government spending will, via the multiplier, lead to the elimination of the income gap Y_1Y_f and bring about full employment. If the income gap is equal to R100 million and the marginal propensity to consume is 0,5 ($=\frac{1}{2}$), this means, according to equation 5.1 above, that the recessionary gap is equal to R50 million. Although the distance EG is precisely the same as ΔG_1, as indicated on the vertical axis, it is customary in graphic work to show the recessionary gap at the full employment level.

Just as there can be a recessionary gap it is possible that there will be an **inflationary gap**. Such an inflationary gap will arise as a consequence of an excess of spending in the economy. Total spending (or aggregate demand) exceeds the full employment production level (Y_f) and, given the production capacity, supply cannot keep up with this demand. Graphically this situation is represented by the TS_3 line in figure 5.2. It is clear that an inflationary gap can exist only if the TS line is positioned above the 45° line *at* the level of income associated with full employment. The inflationary gap is represented by EF in the figure.

If the overheated economic condition is not caused by a situation over which the government has no control, such as a state of war, the required fiscal policy would be to **reduce** government spending by EF (= ΔG_2) so that equilibrium is reached at point E.

Of course, it should always be remembered that the determination of the recessionary and inflationary gaps is no more than a theoretical representation of the problem. In practice no government can determine accurately what fiscal measures should be taken.

5.3 Taxes

In the discussion thus far, government **revenue** has deliberately been ignored. This was done to keep the number of variables in our analysis as small as possible. However, it would be unrealistic to analyse the effect of government expenditure without looking at how this expenditure is financed.

Taxes are the chief source of revenue of the government. In analysing the tax system, it is just as well to note that in its basic approach to financing, the government differs completely from the individual. A private person usually tailors his expenditure to his income; as against this, governments often first determine how much they wish to spend and then they consider how to obtain the required funds. Although the necessary items of expenditure are probably determined with a reasonable measure of conservatism and care, this budgetary procedure on the part of a government shows a very important distinction between the private and public sectors. This procedure can succeed because taxes, in contrast to payments involved in ordinary transactions, are not *voluntary* payments. No one can refuse to pay taxes. Provided the authorities succeed in making a reasonably accurate prediction of the GDP (or, in other words, economic activity) in the next financial year, there is considerable certainty about expected tax revenue.

Direct versus indirect taxes

A government may use a variety of taxes to finance its expenditure programme. Table 5.3 contains a summary of the chief sources of revenue of the government based on the levying of taxes.

In order to determine how the structure of government revenue changed over time, information regarding 1980/81 as well as 1991/92 is provided in the table. The data distinguish between direct and indirect taxes. As indicated by their name, **direct taxes** are levied directly on individuals and institutions, whereas **indirect taxes** are levied on goods and services and therefore only indirectly on individuals or institutions.

Table 5.3

Composition of the tax revenue in South Africa, 1980/81 and 1991/92

Source of income	1980/81		1991/92*	
	R million	%	R million	%
Direct taxes:	**7 833,2**	**57**	**46 669,0**	**57,7**
Income tax:				
Personal	2 090,9	15,2	28 800,0	35,6
Companies	2 417,6	17,6	13 650,0	16,8
Gold mines	2 794,8	20,3	505,0	0,6
Other mines	211,6	1,5	1 259,0	1,5
Other direct taxes	318,3	2,3	2 455,0	3,0
Indirect taxes:	**3 923,8**	**28**	**30 501,0**	**37,7**
Customs and exise	1 477,2	10,7	5 850,0	7,2
Sales tax	1 653,1	12,0	20 320,0**	25,1
Fuel levy			3 987,0	4,9
Other indirect taxes	793,5	5,8	344,0	0,4
Miscellaneous	2 001,3	15	3 715,0	4,6
Total income	13 758,3	100	80 885,0	100

* Provisional estimates.
** This amount also includes VAT since its introduction in 1991.

Source: *Statistical/Economic Review*, Budget 1983/84 and *Budget review*, March 1991.
Government Printer, Pretoria.

Table 5.3 *Taxes can be classified according to direct and indirect taxes. Direct taxes contribute 57 per cent of the total income from taxes.*

In obtaining funds, the government relies mainly on direct taxes, in the form of income tax. Approximately 57 per cent of all taxes in 1991/92 consist of income tax levied on persons, companies and mines. An interesting structural difference that emerges when the two financial years are compared, is the increasing importance of personal income tax and general sales tax (GST). The combined contribution of these two sources of income amounted to 60 per cent of total revenue in 1991/92 compared to a mere 27 per cent in 1980/81. The most important reasons for these substantial increases may be found in (i) the phenomenon of "bracket creeping" which occurred in connection with personal income tax during this period and (ii) the systematic increase in the rate at which GST was imposed.

Bracket creeping occurs when, as a result of inflation (and thus wage increases), a taxpayer finds himself continually in a higher taxable income bracket. As will be noticed from table 5.4, where the personal income tax rates are given, the rates at which individuals are taxed increase as their nominal taxable income rises. If salaries keep pace with the inflation rate, therefore, an individual could well find himself in a much higher marginal tax category after a few years, without his real income having increased in any way. This bracket creeping was, in part, responsible for the fact that the relative contribution from personal income tax increased from a modest 15,2 per cent in 1980/81 to 35,6 per cent in 1991/92 (cf. table 5.3). This matter is also referred to in chapter 9 – see remarks on "fiscal dividend" in section 9.1. The important contribution (roughly 20 per cent) of the gold mining industry to the tax revenue is obvious for the 1980/81 financial year. This was mainly caused by the very high gold price realised during 1980. With the drop in the price of gold in subsequent years, this source of revenue never reached similar levels again and during 1991/92 it contributed only R505 million (0,6 per cent) of the total tax revenue.

The introduction of GST in 1978 led to a considerable increase in the significance of indirect taxes in South Africa. The systematic increase in the rate at which GST is levied (from 4 per cent in 1978 to 13 per cent in 1991) has raised the importance of indirect taxes even more during the 1980s.

In the midst of serious objections from various quarters the government, on 1 October 1991, went ahead to introduce a **value added tax** (VAT) to replace the existing GST. Initially the rate at which this new indirect tax was to be introduced was set at 12 per cent. After threats of strikes and stay-away actions the government relented by scaling down the VAT-rate to 10 per cent. Unlike GST, which is payable only by the end-user (or at the point of purchase), VAT is paid on the increased value of the product or service at every link in the chain of distribution. It is recovered from the purchaser by the seller and is then paid to the tax collector. Like GST, it is in reality also a tax on consumption as, in the final analysis, the end-user pays the tax.

Without GST as a source of revenue, the R20 320 million for the 1991/92 tax year would probably have had to be obtained from increased income tax. Other examples of indirect taxes that make an important contribution to the exchequer in South Africa, are excise duties on goods such as fuel, cigarettes and alcohol, customs duty, and an additional levy on fuel.

Apart from the distinction between direct and indirect taxes, it is also instructive to distinguish between progressive, proportional and regressive taxes:

> A tax is **progressive** if the percentage tax levied **rises** with an increase in the level of income.

> A tax is **proportional** if the tax levied remains a **constant** percentage with an increase in the level of income.
>
> A tax is **regressive** if the percentage tax levied **diminishes** with an increase in the level of income.

Normally indirect taxes are taken to be regressive or proportional whereas direct taxes (usually personal income taxes) are progressive. However, this association does not always apply and each tax has to be considered separately before it can be placed in a particular category. Let us look at some examples.

1. **Personal income tax** is in South Africa, as in most other countries, levied on a progressive basis. That is to say, a larger percentage of tax is paid as income rises. A progressive tax, therefore, diminishes the inequality in the distribution of disposable income.

2. **Company tax** in South Africa is levied on the basis of **proportionality**, since a constant percentage (50 per cent) of company profits is paid to the Receiver of Revenue.

3. A **poll tax**, which levies a certain constant amount on individuals, is a good example of a direct but regressive tax. It is regressive because those with a higher income automatically pay a **lower** percentage of their income in the form of this tax. The poll tax of R2,50 per year levied on Blacks in South Africa was abolished in 1977.

4. The **GST** and **VAT** levied on a wide variety of goods and services falls more heavily on the lower income groups than on the rich and is therefore **regressive**. Although a fixed percentage is levied on all sales, people in the lower income brackets will pay relatively more because a larger part of their income is spent on consumer goods. In other words, the amount paid by the higher income groups on GST or VAT will be a **smaller percentage** of their income.

Personal income tax

When looking at income tax rates in South Africa, the progressive nature of this tax can be clearly seen. Before we do this, the following definitions are relevant:

> The **average tax rate** is that percentage or proportion of income paid out in tax.

> The **marginal tax rate** is the percentage or proportion of each **additional** Rand earned which has to be paid out in taxes.

Table 5.4 gives the average and marginal tax rates applicable in the 1991 tax year to married individuals in South Africa. The marginal rate rises from 15 per cent on a taxable income of less than R5 000 per annum to a maximum of 43 per cent on a taxable income of R80 000 and over. The last column in table 5.4 shows the **lowest** average tax rate in each interval, i.e. the rates are calculated on the first or lowest value in each interval. On a taxable income of R15 000 per annum the tax is R2 550 (17 per cent of R15 000). If taxable income amounts to R15 200, the tax will be R2 550 + (21 per cent of 200) = R2 592.

Table 5.4

Personal income tax rates* in South Africa, 1991

Taxable income	Marginal rate	Lowest average rate in each interval
Rand	%	%
– 5 000	15	
5 000 – 10 000	17	15
10 000 – 15 000	19	16
15 000 – 20 000	21	17
20 000 – 25 000	23	18
25 000 – 30 000	26	19
30 000 – 35 000	29	20,17
35 000 – 40 000	32	21,43
40 000 – 45 000	35	22,75
45 000 – 50 000	38	24,11
50 000 – 55 000	39	25,5
55 000 – 60 000	40	26,73
60 000 – 70 000	41	27,83
70 000 – 80 000	42	29,71
80 000 – +	43	31,25

* Married persons

Table 5.4 *The tax rate levied on the income of persons increase as their taxable income increases. It is thus a progressive tax, e.g. a person with a taxable income of R15 000 pays an average of 17 per cent in tax. If his taxable income increases to R40 000 his average tax rate increases to 22,75 per cent. This marginal rate refers to the percentage tax paid on additional income.*

Once taxable income reaches R80 000, the marginal rate remains constant. However, this does not mean that the average rate also remains at the same level or that progression disappears. As taxable income moves beyond the R80 000 mark, the average tax rate will move closer to 43 per cent. This is illustrated by the following examples:

1.   The tax on taxable income of R100 000 will, according to table 5.4, amount to:

31,25 percent of R80 000	=	R25 000
+ 43,0 percent of R20 000	=	R 8 600
Total tax		R33 600

Therefore, the average tax rate is $\dfrac{33\ 600}{100\ 000} = 33{,}6$ per cent.

2.   The tax on a taxable income of R140 000 will be calculated as follows:

31,25 percent of R80 000	=	R25 000
+ 43,0 percent of R60 000	=	R25 800
Total tax		R50 800

Therefore, the average tax rate is $\dfrac{50\ 800}{140\ 000} = 36{,}28$ per cent.

In other words, even when the marginal rate is constant, the tax remains progressive.

How do taxes affect the level of GDP?

It is obvious that taxes will affect total spending (TS) in the opposite direction of government expenditure. But, because taxes are not part of total spending in a country, they do not affect the level of income in the same direct way as government spending. We saw earlier on that an increase in government expenditure (G) would shift the TS line by the same amount and the effect on the level of income could be deduced via the multiplier (cf. fig. 5.1).

The levying of a tax affects the income level in a more indirect way. From experience we know that taxes reduce our disposable income (Y_d).[§]

§   Taxes can also affect investment, and company tax will affect the expenditure patterns of companies. However, in this section our explanation is confined to taxes on individuals and their effect on consumer spending.

Although it is a simplification, disposable income[§] can be defined as follows:

$$Y_d = Y - T$$
where Y_d = disposable income
Y = the real level of income (or GDP)
T = total taxes.

Before any taxes were levied Y and Y_d were the same ($Y = Y_d$), and the extent of consumption was determined by the level of Y. Once a tax is levied, consumption expenditure becomes a function of Y_d. Because Y_d is less than Y, consumption will also diminish. A lower level of consumption spending will lead to a lower level of total spending (TS) and this will therefore bring about a lower equilibrium level of GDP.

The influence of a lump sum tax

Just as in the case of government spending, the effect of taxation can be represented graphically. In order to keep the problem as simple as possible, we make the assumption that the tax referred to is a lump sum tax. That is to say, a fixed amount is collected from everyone irrespective of income. The poll tax we mentioned earlier on is an example of such a lump sum tax.

Graphically the effect of such a tax is indicated by a parallel downward shift of the consumption function (from C_1 to C_2 in fig. 5.3). Because this is a lump sum tax (and not an income tax) the size of the tax is the same at all income levels so that there is no change in the gradient of the consumption function. The same movement is also seen in the case of the TS line because C is a component of total spending. Again it is clear that there is a multiplier effect (this time in a negative direction). The equilibrium level of income decreases from Y_2 to Y_1.

A more accurate assessment of the effect of such a lump-sum tax on the level of income can be made algebraically. As shown above, the taxation has an effect mainly on consumption spending. This effect is, in other words, exercised on the consumption function in the model. The basic model of three equations can therefore be adapted as follows:

---

§ Transfer payments which may affect disposable income are not taken into account here.

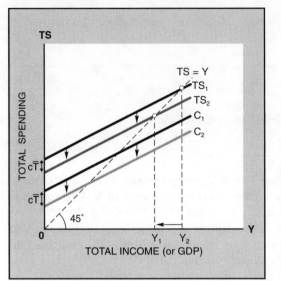

Fig. 5.3 Taxes and the income level

The introduction of a lump sum tax $(\overline{T})$ reduces consumption (from C_1 to C_2) and thus also total spending (TS_1 to TS_2). The reductions in the TS or C lines are only equal to cT.

$$C = \overline{C} + cY_d \quad\text{..}\quad 5.1$$
$$Y_d = Y - \overline{T} \quad\text{..}\quad 5.2$$
$$TS = C + \overline{I} + \overline{G} \quad\text{..}\quad 3.2a$$
$$Y = TS \quad\text{..}\quad 3.3$$

Equation 5.1 shows that consumption now is a function of disposable income (Y_d), which is defined in equation 5.2. The other two equations remain exactly as in the original model. Since it is a lump-sum tax, T is considered to be an autonomous variable in the model. By means of substitution (equation 5.2 in 5.1) the following more workable consumption function is obtained:

$$
\begin{aligned}
C &= \overline{C} + c(Y - \overline{T}) \\
&= \overline{C} + cY - c\overline{T} \\
&= (\overline{C} - c\overline{T}) + cY \quad\text{.................................}\quad 5.3
\end{aligned}
$$

We have now succeeded in defining the consumption function in such a way that we can again distinguish between autonomous consumption ($\overline{C} - cT$) and that portion of consumption that is related to the level of income (cY). The only difference in comparison with the consumption function in the original model is that autonomous consumption (i.e. the intercept on the vertical axis) has been reduced by $c\overline{T}$ as a result of taxation.

Now the model may once again be represented by means of the three familiar equations:

$$C = (\overline{C} - c\overline{T}) + cY \dots\dots\dots\dots\dots\dots 5.3$$
$$TS = C + \overline{I} + \overline{G} \dots\dots\dots\dots\dots\dots 3.2a$$
$$Y = TS \dots\dots\dots\dots\dots\dots\dots 3.3$$

The solution for the level of income is therefore calculated as follows:

$$Y = C + \overline{I} + \overline{G}$$
$$= (\overline{C} - c\overline{T}) + cY + \overline{I} + \overline{G}$$

$$\therefore Y - cY = \overline{C} - c\overline{T} + \overline{I} + \overline{G}$$
$$= \overline{A} - c\overline{T} \qquad \overline{A} = (\overline{C} + \overline{I} + \overline{G}) = \text{autonomous expenditure}$$

$$\therefore Y = \frac{1}{1-c}(\overline{A} - c\overline{T}) \dots\dots\dots\dots\dots\dots 5.4$$

or $\therefore Y = \dfrac{1}{1-c}\overline{A} + \dfrac{1}{1-c}(-c\overline{T}) \dots\dots\dots\dots\dots$ 5.4a

Before the introduction of the lump-sum taxation the solution for the equilibrium level of income was the following:

$$Y = \frac{1}{1-c}\overline{A} \dots\dots\dots\dots\dots\dots\dots 3.5$$

The difference between 5.4a and 3.5 therefore gives the change in the equilibrium income arising from the levying of the tax:

$$\Delta Y = \frac{1}{1-c}(\cancel{A + c\overline{T}})\ (-c\Delta\overline{T})$$
$$= \frac{-c}{1-c}\Delta\overline{T} \dots\dots\dots\dots\dots\dots 5.5$$

This tax multiplier $\left(\dfrac{-c}{1-c}\right)$ **therefore is negative** and also **smaller** than the normal multiplier. This may be illustrated by means of the following example:

Assume that the lump-sum tax that is introduced produces a yield of R10 million and that the marginal propensity to consume is equal to 0,75 (¾). The influence of the two actions may be summarized as follows:

$$\Delta Y = \frac{-c}{1-c}\Delta \overline{T}$$
$$= \frac{-0{,}75}{1-0{,}75} \times 10$$
$$= \frac{-0{,}75}{0{,}25} \times 10$$
$$= -3 \times 10$$
$$= -\text{R30 million}$$

However, unlike expenditure by the government (i.e. an increase in G), an increase in tax causes a **decrease** in the equilibrium level of income. It is particularly interesting that government expenditure and taxes do not have exactly the same opposite effect on equilibrium income. Let us illustrate this point once again by means of an example:

Assume an increase in government spending (ΔG) of R10 million, financed by means of a lump-sum tax. We again assume a marginal propensity to consume of 0,75 (= ¾). The influence of the two actions may be summarised as follows:

Effect of ΔG:

$$\Delta Y = \frac{1}{1-c}\Delta G$$
$$= 4 \times 10$$
$$= \text{R40 million}$$

Effect of ΔT:

$$\Delta Y = \frac{-c}{1-c}\Delta T$$
$$= -3 \times 10$$
$$= -\text{R30 million}$$

The combined effect of these two actions may be represented as follows:

$$\Delta Y = \frac{1}{1-c}\Delta G + \left(\frac{-c}{1-c}\Delta T\right)$$

Because $\Delta G = \Delta T$, it follows that

$$\Delta Y = \frac{1}{1-c}\Delta G - \frac{c}{1-c}\Delta G$$
$$= \frac{1-c}{1-c}\Delta G$$
$$= 1 \times \Delta G$$
$$= 1 \times 10$$
$$= \text{R10 million}$$

Such a balanced budget action therefore, contrary to what one would expect, does not have a neutral effect on the equilibrium level of income. The income level actually increases by the exact same amount as the increase in government spending. That is why we say that **the multiplier effect of a balanced budget action, where ΔG is equal to ΔT, is exactly equal to 1**.

The practical explanation for this somewhat unexpected result naturally lies in the fact that taxes, when they are levied, are not **exclusively** financed by a reduction in spending, but are also partly financed from savings. For that very reason the TS and C lines in figure 5.3 do not decline by the full amount of the taxes, but only by cT. However, as we saw in figure 5.2, the TS line moves by the full amount of the change in government spending.

Hence **taxation** is, regardless of other considerations, an appropriate fiscal measure when it appears that aggregate demand is too high and an inflationary tendency is present in the economy. **Tax concessions** (i.e. a decrease in taxes) obviously have the opposite effect. Disposable income will now **rise** and this will lead to an increase in consumption expenditure which in its turn causes a rise in the equilibrium level of income. Although more realistic forms of taxation such as a proportional or progressive income tax are slightly more involved, the conclusion made in regard to fiscal action is also applicable to these types of tax.

5.4 Policy implications

From the preceding discussion of government expenditure (G) and taxes (T) and their effect on total spending, a number of policy implications became apparent. When analysing these policy implications we cannot, as we did in the previous two sections, consider expenditure and taxation in isolation. The annual budget of the Minister of Finance is, after all, a combination of government expenditure and taxes.

The main policy implications which we found thus far were:

(i)   Total expenditure and therefore aggregate demand can be stimulated by raising G and/or lowering taxes.

(ii) Total spending and aggregate demand can be cut down by decreasing G and/or raising taxes.

The type of fiscal policy or aggregate demand prescribed by (i) implies that the government has to plan for a **deficit** on the budget. In other words, it should be seen to that G > T. Government expenditure can only exceed taxes if the government succeeds in financing its deficit by way of borrowing (domestic as well as foreign). Case (ii) means that the government must act in such a way that there is a **surplus** on the budget (G < T). Spending must therefore not exceed revenue from taxation. Therefore, in principle, the same result can be achieved by changing *either* government spending *or* taxes. The question is: should there be any preference for the one or the other?

Government expenditure versus taxation

Initially, not long after Keynes pointed out the particular advantages of fiscal policy and especially government spending, there was a period when the accent was placed mainly on government expenditure in the management of aggregate demand. More recently, and especially since the sixties, tax changes have gained much prominence as instruments of fiscal policy. Today it is generally accepted that taxes are more flexible than government expenditure in carrying out economic policy. Large projects such as the building of freeways, dams, etc., once they have been started by the state, cannot be suspended as soon as there is a necessity to reduce aggregate demand. The long-term planning required by such projects means they cannot be started at short notice either, when circumstances (from a fiscal policy point of view) would be appropriate. On the other hand, taxes can be changed with considerable effect in a relatively short period. In South Africa tax changes and even a "tax holiday" of several months have been applied in the past. The Minister of Finance is also empowered to announce tax changes between budgets.

Another important reason for the increasing emphasis on changes in taxation rather than government spending, is the mounting suspicion felt in many Western countries in regard to the increasing role of governments. Many people doubt the governments' capacity to spend money as effectively as is done by the private sector. In addition to this, there are some groups who fear that government intervention will take on such excessive dimensions that it will endanger the survival of the free market system.

Fiscal policy and inflation

It is time to have a look at the effect of fiscal policy on the price level. In the preceding sections of this chapter we based our discussion on the "Keynesian cross" diagrams where the general price level is left out. Although we did occasionally refer to concepts such as the "inflationary gap", the discussion did not actually acknowledge the price level as a variable.

In order to take price into account, we use the analysis of aggregate demand and aggregate supply explained in chapters 3 and 4. You will recall that shifts in total spending (TS) were reflected in shifts in aggregate demand (AD). An increase in public **spending** shifts the AD curve to the right, whereas an increase in **taxes** shifts the aggregate demand curve to the left.

Without taking account of the aggregate supply curve we have no complete picture of the state of affairs. It is particularly the **position** and the **gradient** of the aggregate supply curve that will determine what effect

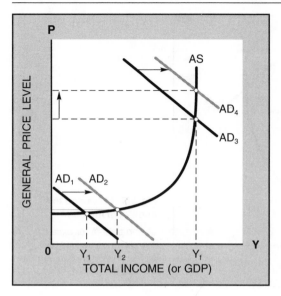

Fig. 5.4 Government spending and the position of the aggregate supply curve

The success of an increase in government expenditure will depend on the position and slope of the AS curve. A shift from AD_1 to AD_2 is very favourable, while a shift from AD_3 to AD_4 has no effect on the level of income.

fiscal policy measures are going to have. Figure 5.4 explains this statement further:

(i)   We first take the case where the economy is in a recession with considerable unemployment and idle capacity. Such a situation is represented by the income level Y_1 (i.e. the intersection of AS and AD_1). If the government decides to stimulate aggregate demand by raising expenditure, there is a shift to, e.g., AD_2. This policy will be very successful because it leads to a *considerable* rise in the level of production but a *minimal* rise in the price level.

(ii) The second case represented in figure 5.4 is a situation of full employment with little or no idle capacity in the economy. An increase in government expenditure (causing a shift from AD_3 to AD_4) at this stage leads to inflation without any increase in real GDP. The additional demand created by government spending only means that an already overheated economy experiences a fresh wave of price increases.

Taxation can be analysed in a similar way. Figure 5.5 shows clearly how successful a rise in taxes can be in combating inflation which may be ascribed to excess demand. The downward shift from AD_1 to AD_2 as a result of the rise in taxes leads to a considerable decrease in the price level without affecting the level of production seriously. It should now be clear that an increase in taxes in a time of recession (where AS follows a relatively flat course) may have extremely detrimental effects, for production will

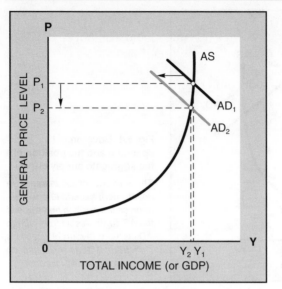

Fig. 5.5 Taxes and the curbing of inflation

During periods of excessive demand an increase in taxation can be successful in bringing down the rate of inflation.

decrease significantly, thus lowering employment further while prices will remain more or less unchanged.

Fiscal policy and the aggregate supply curve

The preceding discussion may have created the impression that fiscal policy is used only to stimulate aggregate demand. Although this certainly is the most important function of fiscal policy, we also have to admit the possibility that fiscal action could hold implications for aggregate supply. In section 1.5 of chapter 1 reference has already been made to the **supply-side economics** which emerged during the 1980s. According to economists who have associated themselves with this school of thought, tax concessions (such as a reduction in the marginal tax rates) could have a positive effect on the supply curve of the economy. The reduction in taxes will, according to this theory, serve as an incentive for people to work harder, increase productivity and improve the general production climate in the economy.

As a result, the AS curve will move to the right, which could have an extremely favourable overall effect on production and on the inflation rate. Such a situation is shown in figure 5.6, where the initial increase in aggregate demand, from AD_1 to AD_2, (as a result of the reduction in taxes), is accompanied by a move to the right in the aggregate supply curve from AS_1 to AS_2. It is clear that this kind of policy action has the ideal effect, as production (level of income) is increased while inflation is reduced. The increase in the level of income from Y_1 to Y_2 is accompanied by a slight drop in the general price level. The proponents of this policy package have further argued that the government's revenue would also not be affected adversely by the reduction in taxes. The economic growth and increased income arising from it would lead to an increase in tax revenue, even at the lower tax rates. The government could therefore continue its programme of expenditure without any funding problems.

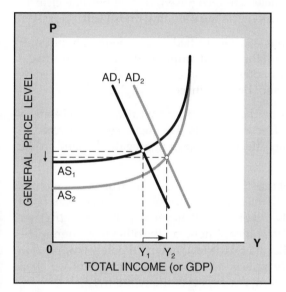

Fig. 5.6 Fiscal policy and the aggregate supply curve

According to some economists, tax concessions could also have a positive influence on the AS curve. A reduction in tax rates could therefore move both the AD and AS curves to the right, which would be favourable for both the level of income and the inflation rate.

When a similar policy was applied in the USA at the beginning of the Reagan administration (1981), it appeared in practice that the above theoretical ideal was not so easy to achieve. The tax reductions did reduce the inflation rate, but were unfortunately also accompanied by a drop in production. The result of this was a particularly high budget deficit in the USA, which is still causing problems for the Americans.

Other factors that hamper government policy

Lags

In the theoretical models used in this chapter it seemed as if any decision related to fiscal policy would be clear and obvious. Whether the government should stimulate or retard the economy could be determined with little difficulty. In practice the position is not always so clear. One reason for this may be found in the delay or **lag** between the time when it becomes necessary to influence aggregate demand and the time when fiscal action becomes effective. This lag or delay can be explained as follows:

(i)   The authorities do not always have the required data or insight to **recognise** the necessity of corrective action. Unfortunately, the growth in the GDP is not constant, but fluctuates irregularly above and below a long-term trend. This results in an irregular cyclical movement within which upward swings are followed by downward swings. Only gradually when data, e.g. on unemployment and prices, come to hand and certain tendencies are recognised, does it become clear in which phase of the business cycle the economy finds itself.

(ii)   When the government has at last identified the problem, it should start taking action. However, the actual **implementation** of the fiscal measure concerned also takes time; after all, tax changes and new expenditure projects cannot be introduced overnight.

(iii) After the fiscal measure has been introduced, a further period elapses before the action has **effective results**. For instance, an increase in taxes will not lead to an effective drop in aggregate demand in the first few months.

If we take account of the fact that the total lag may vary from a few months to almost two years, it becomes clear that the consequences of certain fiscal measures may be completely out of place. Policy may in fact at such a later stage contribute to further instability rather than the other way round. The problems are further complicated by the fact that fiscal policy is applied in combination with monetary policy. In the next two chapters we shall discuss the problems underlying this aspect of the economy.

The balance of payments

Even if we ignore the problem of lags, the choice of fiscal action can also be complicated by the country's **balance of payments**. The unemployment rate could point to the advisability of an expansionary fiscal policy, while the reality of the balance of payments could compel the government to continue its restrictive fiscal action. Stimulating fiscal measures could lead to an unacceptable weakening of the country's foreign exchange reserves. Particularly in a country such as South Africa, where the balance of payments plays such a decisive role in determining the growth potential, the execution of fiscal policy cannot be independent of these considerations. This matter will be discussed in greater detail in chapter 8.

Downward rigidity of prices

It should also be remembered that, although any increase in aggregate demand at an income level close to the full employment level gives rise to

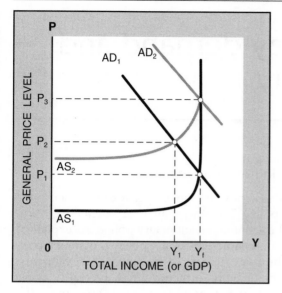

Fig. 5.7 The downward rigidity of prices

Any decrease in aggregate demand from AD₂ to AD₁ does not cause the expected drop in prices because wages and prices tend to be rigid in the downward direction. What is apparently happening here, is that there is a shift from AS₁ to AS₂ so that prices drop only to the level of P₂.

drastic price increases, the opposite does not necessarily happen. In figure 5.7 an increase in aggregate demand from AD_1 to AD_2 (along the AS_1 curve) will lead to an increase in the price level from P_1 to P_3. Should the government then manage, by means of fiscal control, to shift the entire demand curve to the left from AD_2 to AD_1, the inherent downward rigidity of prices could seriously hamper the success of such a policy measure. As the figure shows, it could happen that the effect of such a measure would be reflected in a drop in production rather than in a reduction in prices. The same reduction in aggregate demand therefore reduces prices only to the level of P_2 because the supply curve has apparently moved upwards. This downward rigidity of prices is a phenomenon that appears to be related to the **expectations** of individuals that prices will in future be steadily higher than at present. Such price expectations keep the price level abnormally high in the midst of a decrease in aggregate demand.

Selected references:

Baumol & Blinder: 11.
Dernburg: 5.
Dornbusch & Fischer: 6.
Evans-Pritchard: 10.
Froyen: 18.
Gordon: 3, 17.
Morley: 5, 16.
Shapiro: 6.

6 Money demand and supply

6.1 The role of money – introductory remarks

In the previous chapter we saw how the government can influence the economy by means of fiscal policy. The other main instrument the government can use to influence the economy, is monetary policy. As explained in chapter 1 and in the previous chapter, monetary policy is mainly associated with efforts to control the money supply to the benefit of the economy.

Exactly how changes in the quantity of money affect the real or actual welfare of a country, remains a matter of controversy among economists. It is actually surprising that no certainty (or even any generally accepted theory) exists even today as to exactly how money influences the economy. One could well ask whether it would not be obvious that an increase in the money supply would lead to increased expenditure and hence greater demand, which in turn would lead to an increase in production and/or prices.

Although we have so far assumed a positive correlation between real income and real expenditure, it does not necessarily follow that an increase in the quantity of money will bring about an increase in real expenditure. The important point to remember, is that money is not real income. It should be obvious by now that there can be no mechanical or technical connection between an increase in the quantity of money and a higher production of goods and services. If this were the case, the world's poverty and development problems could have been solved overnight.

Nevertheless, the role of money remains an extremely topical question of our time. Although no simple relation exists between money and real economic growth, economists do in fact accept that the influence of money on the economy is not entirely neutral. The supposed **neutrality of money** was for many years the cornerstone of classical economic theory. It was thought that the amount of money in circulation could influence only the absolute price level (e.g., a doubling of the money stock would lead to a doubling of the price level) without having any real effect on welfare or production.

Today, however, we think differently about money. But before outlining this complex question, we first have to examine a few of the basic characteristics of money. In general, we shall deal with the functions of money,

132

its definition, and with the factors and institutions determining the supply and demand of money. In chapter 7 we shall look at the relation between money and economic activity and see how the government can influence economic activity by means of monetary policy.

6.2 The functions of money

Money as a medium of exchange

Money is such an integral part of our daily lives that its significance is not always appreciated. Just how important money is, can perhaps be understood by imagining an economy that functions without it. In such a barter economy, goods can only be exchanged for other goods. For example, a wheat farmer requiring clothing for his family, first has to find a tailor who needs wheat. Then the exchange can take place. If no tailor can be found who happens to want wheat, the farmer will be obliged to exchange his wheat for something else that the tailor *does* require. In other words, before the exchange of two goods can take place, there has to be a **double coincidence of requirements** between the parties concerned. The barter economy is therefore necessarily characterised by manifold exchange transactions which are cumbersome and inefficient. For each of the farmer's (or anybody else's) numerous requirements, a particular person has to be found who has a specific need for his product.

This obvious inefficiency of the barter economy led, even in early primitive communities, to the use of some form of money. The advantages of a **monetary economy**, where exchange takes place through the medium of money, are just as obvious as the disadvantages of a barter economy. It is no longer necessary that there should be a double coincidence of requirements between parties. The farmer no longer has to look for a tailor who needs wheat. As long as a **buyer** can be found for his product, the money yielded by such a transaction can be used to buy clothes. Money therefore serves as a lubricant or **intermediary** to facilitate the process of exchange and to make it more efficient. This is the first and foremost function of money, namely its function as a **medium of exchange**. When the other functions of money are discussed, we shall see that the medium of exchange function is the only one which is unique to money.

> In terms of this function; money can be broadly defined as **anything that is generally accepted as payment for goods and services or which is accepted in settlement of debt.**

This definition, which is probably the most acceptable definition of money today, testifies to the problems experienced over many years in defining this elusive concept. If you look carefully at the wording of the definition, you will realise that it actually says that **money is what money does**. The meaning of money is so difficult to capture in words, that we are obliged to define it in terms of its main function. It is therefore true that if money loses this property of being a **generally acceptable means of payment**, none of its other functions remains valid. Money is accepted as payment because people believe that it will be accepted as payment by other people.

Money as a measure of value or accounting unit

If money is to fulfil its role as a means of exchange, it follows that it must also fulfil the function of a **measure of value** or an **accounting unit**. It is precisely this function of money which enables us, in chapter 2, to work with overall totals such as the GDP or the NNI. Money has made it possible to compare the relative value of different goods and services and to express this value in terms of a common accounting unit.

The function of money as a unit of account is closely related to its function as a medium of exchange. Obviously, what serves as a medium of exchange will necessarily also fulfil the function of an accounting unit. The accounting unit function can however be seen as secondary to the medium of exchange function.

Money as a store of value

A further function of money is that of being a store of value. In any society a need exists to conserve wealth (or surplus production) in some form or other. The most common form for conserving wealth, is money, since it can be used in exchange for other goods and services. Wealth can however also be conserved in more specific forms, such as fixed property, real assets, stocks and shares. The advantage of using money as a store of value lies in the fact that it is usually more convenient and can be used immediately in exchange for other assets. We therefore say that money is the most **liquid** form in which wealth can be conserved.

Yet, it is not always advantageous to use money as a store of value. In times of high inflation, when money loses its purchasing power, it cannot be successfully utilised as a store of value. A person who keeps all his wealth in the form of money, will soon realise that his wealth is not retaining its value. If the price level is unstable, as in our present inflationary climate, there will be a tendency to use other objects as stores of value, e.g. fixed property, shares, works of art, postage stamps, etc. The store of value function, unlike the medium of exchange function, is therefore not unique to money. The more stable the value of money, the more attractive it becomes as a store of value. It should however always be borne in mind that the store of value function is derived from the medium of exchange function. If money did not fulfil the function of a medium of exchange, it would not be able to serve as either accounting unit or store of value.

Just as the medium of exchange function implies the accounting unit function, so the store of value function implies that money serves as the **standard of deferred payments**; i.e. it is the measure of value for payments which only take place after the lapse of a considerable length of time. This means that money has pre-eminently become the means whereby the granting of credit is made possible.

6.3 Different kinds of money

Through the ages various goods have from time to time served as money. For example beads, tea, cattle, silver and cigarettes (in modern prisoner of war camps) have served as money at one time or another. The evolutionary process whereby various forms of money were developed, runs from commodity money right through to the modern cheque book account with a bank.

The earliest form of money was **commodities**, where the intrinsic value of the commodity was equal to the exchange value assigned to it. Naturally, certain commodities were more suitable to be used as money than others. Properties such as **uniformity, durability, divisibility** and the ability to be **carried** (which is determined by size and weight) were not to be found in all commodities. For example, cattle are not divisible into "change", nor can they easily be carried about.

This type of commodity money in due course made way for the more efficient **coins** made of various kinds of metal. Initially iron and copper coins were very popular as money but they soon lost their value because of their abundance and were replaced by scarcer, more durable metals such as silver and gold.

In time, however, the exclusive use of coins as a medium of exchange also became inconvenient as a result of increasing specialisation of production and the resultant greater dependence on trade. Particularly in large transactions, the coins became unwieldy and difficult to handle. This in turn led to the use of **paper money**, which made its first appearance in England in the 16th century. What happened was that the owners of gold (or silver) **deposited** it with certain institutions, for instance the goldsmiths of that time. In exchange for such **deposits** they received certificates of deposit, and these certificates could be transferred to another person to pay for a transaction. The certificate of deposit was the first form of paper money which was fully covered by the coins it was supposed to represent.

The next step in the evolutionary process was the replacement of this entirely representative paper money (i.e. 100% coverage) by notes which were only partially covered by a commodity (e.g. gold). The gold standard, which applied in most countries up to the 1930s, functioned under such a partial coverage of gold. This form of money therefore had an exchange value which was much higher than its commodity value. Such money is called **fiduciary** or **credit money**.

The modern bank note which is in use today, bears no relationship to any commodity and its value is based solely on **confidence** in the government or monetary authorities to control the supply of notes in such a way that their purchasing power will not disappear completely. As long as one is assured that goods and services can be obtained in exchange for bank notes, the confidence in and acceptability of such paper money will not be affected.

This confidence is further supported by the fact that the notes and coins issued by the Central Bank have been declared by law to be **legal tender**. (In South Africa these are notes and coins issued by the South African Reserve Bank). This means that such notes or coins cannot be refused if they are tendered in payment of a debt. With a view to the convenience of the receiver, it has been stipulated that payment in nickel coins shall be restricted to an amount of R4, and payment in bronze to a total of 10 cents.

The next important development in the evolution of money, is the use of cheque books by banks. In any developed country this form of money constitutes the greater part of the money stock. Before looking at the factors determining the size of the money supply of a country, it is necessary to determine more specifically how money is defined in South Africa.

6.4   The money supply in South Africa

When we talk about the money supply (or quantity of money) in a modern economy such as that of South Africa today, we may be referring to any one of several measures. Naturally the different measures have to relate to the general descriptive definition of money identified in section 6.1.

The conventional measure (M1)

According to this measure, money is defined solely on the basis of its function as a medium of exchange. The money supply is therefore measured on the basis of those articles which are regarded as general means of exchange. In South Africa these are

> **coins and notes (in circulation outside the monetary sector) as well as all demand deposits (including cheque and transmission deposits) of the domestic private sector with monetary institutions.**

This definition of M1 is very important for our purposes and its meaning must be thoroughly understood. The concept of **demand deposits** refers to deposits (money which has been deposited) that can be withdrawn immediately, for example, by means of a cheque in the form of cash. It is therefore simply a more scientific term for the money for which cheques may be written out in a country. The value of these accounts forms part of the money supply since it is immediately available and is also generally accepted as payment in South African society.

Since only demand deposits of the **domestic private sector** are taken into account, it may be assumed that such deposits of the government and the foreign sector are not included. It appears moreover that only coins and notes **in circulation outside the monetary sector** constitute a part of the money supply. The reason is that only cash in the hands of the public can be used as a means of payment. The cash in the bank vaults and in the hands of other institutions obviously cannot be used in the money-goods flow and is consequently excluded.

To summarise, we can see that everything that serves and is available to the domestic private sector as a means of payment in the normal course of events is included in the definition of M1.

This definition of money can be written as an equation, as follows:

$$M = C + D \dots\dots\dots\dots\dots\dots\dots\dots\dots\dots\dots\dots\dots\dots\dots\dots\dots\dots \quad 6.1$$

where M = money supply
where C = cash (coins and notes in circulation outside the monetary
               sector)
        D = demand deposits.

Contrary to what may have been expected, D forms far and away the largest part of the M1 measure of money. In South Africa the composition of M1 in 1991 was as follows:

	R *million*
Coins $\Big\}$ (C) Banknotes	8 834
Demand deposits (D)	52 076
Total (M1)	60 910

About 86 per cent of the money supply therefore consisted of demand deposits. There has been little change in this percentage over the past few years.

A broader definition of money (M2)

According to this definition money is:

> **M1 *plus* all short- and medium-term deposits of the domestic private sector with monetary institutions.**

As the name indicates, these short and medium-term deposits are not immediately available as a medium of exchange. They are deposits invested for a certain period (less than 30 days for short-term deposits and less than 6 months for medium-term deposits) and can only be withdrawn at considerable cost in the interim. Since the maturity of these deposits is not very long, they are very similar to M1 money and are known in South Africa as **quasi money**. Together with M1, this quasi money forms the M2 measure of money.

The most comprehensive measure of money (M3)

For many years M1 and M2 were the only measures used to measure the money supply, but today great significance is attached to the M3 measure, which gives money an even broader definition than M2. It is defined as follows:

> **M2 *plus* all long-term deposits of the domestic private sector with monetary institutions.**

Over and above the short and medium-term deposits included in M2, long-term deposits (with a currency of longer than 6 months) are added to form the M3 measure. The monetary authorities today use this broad measure of the money supply to evaluate the success of monetary policy since they are of the opinion that this is the most reliable indicator of developments in the monetary (or financial) sector of the economy.

Table 6.1 gives a summary of the relative values of the various measures discussed above.

Although the money supply shows a tendency to increase in respect of all the measures, table 6.1 also indicates that the rate of increase in the various totals has been fairly divergent. As can for instance be seen, the M1 measure showed an increase of 10 per cent from 1988 to 1989 and the M3 measure an increase of 22 per cent. During the same period the M2 measure increased by 27 per cent.

Table 6.1

Monetary aggregates in South Africa, 1987–1991

End of:	R millions						
	Coins and banknotes	Demand deposits	M1	Quasi-money	M2	Long-term deposits	M3
1987	4 786	29 232	34 018	35 273	69 291	23 856	93 147
1988	5 941	35 597	41 538	51 584	93 122	24 810	117 931
1989	7 171	38 590	45 761	72 603	118 364	26 014	144 378
1990	8 064	44 983	53 048	80 825	133 873	28 181	162 054
1991	8 834	52 076	60 910	94 453	155 363	27 252	182 615

(handwritten annotations: M1, C+DD, M1+SMD; exchange, store value, accounting unit)

Source: South African Reserve Bank: *Quarterly Bulletin*, December 1988 and March 1992.

Table 6.1 *The narrow definition of money (M1) consists of only (i) coins and bank notes, and (ii) demand deposits. The broader definition, M2, includes short-term deposits (quasi money) and is about twice the value of M1. M3, which includes long-term deposits, is regarded as the best measure of developments in the monetary sector.*

Medium of exchange as against store of value

Looking at the above three measures, it is clear that M1 is the only one that takes only the medium of exchange function as its point of departure. As more and more financial assets (other than C and D) are added to this measure, the emphasis placed on the medium of exchange function becomes less distinct. As we move from M1 to M2 to M3, the emphasis on the store of value function grows. It is evident that a deposit with a banking institution having a currency of more than 6 months, can hardly be regarded as an available means of payment today. Such a deposit is much closer in kind to the store of value function.

Money and other related concepts

Money is such a commonplace phenomenon that it is often confused with other concepts. It should not, for example, be confused with concepts such as **income** or **wealth**. A person in possession of great wealth does not necessarily possess a great deal of money. This wealth can take many other forms, such as shares or fixed assets. Nor is a person's income equivalent to the money he possesses. This confusion between the three concepts **money, wealth** and **income** arises from the fact that all three can be expressed in terms of a particular monetary unit (e.g. rands, dollar, pounds, etc.)

Money supply and wealth are both **stock concepts** which can be measured at a particular point in time. As we saw in table 6.1, the amounts given relate to the money supply at the end of the respective years, i.e. on 31 December of each year. Wealth is however a far more comprehensive measure and includes other assets in addition to money. In contrast, income is a **flow concept** which can be measured over a period of time, e.g. R1000 **per month** or R12 000 **per annum**.

From a macro-economic point of view, the difference between income and money can best be illustrated when we consider that the GDP, which is a measure of income, amounted to approximately R296 667 million in 1991, while the money in circulation during the same year only came to R60 910 million (M1). M1 as a percentage of the GDP therefore amounted to around 20 per cent. This ratio between the narrower definition of money (M1) and the value of total production (GDP or GNP) varies considerably from one country to another and also gives an indication of the velocity of circulation of money.

6.5   The role of financial intermediaries

With the rise of the monetary economy referred to above, a new sector of the economy came to the fore. With the advent of money, a group of institutions emerged which specialised in purely financial transactions. These transactions may be distinguished from normal or real transactions by the fact that no actual goods or services are involved as a quid pro quo. The goldsmiths of earlier times were probably the first institutions to earn their living on a purely financial basis. But even this could be disputed, since gold was actually exchanged, i.e. there was a real good involved in the transaction. As a result of the development of pure credit money, examples abound today of different kinds of institutions making their living without any real goods (apart from bits of paper!) changing hands.

On the basis of this clear distinction between **real transactions** and **financial transactions**, it is possible to divide the economy into a real and a financial sector. Today a multitude of different kinds of institutions can be distinguished within the financial sector, each one specialising in a particular service or segment of the market. In spite of this specialisation, the overall function of all these institutions is **to act as an intermediary between the surplus units and the deficit units of the monetary economy**.

At any particular stage there are surplus units (usually households which have saved money) disposing of funds that can be invested and deficit units (e.g. entrepreneurs wishing to start new business enterprises) who are in search of funds. Although it is possible, and does in fact happen, that such parties can contact each other directly, it has been shown in practice that the vast majority of business transactions take place through the agency of financial intermediaries. These institutions therefore specialise in the acceptance and granting of credit.

Credit is granted when a person or institution lends funds to another person or institution. In exchange for the funds a piece of paper (or credit instrument) is normally issued which stipulates the **interest rate**[§] at which the funds are loaned and when and how the amount is to be paid. Examples of such credit instruments are bills of exchange, promissory notes and bankers' acceptances. When the government lends money it makes use of treasury bills and government stock.

For our purposes the activities of the financial sector are largely ignored. This is a highly specialised field of study which is dealt with in greater depth in monetary economics. In the rest of this chapter we shall confine ourselves to some of the aspects of banks which have a direct bearing on the money supply of the country. The money supply and its effect on the economy are, after all, our primary interest.

The Deposit-taking Institutions Act

The implementation of the Deposit-taking Institutions Act on 1 February 1991 introduced a new era for financial institutions in South Africa. This Act consolidated into one single act, the rules and regulations which apply to all institutions accepting deposits from the general public. The artificial distinction between banks and building societies that was upheld by the old Banks Act (Act 23 of 1965) and the Building Societies Act (Act 82 of 1986) was finally done away with.

According to the Deposit-taking Institutions Act all banks (previously commercial, merchant and general banks), equity building societies and discount houses are subject to the same set of rules and regulations. Because the same rules and regulations now apply to all these institutions it means that the traditional demarcation lines between the services provided by each type of institution have disappeared. For a number of years we have witnessed the convergence of the business of banks and building societies in the form of mortgage facilities (provided by banks) and cheque book facilities being offered by building societies. Where legislation in the past has concentrated on accommodating **institutional** differences the new Act endeavours to regulate institutions in terms of **functional** guidelines. The emphasis is placed on the function of accepting deposits rather than on the institutions acting as deposit-taking institutions.

Any unfair advantage that one group might have had, over another

---

§   The interest rate is calculated as a percentage per annum.

group in terms of, for example, cash reserve requirements, has now been eliminated to establish equitable competition between all deposit-taking institutions. Insurers are, however, not subject to the regulations of the Deposit-taking Institutions Act. The activities of mutual building societies (non-equity building societies) are also regulated by a separate act.

6.6 The supply of money

We can now spend some time on the factors that determine the size of the money supply. To keep the analysis as simple as possible, we shall make the following assumptions:

(i)   There is only one definition of the money supply, viz.:

$$M = C + D \dots\dots\dots\dots\dots\dots\dots\dots\dots\dots\dots\dots\dots\dots\dots\dots\dots\dots\dots\dots\dots\dots \quad 6.1$$

According to this, we accept only the narrow, M1 definition of money. Time deposits therefore play no part in our analysis.

(ii)   Although the M1 definition of money includes demand deposits with other monetary institutions, we are going to assume that only banks are authorised to hold such deposits. This is a legitimate assumption in view of the fact that almost 80 per cent of all demand deposits (D) are held by banks.

(iii) We further assume that there is a central bank which exercises control over the activities of banks. Exactly how this control is exercised, will be explained further on.

From the definition of the money supply (M = C + D) we have already deduced that D constitutes the major portion (85%) of the quantity of money. In any analysis of the money supply it is therefore essential to establish what determines the size of these deposits.

The most important services rendered by banks are: (i) The acceptance of deposits (demand as well as time deposits); (ii) the transfer of payments, usually by means of cheque facilities; and (iii) the granting of credit, *inter alia* in the form of **overdraft facilities**. The most striking feature of banks, however, is the fact that their clients can open cheque accounts and therefore have the right to demand deposits.

How are demand deposits created?

The most important characteristic of demand deposits is the fact that the bank is obliged to pay out the deposit in cash (bank notes) or to transfer it to another bank or account holder in full or partially immediately on demand. The cheque account can therefore be treated like money (hence it forms part of M1). For this reason, and its consequent convenience to account holders, the interest paid by banks on these accounts is particularly low and they even debit account holders with bank charges for payments they have to make in terms of these accounts.

Demand deposits (D's) can be created in the following ways:

(i) Provided a person possesses a reasonably good name and has a reasonable amount of money at his disposal, any bank will be prepared to create a demand deposit in favour of that person in exchange for cash. If you deposit R1 000 in bank notes with Bank A, the bank will issue you with a cheque book which will give you the right to write out cheques to the value of R1 000.

(ii) This is not, however, the only way in which D's can be created. Because the banks, like the goldsmiths in earlier times, noticed that the D's held by them were not all withdrawn immediately or simultaneously, they got into the habit of lending some of these funds to deficit units in the form of overdraft facilities. Provided that the bank can be convinced of your creditworthiness, a demand deposit can therefore be created in your favour without any cash deposit.

It is clear that there is a considerable difference between the two ways in which D's are created. In the *first case* the bank's role is fairly **passive** since nothing has been done to change the money supply in the country. You will recall that the definition of M1 makes it clear that only cash that is in circulation outside the banking sector can be regarded as part of the money supply. In other words, the creation of the D's has been accompanied by a corresponding decline in C. The change in M can therefore be expressed as follows:

$$\Delta M = \Delta C + \Delta D$$
$$= -R1\ 000 + R1\ 000$$
$$= R0.$$

In the *second case* the conduct of the bank is more **active**. The bank has deliberately lent money and thus **created credit** and, more importantly, the money supply in the country has been increased. According to our equation, the change in M can be expressed as follows:

$$\Delta M = \Delta C + \Delta D$$
$$= 0 + R1\ 000$$
$$= R1\ 000.$$

The reserve position

The credit creation referred to above can lead to certain eventualities for which banks have to be prepared.

In the **first** place, it must be remembered that D's may be withdrawn at any time. Cash and demand deposits can be arbitrarily substituted for each other. Each bank must therefore at all times ensure that it has sufficient **cash reserves** available to provide for **cash withdrawals**.

In the **second** place, the bank, which forms part of a larger banking system, must provide for the claims of other banks, which may exceed its own claims. This happens when a bank's clients (including those who have obtained overdraft facilities) write cheques in favour of persons who have accounts with other banks. Such transfers to other banks may be larger than the transfers received by the bank for similar cheques.

The banks very soon learned what percentage of the total deposits received by them should be set aside in the form of **cash reserves** for the abovementioned eventualities. Today this discretionary judgement based solely on experience is no longer left to the individual banks. In any business enterprise it is of the utmost importance that the confidence of creditors should be maintained. In the business of banking the creditors are the multitude of depositors – the holders of current accounts, savings accounts and time deposits – and here it is even more important than elsewhere to maintain trust. The slightest crack in the banks' image of creditworthiness could give rise to a snowball effect that could disrupt the entire financial system.[§]

For these very reasons the monetary authorities (which in South Africa were established by the creation of the central bank in 1921) laid down legal requirements right from the start, stipulating the amount of cash reserves to be held against the total liabilities (demand deposits) of a bank.

It was further stipulated that such cash reserves should be held without interest by the Reserve Bank (our central bank). The purpose of the **cash reserve requirement** was to ensure that banks would not be guilty of extravagant credit creation. Since the cash reserves remain in the central bank without bearing interest, a sound balance is created between the **liquidity motive** on the one hand and the **profit motive** (by lending money) on the other.

On the basis of the following example, we shall endeavour to show how the cash reserve requirements imposed by the central bank affect the level of demand deposits:

(i)   Suppose Mr X deposits R1 000 with Bank A. Bank A's cash reserves increase by R1 000 and in exchange it creates a demand deposit to the

---

§   An example of a "run on cash" in banks occurred in the USA in 1929 and contributed to the depression of the thirties.

amount of R1 000 in favour of Mr X. As we have seen, this does not increase the money supply.

(ii) Suppose further that the **legal reserve ratio** that banks have to maintain with the central bank against their demand deposits is equal to 20 per cent. The additional R1 000 in D's created in favour of Mr X therefore requires a cash reserve of R200 which has to lie interest free in the central bank. !§   This leaves Bank A with R800 in cash reserves which can go out on loan. These reserves may be regarded as **excess reserves**, i.e. reserves in addition to those it has to or wants to maintain.

(iii) Without in any way exceeding the reserve ratio (20% or $\frac{1}{5}$) which has to be maintained, Bank A can now grant R800 to Mr Y in the form of overdraft facilities.

(iv) The next step is that Mr Y makes use of his overdraft facilities. Suppose he writes a cheque for R800 in favour of Mr Z, who deposits it with his own bank, Bank B.

(v) The original cash deposit of R1 000 has now increased to R1 800 in demand deposits. (R1 000 in favour of Mr X and R800 in favour of Mr Z at Bank B.) The money creation process by banks has begun.

(vi) If the process stopped here the extent of credit creation would not have been so great. The deposit of R800 however increases Bank B's cash reserves. As in the case of Bank A, Bank B is now in possession of excess reserves. If the same reserve requirement applies to Bank B, it means that 20 per cent of the additional reserves (20% of R800 = R160) will be retained and the remaining R640 will go out on loan, for instance to Mr W.

(vii) The process begun by Mr X's deposit of R1 000 continues in this way until it has "worked itself out".

(viii) For every rand received by a bank in the form of a cash deposit, 80c can therefore go out on loan while 20c has to be kept as a cash reserve with the central bank. If the cash reserve ratio is represented by the symbol b, this means that $(1 - b)$ of the amount may be loaned while b of the amount must be held in reserve.

(ix) The total increase in demand deposits is the sum of:

Bank A	Bank B	Bank C	Bank D
$\Delta D = 1\ 000 + (1-b)1000$		$+ (1-b)\{(1-b)1\ 000\}$	$+ 1-b\{(1-b)(1-b)1\ 000\}$ ..+..
$= 1\ 000 + (1-0,20)1000$		$+ (1-0,20)^2 1\ 000$	$+ (1-0,20)^3 1\ 000+$ ....
$= 1\ 000 +$	800	$+ 640$	$+ 512 +$ ....

§   To keep the argument as simple as possible, we may assume that the vault cash that the bank has to keep on hand for normal day-to-day cash withdrawals is included in this R200.

If this series is followed through to its ultimate conclusion,[§] the total increase in demand deposits (ΔD) will be equal to R5 000. It can also be demonstrated that the above equation may be reduced to the following:

$$\Delta D = \frac{1}{b} \times R1\ 000$$
$$= \frac{1}{0,2} \times R1\ 000$$
$$= 5 \times R1\ 000$$
$$= R5\ 000$$

In more general terms we can say that the ratio between an increase in a bank's cash reserves (ΔR) and the consequent increase in demand deposits (ΔD) is as follows:

$$\Delta D = \frac{1}{b} \Delta R \quad \dots\dots\dots\dots\dots\dots\dots\dots\dots\dots\dots\dots\dots\dots\dots \quad 6.2$$

where ΔD = increase in demand deposits
ΔR = increase in cash reserves
b = cash reserve ratio

The whole process of credit creation therefore indicates that a multiplier effect is involved here as well. This is known as the **credit multiplier** which in equation 6.2 is equal to $\frac{1}{b}$.

The position of the individual banks

What applies to the banking system as a whole, does not however apply to individual banks. Especially in the past, bankers were often surprised when it was said that they could create credit and therefore money practically out of nothing. They could, in fact, point out with some justice that they never loaned more than a certain part of the deposits they received. This (microeconomic) point of view can be explained from the bank's point of view by means of the following example:

Bank A receives R1 000 in cash of which R200 is held in reserve and R800 loaned to Mr Y *via* an overdraft. Bank A's balance sheet will reflect these transactions as follows:

§   I.e. if the increment of each additional deposit becomes so small that it can eventually be ignored. In the equation such a point will be reached where the term $(1 - 0,20)^n$ applies and n is infinitely great; i.e. where $n \to \infty$.

Bank A

Liabilities		Assets	
Deposit (by X)	R1 000	Reserve	R200
		Loan to Y	800
	R1 000		R1 000

There is no question of credit creation here. The bank merely loans what it has received in funds. Banks B and C will present a similar picture:

Bank B

Liabilities		Assets	
Deposit (by Z)	R800	Reserve	R160
		Loan (to W)	640
	R800		R800

Bank C

Liabilities		Assets	
Deposit (by V)	R640	Reserve	R128
		Loan to ...	R512
	R640		R640

It is clear that the individual bank's credit creation possibilities are restricted to only a part of the deposits (or cash reserves) received. What in fact happens, is that the system **as a whole**, via the credit multiplier, can convert the amount received in the form of a deposit (R) by a multiple thereof into demand deposits.

If we desired to analyse this process still further, we could demonstrate that the multiplier effect of 5 (with a cash reserve ratio of 20%), derived above, would probably in practice have been much smaller. In section 6.4 we pointed out that approximately 85 per cent of the total money supply consists of demand deposits. This is the same as to say that approximately 15 per cent of the money supply consists of notes and coins; in other words, the public will keep approximately 15 per cent of its receipts in the form of notes. In our case it would for instance mean that Z would keep R120 of the R800 paid to him in cash (as would the other recipients coming after him), with the result that he would only deposit R680 with Bank B. Although this would decrease the credit multiplier, it does not detract from the principle of money and credit creation.

The extent of demand deposits

(i) Changes in the cash reserve ratio

The next step in the development of modern banking was that the authorities realised the money supply could be influenced by changing the **legal cash reserve ratio** and that this could form an important instrument of monetary policy. Any change brought about in the reserve requirement by the monetary authorities will, in fact, immediately change the value of the credit multiplier. A **decrease** from 20 per cent to 10 per cent in the legal reserve ratio requirement leads to an **increase** in the credit multiplier from $5 (= \frac{1}{0,2})$ to $10 (= \frac{1}{0,1})$. In the example above this would mean that the R1000 deposited would lead to an increase of R10 000 in demand deposits.

$$\begin{aligned} \Delta D &= \frac{1}{0,1} \times R1\ 000 \\ &= 10 \times R1\ 000 \\ &= R10\ 000 \end{aligned}$$

From this it can be seen that the central bank, which is authorised to vary the reserve requirements within limits, is in possession of a powerful instrument to either extend or curb the possibility of creating demand deposits.

The success of such a policy will depend on the existence of **excess reserves**. Although the banks normally endeavour to keep only the minimum cash reserves (which are required by law) with the central bank (since they do not bear interest), it can sometimes happen that banks prefer to keep more than this minimum amount in their current account with the central bank. Business conditions may be of such a nature that banks prefer to consolidate their position rather than to participate in further credit extension. In such circumstances a lowering of the cash reserve ratio (b) by the authorities (in order to increase M) would not have the desired effect since banks would prefer to allow **excess reserves** to accumulate with the central bank rather than creating demand deposits (D). The business climate reigning in the economy is probably of decisive importance in this case.

(ii) The level of cash reserves

Just as a change in the credit multiplier can lead to a change in the level of demand deposits, a change in the reserves (R) available to banks can also lead to changes in D. In other words, the reserves form the basis on which credit creation is possible. Any change in this **monetary base** can therefore give rise to a much greater change in demand deposits. The same conclusion can also be drawn from equation 6.2:

$$\Delta D = \frac{1}{b} \Delta R \ldots\ldots\ldots\ldots\ldots\ldots\ldots\ldots\ldots\ldots\ldots\ldots\ldots\ldots\ldots\ldots \quad 6.2$$

In other words, any change in total reserves (R), i.e. in the monetary base, can lead to a greater change in D (D). In the next chapter we shall see how the monetary authorities can alter the cash reserves (and therefore the monetary base) of banks by means of open market transactions in order to influence the money supply.

The demand for cash

It is interesting to note that the extent of the quantity of money is also affected by the demand for cash (i.e. the demand of the private non-banking sector). The more money the public keeps in the form of cash, the smaller the banks' cash reserves and the smaller the amount of demand deposits that can be created. In the foregoing example it should be remembered that the R1 000 that was in Mr X's possession before he deposited it with Bank A, only represented "ordinary" money. When the money was paid into the bank it no longer formed a part of the money supply, but the same R1 000 has now become the basis on which the banks can create further credit. Although this may seem strange, it means that if the public could get along without any cash (C), the potential money supply (M) would be greater because the potential for creating D would be enhanced.

6.7 Factors that can influence the money supply

The above account of the process of money creation enables us to identify the market participants and types of transactions on the money market that have an influence on the quantity of money.

Market participants

From our discussion in section 6.6 the following market participants can be distinguished:

(a) Firstly, the **central bank**, which determines the conditions and level of the cash reserves to be held by the banks against their demand deposits.

In South Africa changes in the reserve ratio (b) are seldom used nowadays to influence the money supply. The main influence of the monetary authorities lies in their ability to change the magnitude of the actual cash reserves (R).

(b) Secondly, the **banks**, which exercise an independent influence on the money supply since they decide, on the basis of business considerations, on the quantity of excess reserves to be held. If the banks have a high level of excess reserves, a change (e.g. an increase) made in the legal reserve requirement in order to bring about a change in the money supply may be a total failure. In such a case the banks could simply reduce their excess reserves in order to meet the increased requirement without the money supply changing at all.

(c) We have shown above how the **public** (you and I) exert a significant influence on the extent of the money supply. Every person decides for himself how he is going to apportion his money between cash and demand deposits. The greater our need for cash, the smaller the banks' credit creation capacity becomes. Each bank note or coin in the public's possession means fewer cash reserves in the hands of the banking system.[§]

The variety of market participants (central bank, banks and the private non-banking sector) and the complex part each one plays in the process of money creation, make it extraordinarily difficult for the monetary authorities to control the money supply efficiently. In particular, the supply of demand deposits, which is subject to a multiplier effect, complicates the process of control.

Foreign transactions

The money supply of a country may also be influenced by transactions with foreign countries. In South Africa foreign trade and international capital movements (see chapter 8) are of particular importance and can exert a significant influence on the domestic money supply.

If a local exporter earns foreign currency (in payment for exports) and exchanges it at his bank for a demand deposit, the money supply will be directly increased. The bank which deposits the foreign currency with the Reserve Bank (as guardian of our gold and foreign exchange reserves), at the same time increases its own reserves. On the basis of these reserves, the bank can then create further demand deposits, whereby the credit multiplier is put into operation and the quantity of money is increased.

§   Although **credit cards** do not form a part of the money stock, their use can definitely reduce the public's demand for actual cash. They are therefore an indirect cause of an increase in the potential money supply.

On the same principle, local importers who have to pay for imports will have a negative effect on the quantity of money. Gold sales to foreign countries undertaken by the Reserve Bank on behalf of the gold mines, increase the monetary base and the money supply of the country in the same way as exports do.

To summarise:

> A country's money supply generally increases when its gold and foreign exchange reserves increase and falls when the gold and foreign exchange reserves decrease.

In other words, the domestic money supply is not independent of the country's foreign transactions.

Government transactions

In the previous chapter we saw that fiscal policy is related to the regulation of the state's income (from taxes and loans) and its expenditure (on current and capital projects). The financing of the latter from sources other than taxes exerts a particularly strong influence on the money supply.

When the government levies taxes, its deposits with the Reserve Bank (as government banker) increase and the money supply decreases. When the government spends this money, e.g. on salaries to public servants, its cash balance with the Reserve Bank is decreased and the money supply in the country increases.

To summarise:

> If the government's current income is exactly equal to its current expenditure there is no change in the cash reserves and the money supply of the country. If the government's current income exceeds its current expenditure there is a decrease in cash reserves and in the money supply; if, on the other hand, current expenditure exceeds current income, the country's monetary base, and consequently the money supply, increases.

If the government does not dispose of sufficient funds in the form of deposits with the Reserve Bank to compensate for the deficit (created when expenditure exceeds income), it can finance the deficit by contracting a loan with the Reserve Bank. Such a loan will lead to an increase in the economy's monetary base and, via the credit multiplier, to an increase in the money supply. This type of financing is usually referred to as **inflationary financing**.

6.8 The demand for money

The interaction between demand and supply determines the price of any good or service. This rule also applies to **interest rates**, which can be regarded as the "price" of money. It is therefore necessary that we now look at the factors which determine the demand for money.

While the supply of money (see previous section) actually refers to the amount of money *available* in the country at any time, the demand for money represents the amount of money people would like to have at any time. It is in other words **that component of an individual's total wealth which he/she wishes to keep with a financial institution in the form of cash and/or demand deposits.** It involves the demand for cash or cash balances in contrast to other forms of wealth such as fixed assets, shares, stocks, etc.

As may be expected, the demand for money arises from the functions fulfilled by money. Were it not for these useful functions, there would be no reason for wanting to hold money. On this basis the following components of the demand for money may be distinguished:

(i) The **transactional demand** for money, arising from its medium of exchange function; and

(ii) the **demand for money as an asset**, arising from its store of value function.

Classical thinking on the demand for money

The classical economists recognised only the medium of exchange function of money, consequently their theories emphasized the transaction demand for money. None of these economists considered the possibility that money could be in demand for any other purpose (than performing transactions). In their opinion the demand for money was determined by the **level of income**, i.e. the quantity of goods and services produced, as well as the **prices** paid for them. A need for money therefore exists in order to make the daily purchase and sale of goods and services possible. The higher the prices of these products, the more money would be required to perform the transactions. This conclusion can be summarised as follows:

$$M_d = f(Y \text{ and } p)$$

where M_d = demand for money
$\qquad$ Y = level of income (or real GDP)
$\qquad$ p = the general price level.

According to the equation, the demand for money (M_d) is a function (f) of the level of income (Y) and the general price level (p). If either of the latter rises, the demand for money will also rise. In other words, there is a **positive** relation between both of these variables and the demand for money.

Keynes's three motives for holding money

The above classical point of view that the total demand for money consisted only of the transaction demand, remained the prevailing theory about the demand for money for many years. It was only in the 1930's that Keynes formulated a new theory which recognised the fact that money could also be kept as an asset or as a form of wealth. According to Keynes three motives for the demand for money could be distinguished.

(i) The **transaction motive**, which is closest to the classical point of view. According to this theory, a need to hold money arises because a person's payments and receipts of money do not always coincide. Wages and salaries are normally paid by the week or month, while purchases of goods and services take place on a more regular basis. Obviously, the **income level** and the **price level** are the most important factors influencing the transaction demand for money.

(ii) The **precautionary motive** for the demand for money arises because a person's expenditure pattern may not be entirely predictable. Over and above the normal transaction balances, provision should also be made for unforeseen expenditure. Here it is once again reasonable to assume that the **income level** and the **price level** will have a decisive effect on the precautionary demand for money.

(iii) The last motive for the demand for money distinguished by Keynes, is related to the store of value function of money. This component of the demand for money arises from the **speculative motive**. The identification of the speculative demand for money was Keynes's most important contribution in the monetary field. In contrast to the first two motives, where the funds are **actively** employed, the speculative demand can rather be associated with **passive balances**. These speculative funds are influenced mainly by the interest rate and interest rate expectations.

$\qquad$ Since these speculative (or passive) funds are only one of several alternative stores of value used to conserve wealth, the costs (or

advantages) of keeping the money will naturally be weighed against
the costs (or advantages) of keeping alternative stores of value. The
most important difference between money and other stores of value,
such as securities, is the fact that money normally earns little or no
interest whereas securities do. If interest rates are high, the opportunity
cost of money is also high (since an interest yield is lost) and consequently the demand for speculative balances will be low. But if interest
rates are low, the cost of holding money (relative to securities) will also
be low and the demand for speculative funds will rise.

Our conclusion is therefore that there is a **negative relation
between the interest rate level** and the **speculative demand for
money.**[§]

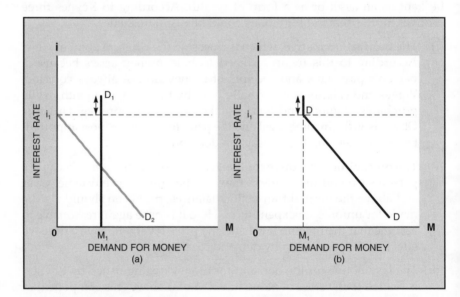

Fig. 6.1 The demand curve for money

*The demand for money consists of the demand for active balances (D₁) and the demand for
passive balances (D₂). The former is determined by the income level and the price level, while
the latter is a function of the interest rate. Shifts in the total demand for money (DD) occur as
a result of an increase or decrease in the income level and/or the general price level.*

§ In this analysis interest rate expectations have not been taken into account. The latter
   however reinforce the negative relation between the interest rate and the speculative
   demand derived.

In view of all these factors, the demand curve for money may be represented as in figure 6.1. In the (a) part of the figure the demand for **active balances** (transaction and precautionary motives) and for **passive balances** (speculative motive) are shown separately. The former (D_1 in the diagram) is a vertical line which is not sensitive to interest rate variations measured on the vertical axis. The position of D_1 at OM_1 is determined by the income level and the price level. The higher the income and price levels, the further to the right D_1 will be situated. The D_2 demand curve clearly demonstrates the negative relation between interest rates and the speculative demand for money. At a certain interest rate level (i_1) there will be no demand for funds to be used for speculative purposes.

In the (b) part of figure 6.1 the joint or **total demand curve** (DD) of money is represented. This is merely the horizontal addition of the two individual demand curves in the (a) part of the diagram. The properties of the demand curve can be summarised as follows:

(i)   The negative **slope** reflects the negative relation which exists between the interest rate level and the speculative demand for money.

(ii) The **position** of the demand curve is mainly determined by the demand for active balances. As we have seen, the latter are determined by the income level and the general price level. Consequently, any increase in income and/or the price level leads to a shift to the **right** in the total demand curve, while a decrease in the income and/or price level will cause the DD curve to shift to the left.

In general terms the factors that have an influence on the demand for money may be expressed in an equation as follows:

$$M_d = f(Y, p \text{ and } i)$$

where i represents the interest rate and the other symbols have the meanings previously attached to them.

The equation therefore states that the demand for money is a function of (i) the **income level**, (ii) the **price level** and (iii) the **interest rate level**. The former two factors influence the demand for money positively (position), while the latter has a negative impact (slope) on the demand for money.

The interest rate

The interest rate level referred to in the above analysis probably needs further clarification. Here as well as in the rest of the book, we shall often refer to "the interest rate" or "the interest rate level" as though there were only one such rate in the economy. This is certainly not the case, since there are numerous different kinds of interest rates, each associated with the borrowing and lending of specific funds.

For example, there is the bank rate, the prime lending rate of banks, the bankers' acceptance (BA) rate and the rate on government stock, to mention only a few that are regularly discussed in the media.

Although all these rates are different and there are sound economic reasons for these differences, the rates nevertheless tend to move in harmony with each other. When we therefore refer to "the interest rate" in macro-economics, it should be regarded as a representative rate for all the individual rates encountered in practice. In other words, the general rate of interest agrees to a large extent with the general price level, which is another important variable in macro-economics.

6.9   The interaction of the demand for money and the supply of money

The supply curve of money

The greater part of this chapter has been devoted to the factors determining the demand for money. We have seen that the whole process of money creation and the supply of money is influenced and controlled by a variety of participants and institutions. The complex nature of the process of money creation (which is also influenced by the demand for cash) makes it particularly difficult to derive a generally applicable supply curve of money. To what extent, for example, the supply of money is affected by interest rates, is not quite clear. It could be argued that banks will be inclined to make more credit available as interest rates rise. In such cases one would have a supply curve that normally rises from bottom left to top right, i.e. a supply curve that is elastic with respect to the rate of interest. In order to avoid the unnecessarily complex influences that could have an impact on the supply of money, it is however advisable to represent the supply curve of money as a vertical straight line which is entirely inelastic as far as the ruling interest rate is concerned.

Equilibrium in the money market

Such a supply curve (M_1M_1 in fig. 6.2), together with the demand curve (DD), determines at which rate of interest equilibrium will be reached in the money market. Any expansionary monetary policy by the monetary authorities will increase the supply of money (e.g. from M_1 to M_2 in the diagram) while the equilibrium interest rate will fall from i_1 to i_2. Such an

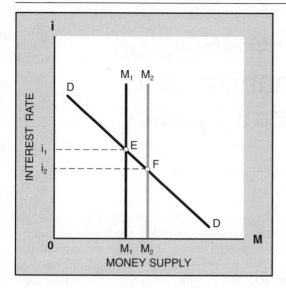

Fig. 6.2 Equilibrium on the money market

Equilibrium on the money market is established at the point of intersection (E) of demand and supply. An increase (decrease) in the supply of money leads to a drop (rise) in the interest rate.

extension could, for instance, be brought about if the Reserve Bank were to lower the minimum reserve ratio of banks. On the other hand, any action that reduces the excess reserve position of banks would lead to a drop in the supply of money (a shift to the left of the supply curve) and a consequent increase in the rate of interest.

The graphic presentation in figure 6.2 provides a concise summary of the variables involved in the implementation of monetary policy. Monetary policy is aimed at changing an equilibrium position as represented by E by altering either the supply of money or the interest rate. How and why this is done, forms the subject of our next chapter.

Selected references:

Baumol & Blinder: 12.
Dernburg: 7, 8.
Dornbusch & Fischer: 4.
Evans-Pritchard: 9.
Froyen: 9, 15.
Gordon: 15, 16.
Morley: 5.
Shapiro: 10, 11.

7 The transmission mechanism and monetary policy

In the previous chapter the demand and supply of money were discussed. The interaction between demand and supply takes place on the money market, where the interest rate is determined. The determination of the quantity of money and the interest rate are not however the primary reason for our interest in the money market. Our interest in money is mainly due to the fact that there is a link between the money market (monetary or financial sector) and the goods market (real sector). Money as such cannot satisfy any need directly and unless changes in the quantity of money lead to changes in the production of real goods and services, the money market is of no particular interest.

Although people are generally agreed upon the **existence** of such a link between the monetary and the real sectors of the economy today, there is considerable disagreement as to **how** this **transmission mechanism** actually works. In the previous chapter we said that the classical economists did not recognise the existence of such a link between the two sectors. This complete segregation between the two sectors (i.e. the absence of any link) is known as the **classical dichotomy** (or duality). The only link recognised by the classical school was the proportional relation between a change in the quantity of money (ΔM) and the change in the price level (ΔP). A ten per cent increase in the quantity of money would lead to a ten per cent rise in prices. Money as such is therefore simply a lubricant which facilitates the process of exchange but in itself has no impact on production, consumption and other real variables.

Today there are two main schools of thought regarding the manner in which changes on the money market are transmitted to the real sector. Firstly, there are the *monetarists*, who believe in a *direct* link between the quantity of money and total expenditure. Then there are the *Keynesians*, who believe that a change in the money supply will influence the financial climate, particularly the level of the interest rate, which affects the borrowing and lending of funds, and in this *indirect* way the real economy will be

158

affected. These two points of view are not always as divergent as some of the more extreme arguments of the two schools would lead us to believe. Nevertheless, an analysis of their premises provides a useful overview of the critical decisions that have to be taken by economic policy-makers.

7.1   The transmission mechanism: Keynesian explanation

Since Keynes's ideas were regarded as the most important school of thought up to and including the 1960s and even today have many supporters among economists, we shall begin our analysis of the transmission mechanism with the Keynesian explanation.

Our point of departure will be the demand and supply mechanism developed for the money market in the previous chapter. It has been seen (cf. fig.6.2) that equilibrium is reached on the money market at the intersection of the demand and supply curves.

What happens when **a change in the supply of money takes place?** Suppose the quantity of money is increased as a result of a lowering of the legal reserve requirement of the Reserve Bank.[§] In figure 7.1(a) the supply of money shifts from M_1 to M_2 and the interest rate consequently falls from 16 to 12 per cent. This fall in the interest rate has interesting implications.

Investment and the interest rate

The next link in the Keynesian explanation is the relation between the interest rate and the level of investment. When a person considers investing in a capital asset, the costs have to be carefully compared with the expected yield from it. Any investment is undertaken with a view to realising a profit in the future. If the funds to purchase the capital goods (machinery, factories, apartment blocks, etc.) are borrowed, the costs involved are equal to the ruling interest rate.[§§] The higher the interest rate, the more must be subtracted from the yield before the year's profit can be calculated. The higher the interest rate therefore, the lower the profit and the less investors will be prepared to invest. The lower the interest rate, the greater the number of projects that will realise a profit and consequently the greater the demand for capital goods. A drop in the interest rate from 16 per cent to 12 per cent (as in fig. 7.1(a)) will mean that projects previously regarded as unprofitable can now be undertaken. In the same way, a rise in interest rates will lead to a decrease in the demand for capital goods. It is therefore

§   As we shall see later in this chapter, the money supply can also be increased by other means.
§§ If the entrepreneur owns the necessary funds himself, the opportunity costs involved are equal to the interest that could be earned on this money if it were invested with a bank or building society.

clear that a negative relation exists between changes in the interest rate level on the one hand and investment on the other hand. This relationship is illustrated in the form of a graph in figure 7.1(b) where the drop in the interest rate from 16 per cent to 12 per cent leads to an increase in investment from R300 million to R500 million.

Since investment is one of the components of total expenditure (TS) and therefore of total demand, this rise in investment will lead to an upward shift in the TS line in figure 7.2, which in turn will result in an increase in the level of income.

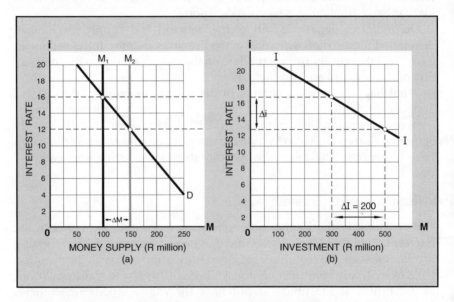

Fig. 7.1 The effect of a change in the money supply on investment

An increase in the money supply from M₁ to M₂ leads to a drop in the interest rate from 16 to 12 per cent (fig. 7.1(a)). Since a negative relation exists between interest rates and investment (I), this lowering of the interest rate will increase the level of investment from R300m to R500m (fig. 7.1(b)).

Keynesian skepticism about the effectiveness of monetary policy

According to the above discussion, it would appear as though monetary policy could be very effectively used to bring about changes in the income level and in employment. But Keynes questioned the effectiveness of monetary policy as a **means of stimulating** the economy and favoured fiscal policy as a stimulus to total demand. This scepticism about monetary policy on the part of the Keynesians was based on two sets of considerations:

(i)   The demand for money is, according to them, far **more** elastic than is indicated by figure 7.1(a); and

(ii)   The demand for investment is far **less** elastic than is indicated by figure 7.1(b).

The implications of this way of thinking may be illustrated by figs.7.3(a) and (b): In figure 7.3(a) the demand for money (D_kD_k – where the k's refer to Keynes) is represented, in accordance with the Keynesian point of view, as being **more** elastic. The same increase in the supply of money (M_1 to M_2) now leads to a drop of only 2 per cent in the interest rate. In figure 7.3(b),

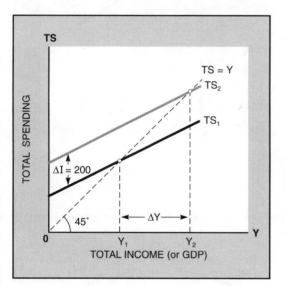

Fig. 7.2 The effect of increased investment on the income level

Since investment is a component of total expenditure (TS), an increase in investment of R200m (cf. fig. 7.1(b)) causes a rise in the income level.

on the other hand, where the I_kI_k curve is represented as being **less** elastic, the effect of interest rate variations on investment is practically eliminated (investment rises by a mere R30 million from R300 million to R330 million). A less elastic investment curve (such as I_kI_k) implies that decisions on investment are less sensitive to changes in the interest rate. According to the Keynesians, empirical studies in many Western countries have confirmed this inelastic demand curve for investment. In South Africa, however, we have seen that at very high rates of interest, such as prevailed for a period in the 1980's, the level of investment (and hence of capital-formation) was seriously impaired. If the adjustments made by the Keynesians with regard to the curves in figs. 7.3(a) and (b) are correct, it can be seen that monetary policy may be ineffective as an instrument to influence the level of income. Compare, in this connection, the slight increase in the income level of figure 7.3(c) with that of figure 7.2.

Whatever the effectiveness of monetary policy may be, it is clear that the **interest rate** plays a decisive part in the Keynesian transmission mechanism. Monetary policy which does not at the same time succeed in changing the interest rate has, according to this explanation, no chance of success.

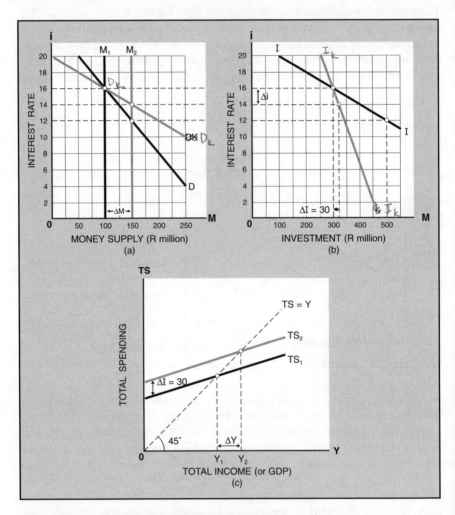

Fig 7.3 Keynes questions the effectiveness of monetary policy

Since the demand for money (cf. D_kD_k in (a)) is more elastic and the demand for investment (I_kI_k in (b)) is less elastic than is normally supposed, monetary policy is less effective in influencing the level of income (cf. ΔY in (c)).

Only through this **indirect way** can there be any question of a link between the monetary and the real sectors of the economy.

Historical perspective

During the Depression the world's most important economies found themselves in a sea of liquidity and no expansion of the money supply by the authorities had any significant effect on the level of income. This fact, together with the success of fiscal policy during and after World War II, lead to a general distrust of monetary policy. Extreme Keynesians took the view that the quantity of money as an instrument of economic policy could have no effect on the real sector.

This point of view prevailed for some time. During the sixties, however, a school of thought known as **monetarism** emerged, which re-emphasised the importance of the quantity of money as an instrument of policy.[§] The monetarists, under the leadership of Milton Friedman (winner of the 1976 Nobel Prize for Economics) began to propagate the merits of monetary policy against those of fiscal policy. Just as the Keynesians had criticised the effectiveness of monetary policy, the monetarists in turn raised doubts about the success of fiscal policy. The controversy between the Keynesians and the monetarists continues, and today has an ideological base as well. Where the Keynesians have definite opinions on the importance of the role the government ought to play (via fiscal policy) in the economy, the monetarists place greater emphasis on private initiative and the operation of the market mechanism with a minimum of permissible interference from the authorities. We must now look at the monetarists' view of the transmission mechanism.

7.2 The transmission mechanism: monetarist explanation

The point of reference for the monetarist account of the working of the transmission mechanism is to be found in the equation of exchange formulated by Fisher early in this century.

The equation of exchange

The equation of exchange may be stated as follows:

§ The designation "monetarism" should not be confused with people who implement monetary policy. Both the Keynesians and the monetarists have definite views on what can and what cannot be achieved by means of monetary policy.

$$MV = PY$$

where M = the quantity of money
       V = the velocity of circulation of money
       P = the average (or general) price level
       Y = the real GDP or the physical quantity of goods
             and services produced.

What this equation says is that the quantity of goods and services produced during a year (Y), multiplied by their prices (P), is equal to the money supply (M), multiplied by the velocity of circulation of money (V). Let us look at the meaning of the equation and particularly at the concept of **velocity of circulation** in greater detail.

In the previous chapter it was mentioned that the quantity of money in circulation is not the same as the income (or GDP) generated in the economy. According to the equation of exchange, the monetary value of the GDP (PY) is greater than the value of the quantity of money (M). It is greater than the quantity of money because the money is used more than once during the year to accommodate the transactions represented by the GDP. V is therefore an indication of the number of times the average rand (either in the form of cash or in that of demand deposits) changes hands (or circulates) during a given period. The value of V can be derived from the equation of exchange:

$$MV = PY$$
$$\therefore \quad V = \frac{PY}{M}$$

In other words, if the money supply is equal to R100 and we assume that Y is equal to 200 units of physical products and services, and also that the average price of each unit is R2, we get the following result:

$$V = \frac{200 \times R2}{R100}$$
$$= \frac{R400}{R100}$$
$$= 4$$

This means that each rand had to be used in transactions approximately four times in order to accommodate a GDP of R400. More realistic figures for South Africa during 1991 provide the following information with regard to the velocity of circulation of the rand:

$$V = \frac{GDP}{M1}$$
$$= \frac{R296\ 667}{R60\ 910}\ \text{million}$$
$$= 4{,}87$$

The average rand therefore had to pass from hand to hand approximately 5 times during 1991 in order to accommodate the monetary value of the final goods and services produced.

The equation of exchange formulated above is no more than an **identity** or a **tautology**. By definition the equation is always true. The value of PY must necessarily be equal to MV. The question is how the monetarists converted this exchange equation into a theory to forecast what would happen to the economy if the quantity of money is changed.

The quantity theory of money

The equation of exchange was converted by the monetarists into a theory by assuming that the velocity of circulation of money (V) was relatively constant. If it is accepted that V is a constant, the equation of exchange is converted from an identity or a definition into a theory because we are then able to forecast or explain the effect on the nominal value of GDP if the quantity of money changes. This theory, which is known as the **quantity theory of money**, says that if the quantity of money changes by a certain percentage, the monetary value of the GDP (or PY) will change by approximately the same percentage. In the simple example given above where the velocity of circulation is equal to four $(V = \frac{R400}{R100})$, an increase in the money supply from R100 to R150 (i.e. 50%) would lead to an increase in PY from R400 to R600 (i.e. also 50%) provided the velocity of circulation remains constant.

This analysis therefore agrees to a certain extent with what we have said above about classical thinking (on the role of money). In contrast to the classical economists, who believed that a change in the money supply (ΔM) would lead to a proportional change in the general price level (ΔP),[§] the monetarists maintain that ΔM will lead to a proportional change in the nominal value of income (ΔPY). Exactly how ΔP and ΔY will react individually cannot be determined with any degree of accuracy. It is nevertheless accepted that in the long run changes in the money supply are solely responsible for price changes.

The monetarists therefore argue that an increase in the supply of money

§   There is therefore no possibility that Y could change.

in the short term will mean an excess supply of money. This excess money will increase the aggregate demand as well as the monetary value of the GDP. By the same token, a sudden drop in the money supply will lead to an excess demand for money, which can only be satisfied by curbing expenditure on goods and services. This will cause aggregate demand to decline and the monetary value of the GDP to be reduced.

The monetarist explanation of the transmission mechanism is far more **direct** than the Keynesian explanation, whereby the quantity of money exerts an influence on investment and hence on total expenditure *via* the interest rate. Monetarists believe that because of a direct relationship, stability in the economy is directly dependent on a **stable money supply**.

Summary of various explanations

At the risk of oversimplification, the divergent points of view of the different schools of thought on the transmission mechanism may be sum-marised as follows:

(i)   **The Classical economists**
      Direct transmission mechanism

$$\Delta M \rightarrow \Delta TS \rightarrow \Delta P$$

In other words, an increase in the money supply (ΔM) leads to an increase in total expenditure (ΔTS) which gives rise to a proportional change in prices (ΔP). No real change in the income level (Y) is therefore involved, hence no transmission mechanism exists.

(ii) **The Keynesian explanation**
      Indirect transmission mechanism

$$\Delta M \rightarrow \Delta i \rightarrow \Delta I \rightarrow \Delta TS \rightarrow \Delta Y$$

A change in the money supply (ΔM) gives rise to a change in interest rates (Δi) which in turn leads to a change in investment (ΔI). Since investment is a component of total expenditure, TS will also change (ΔTS) and consequently the income level (ΔY) will be influenced. For various reasons this link between ΔM and ΔY will not, according to the Keynesians, be very strong.

(iii) **Monetarist explanation**
Direct transmission mechanism

$$\Delta M \rightarrow \Delta TS \begin{cases} \rightarrow \Delta P \\ \rightarrow \Delta Y \end{cases}$$

The increase in the money supply (ΔM) leads to an increase in expenditure, which then affects either the price level (ΔP) or the income level (ΔY).

7.3 Coordination of fiscal and monetary policy

Because the two schools (Keynesians and monetarists) differ with regard to the working of the transmission mechanism, they also have differences of opinion in respect of the application of monetary policy.

(i) The adherents of the **Keynesian school** would normally prefer to use fiscal policy to influence aggregate demand. Any monetary policy measure which might in fact be used, had to be aimed at influencing the **interest rate**, since the transmission mechanism worked indirectly (via the interest rate). The Keynesians' preference for fiscal policy also implies that they are in principle in favour of government intervention in the economy because they believe the free-market mechanism to be inherently unstable.

(ii) In contrast, the **monetarists** generally profess a free-market economy to be intrinsically stable and functioning in the most effective way. Government action should preferably be restricted to the minimum. Since a direct relation existed between changes in the money supply (ΔM) and the nominal income level (ΔPY), monetary policy could and should play a significant part in stabilising the economy. In this respect the effect on the general price level should be noted. The growth in the money supply should preferably be so regulated that it merely kept abreast of the growth in real production. Such action would have the least disturbing effect on the efficient functioning of the free-market economy.

The distinctions between these two schools of thought may create the impression that policy-makers use either monetary or fiscal policy to guide the economy in a certain direction. What actually happens, is that the two instruments of policy are generally used in conjunction to combat recession or inflation. Most economists today find themselves somewhere in the "gap" between Keynes and Friedman. In general, recognition is therefore given to the view that fiscal and monetary policy are both important instruments in the stabilisation of aggregate demand.

In spite of the viewpoint that the two kinds of policy instruments should be used together to promote general economic welfare, it has nevertheless been proved in practice that in certain circumstances the one instrument may be more successful than the other. **Fiscal policy** has generally been more successful in **stimulating** the economy, while **monetary policy** can be employed with greater assurance to **dampen** an overheated economy.

When the economy needs to be stimulated during a depression, the obvious instrument to use, would be fiscal policy. Such a situation is shown in figure 7.4, where aggregate demand is shifted towards the right by means of fiscal policy (from AD_1 to AD_2). In the same diagram a condition of virtually full employment may be seen, where a restrictive monetary policy would probably be the best way of shifting aggregate demand to the left (from AD_4 to AD_3) in order to bring inflation under control. The position of the economy on the aggregate supply curve will therefore largely determine the instrument of policy to be used.

The institutional nature of the two policy instruments serves to emphasise this point still further. As we saw in chapter 5, fiscal policy is subject to parliamentary approval and the decisions in this respect are normally taken by politicians. Monetary policy, on the other hand, is formulated by the Reserve Bank, which enjoys a greater degree of autonomy. The pressure on politicians to act in the interest of voters has also led to fiscal policy being generally more attuned towards stimulating aggregate demand, while the

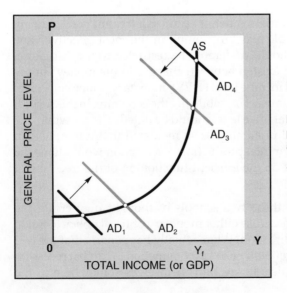

Fig. 7.4 Fiscal and monetary policy and the position of the aggregate supply curve

Although no general rule may be formulated, fiscal policy is probably more successful as a stimulating measure (shift from AD_1 to AD_2), while monetary policy is more effective as a restrictive measure (downward shift from AD_4 to AD_3).

Reserve Bank and other central banks traditionally take a more conservative and restrictive attitude towards economic policy.

In most cases it is nevertheless necessary to find a suitable combination of the two policy instruments to combat certain problems occurring in the "trade-off" area of the AS curve. In this connection, continual consultation between authorities such as the Reserve Bank, the Department of Finance and other government departments is of the utmost importance.

7.4 The South African Reserve Bank

Before discussing the instruments of monetary policy in South Africa, it is necessary to take a brief look at the main functions of South Africa's central bank. South Africa's central bank is the South African Reserve Bank (SARB) which was established in 1921. It is the most important single institution when it comes to the implementation of monetary policy in South Africa. Together with the Treasury, the Reserve Bank forms the **monetary authority** in South Africa.

Five main functions undertaken by the Reserve Bank may be distinguished:

- Controller of note issues.
- Banker for other banks.
- Banker for the government.
- Custodian of the country's gold and other foreign exchange reserves.
- Responsible for the formulation and implementation of monetary policy in South Africa.

In the execution of these functions the SARB uses its powers to exercise control over the money supply and credit creation.

Controller of note issues

Since its inception the Reserve Bank has had the sole right to the issue of bank notes and coins. This cash comes into general circulation through the purchase of assets (usually financial assets) by the bank. By the purchase of government stock and assets from banks, credit is actually made available by the Reserve Bank to the government and banks. The Reserve Bank is largely guided by the public's cash requirements ("till money requirements") in its issues of notes and coins.

Bankers' bank

In its capacity as bankers' bank the South African Reserve Bank is the holder of the minimum (compulsory) cash reserves required of banks. On the grounds of this **monetary base**, the banks can create the demand deposits (D) which constitute the largest part of the quantity of money. By exerting control over the level and composition of these reserves, the Reserve Bank can to a large extent control the quantity of money. These reserves are simultaneously used to clear the banks' mutual claims and obligations, i.e. the Reserve Bank also acts as **clearing bank**. Banks' reserve positions change all the time in that one bank's debit clearance balance is cleared against other banks' credit balances.

As bankers' bank the Reserve Bank also acts as **lender of last resort**. This basically means that any cash balance shortage experienced on the money market by the Corporation for Public Deposits (formerly the National Finance Corporation), the discount houses and the banks themselves, can be obtained from the SARB. What normally happens is that the discount houses obtain the necessary cash balances from the Reserve Bank on behalf of the banks by rediscounting land bank bills, treasury bills, bankers' acceptances, etc. The fixing of the rates and the terms and conditions under which the SARB executes its rediscounting are called its **discount policy**.

Banker for the government

As government banker the Reserve Bank handles all financial receipts and payments of the state. The bank-client relationship in this case also includes the granting of credit. In the previous chapter we dealt with the influence of government transactions on the money supply. The Reserve Bank also deals with the weekly issues of treasury bills on behalf of the Treasury, advises the government with regard to monetary and financial matters and is responsible for the administration of all exchange control regulations.

Custodian of gold and other foreign exchange reserves

With the exception of smaller necessary balances held by banks and the Treasury, the Reserve Bank keeps all the country's gold and foreign exchange reserves. Gold coins and gold bullion are added to the reserves at a market-related price. The level of South Africa's gold and other foreign exchange reserves is one of the main barometers of the state of the economy and of prospects for future economic growth (cf. chapter 8).

Formulation and implementation of monetary policy

The SARB, in cooperation with the Department of Finance, is responsible for formulating and implementing monetary policy. The way in which the bank's other functions are fulfilled, will mainly be determined by the goals of monetary policy at that juncture. In this regard it should be mentioned that the Reserve Bank has accepted the protection of the domestic and external value of the rand as its most important goal. In the next section the main instruments of monetary policy are discussed.

7.5 The instruments of monetary policy in South Africa

As we have said, the monetary authorities endeavour to achieve broad policy objectives by exercising control over the financial system in general and more specifically by influencing certain variables such as the money supply, the level and structure of interest rates and the general availability of credit in the economy.

The early 1980's in South Africa were characterised by continuous change and reform in monetary policy. This period of reform was heralded by the appointment in 1977 of a commission to inquire into and submit recommendations on the monetary system in South Africa. Although the final report of this commission (the so-called De Kock Commission) was only released in 1985, the activities of the commission gave rise to the implementation of new measures over a broad financial front from as early as 1979. The implementation of the Deposit-taking Institutions Act in 1991 may also be regarded as part of the reform process which was started by the De Kock Commission.

The changes that took place during this period of reform altered the framework of monetary policy so extensively that a discussion of the instruments of monetary policy today would differ considerably from one taking place in the seventies. Because the reform placed greater emphasis on market-oriented policy measures (in contrast to direct measures), it is important that greater clarity should be obtained on the difference between the two kinds of policy measures.

Market-oriented and non-market-oriented policy instruments

Non-market-oriented (or direct) policy instruments essentially mean that the monetary authorities instruct the banks and other financial institutions to do or to refrain from doing certain things with regard to their lending and borrowing activities.[§] Failure to comply with such instructions may lead to a fine or some other penalty. Examples of non-market-oriented policy instruments are the placing of quantitative restrictions on bank credit (the so-called **credit ceilings**) and **deposit rate control**. In the case of credit ceilings, the banking institutions are informed by means of a proclamation in the Government Gazette than their outstanding loans to the

§ Cf. J.H. Meijer in Meijer, Falkena and Van der Merwe. 1991. *Financial Policy in South Africa.* Southern Book Publishers, p.107.

public should not exceed a certain limit at a specified date. In the same way, deposit rate control is enforced when financial institutions are instructed as to the rates they may pay or may require clients to pay on deposits. Clearly, these measures allow the market no margin of discretion. Both these measures have been abolished during the reforms of the past few years.

Market-oriented policy measures, on the other hand, seek to guide or encourage financial institutions to take certain actions on a voluntary basis. In this case the authorities create price and/or interest-rate incentives to encourage private enterprise, and hence financial variables, to move in a desired direction.

What happens, is that the monetary authorities create such incentives through their own buying and selling activities on the financial markets or by varying the terms on which they are prepared to offer credit. A good example of such a policy instrument is the change in the **bank rate** which is announced from time to time. The bank rate represents one of the rates at which the Reserve Bank is prepared to grant financial assistance to the banking sector and should be regarded as the cost of credit to the banking sector.

As indicated above, a high priority is currently given to market-oriented policy instruments. The instruments mainly used to enforce monetary control in South Africa are:

– public debt management;
– open market policy;
– discount policy; and
– reserve asset requirements.

Without going into detail, the meaning of each of these policy instruments will be briefly discussed.[§]

Public debt management

The concept of "public debt management" is defined as the decisions and actions taken by the authorities to exercise a planned influence on the **size, composition** and **maturity** of the central government's debt. Changes in the size of the central government's outstanding debt result from the budget deficits and surpluses realised annually. The **manner** in which, for example, a budget deficit is to be financed will have important consequences for the composition and maturity of the public debt. The financing of a budget deficit, in particular, has direct monetary implications. Public

§   For a more detailed discussion of the framework of monetary policy in South Africa, see Meijer in Meijer, Falkena and Van der Merwe. *op.cit.*, pp.107–164.

debt management may therefore justifiably be regarded as the meeting ground of a country's fiscal and monetary policy.

The following are examples of the application of public debt management as an instrument of monetary policy:

(i)   The government's domestic borrowing in a particular financial year may be made to exceed its budget deficit in order to achieve a net withdrawal of cash reserves from the banking sector, which will be matched by an increase in the government's cash balances with the Reserve Bank.

(ii) Alternatively, the government's borrowing may be insufficient to finance the budget deficit so as to lead to a net flow of cash reserves to the banking system and a corresponding drop in the government's cash balances with the Reserve Bank.

(iii) Public debt management also entails decisions on the combination of short and long-term debt to be adhered to in the financing of government expenditure. Because monetary control in South Africa is achieved partly by the imposition of liquid asset requirements (the meaning of this will be explained below), the excessive issuing of any short-term debt (e.g. treasury bills and short-term government stock which qualify as liquid assets) leads to an excessive expansion of bank credit and the quantity of money.

Open market policy

Open-market transactions as an instrument of monetary policy consist of the sale or purchase of domestic financial assets (mainly treasury bills and government securities) by a central bank in order to exert a specific influence on interest rates and the supply of money in the country.

For example, when the central bank wishes to **increase** the money supply, it **buys** government securities on the open market from a broker or an institution such as a bank. If the securities are purchased from a bank, the central bank will normally pay for them by raising the cash reserves of the bank concerned by means of a book entry. The bank will now have excess reserves which may be used to create demand deposits. In this way the monetary base is increased and the initial aim of the central bank is achieved. This procedure is primarily used in the USA where the 'discount window' (see next chapter) is not always available to banks. Under these circumstances it is possible to use open market operations in a direct way to influence the money supply.

The procedure followed when the intention is to **decrease** the quantity of money, is exactly the opposite of the above. Now the central bank **sells** government stock on the open market and so reduces the cash reserves of banks (directly or indirectly), which in turn leads to a reduction of the money supply.

The question is of course how the central bank persuades the various market participants (e.g. banks and other financial institutions) to buy or sell bonds (such as government stock, land bank bills and municipal stock) at a specific moment. In order to encourage people to buy securities, their prices have to be made attractive (i.e. lowered). Paying a lower price for a bond (or any similar security) implies that a higher yield will be realised on it.

The *relation* between the price of a bond and the yield (interest rate) that can be earned on it, may be illustrated by the following example:

Suppose a negotiable bond of indeterminate maturity (i.e. the date of repayment is not explicitly stated), is issued for an amount of R1 000. Suppose further that the holder of such a bond is entitled to receive R120 interest per annum. For as long as this bond is held, the holder is assured an income of R120 or a nominal yield rate of 12% ($\frac{R120}{R1\,000} \times \frac{100}{1}$). If the bond is sold to someone else for R800, then the market yield rate for the new bond holder will be raised to 15% ($\frac{R120}{R800} \times \frac{100}{1}$). Since the annual interest payments remain constant, any change in the price of the bond will have a direct effect on the yield or effective interest rate. **A higher bond price will bring about a lower market interest rate (yield rate), while a lower bond price will lead to an increased interest rate**. An inverse relation therefore exists between the price of a bond (or other type of security) and the interest rate.

When the central bank buys securities (i.e. increases the quantity of money), the price of securities will tend to rise and interest rates to drop. Open-market transactions consequently affect not only the quantity of money but also the **interest rate pattern.** They can therefore be used to support the discount policy (see next section) of the Reserve Bank. An increase in the bank rate should be accompanied by the sale of securities, whereas a decrease in the bank rate should be supported by the purchase of securities.

The main facet of open-market policy as it is applied in South Africa, is that the sale of government stock may be undertaken in order to bring about a shortage of cash reserves in the banking system so that banks will be forced to make use of the rediscounting facilities of the SARB – thus rendering the discount policy to be discussed below more effective.

Discount policy

When a bank experiences liquidity problems, it can either change liquid assets into cash or borrow to supplement the shortage. The funds required are obtained from other institutions (including other banks) who have excess funds at their disposal. If all banks have the same liquidity problem (e.g. at the end of the month or as a result of an unusually high demand for credit), the Reserve Bank, as bankers' bank, acts as **"lender of last resort"**. The credit may be obtained at the **'discount window'** of the SARB. At present two methods are in use to make refinancing available through the "window":

(i) The **rediscounting** of treasury bills, land bank bills and certain bankers' acceptances which are offered at the "window" by banks. The **bank rate** is the least expensive form of financing by the SARB and is equal to the rate at which treasury bills are rediscounted for banks. All rediscount rates on other bills and acceptances are more expensive.

(ii) The granting of **overnight loans** to banks against security of various kinds of approved securities. The interest costs of overnight loans are higher than the rates of rediscounting.

The discount policy of the Reserve Bank, which entails changes in the bank rate and other conditions on which cash is made available to banks, is therefore an instrument by which the quantity of money is regulated through variations in the **cost of credit**. The reason is that changes in the bank rate lead to adjustments in the interest rates at which credit is made available at other levels; the cost of credit is therefore directly linked to the bank rate of the Reserve Bank. Other interest rates will move in sympathy with the Reserve Bank's discount rate. Today the bank rate constitutes the most important policy instrument of the monetary authorities.

Reserve asset requirements

As we have mentioned, banks in South Africa have always, since the inception of the SARB in 1921, been subject to some form of reserve asset requirements. In contrast to the three policy instruments discussed so far, changes in the reserve asset requirements cannot really be regarded as a market-oriented policy instrument. This instrument is applied in a way that has more in common with a direct policy measure.

The reserve asset requirements in South African consist of (i) a cash reserve requirement, and (ii) a liquid asset requirement. In the previous chapter, where we dealt with credit creation by banks, it became clear that any change in the legal reserve requirements could have a significant effect on the quantity of money.

In that discussion we assumed that the system used only cash reserve requirements to control the quantity of money. We explained that a lowering of the legal (cash) reserve requirement from 20 per cent to 10 per cent would mean that a bank would be enabled to raise the level of its demand deposits and hence increase the money supply significantly. Whether such a measure would in fact lead to an increase in the supply of money would depend on the banks' desire to increase their loans and demand deposits. As we saw in the previous chapter, no one can prevent the banks from preferring to allow their excess reserves to accumulate. Similarly, the Reserve Bank could try to lower the money supply by increasing the legal (cash) reserve requirement. Such a restrictive measure would probably have a better chance of success than one aimed at stimulating the economy.

As we have pointed out, in South Africa the cash reserve requirement is supplemented by a liquid asset requirement. This means that banks are required to hold a certain percentage of their demand deposits and other liabilities in the form of prescribed liquid assets. Apart from cash reserves, liquid assets include cash deposits with the Corporation for Public Deposits, treasury bills, land bank bills, etc.

In principle an increase in these required liquid assets will affect the money supply in the same way as an increase in the cash reserve ratio, although a change in the latter will have a more direct effect on the quantity of money.

Other instruments

In addition to the above four policy instruments, there are a number of other measures that may be used by the monetary authorities to achieve their aims. We have already mentioned the non-market-oriented measures such as **credit ceilings** and **deposit rate control**, which have been discontinued for some years. Other monetary policy measures, which are in fact used, are changes in the **terms of hire purchase agreements, changes in exchange control regulations** and Reserve Bank **intervention in foreign exchange markets.**

A final instrument at the Reserve Bank's disposal is the informal measure of **moral suasion.** Although moral suasion is not a policy instrument in the strict sense of the word, the Reserve Bank can nevertheless, by means of consultation and persuasion, influence the banks in a certain direction when it does not wish to or cannot use actual policy instruments.

Selected references:

Baumol & Blinder: 13, 14.
Dernburg: 9, 10, 11.
Dornbusch & Fischer: 6, 10.
Evans-Pritchard: 9.
Meijer, JH, Falkena, HB, & Van der Merwe, EJ (Eds) 1991. *Financial Policy in South Africa.* Southern Book Publishers. Chapter 5.
Froyen: 19.
Gordon: 16.
Morley: 14, 17.
Shapiro: 10, 26.

8 The external sector

After the introductory chapter 1, the next three chapters (2, 3 and 4) contained an explanation of the working of the macro-economic supply and demand system. In the next chapter we presented the basic principles according to which the government can influence aggregate demand by means of taxation and expenditure. The subject matter of chapters 6 and 7, which can be taken as a unit, was the nature and working of money and the monetary system – again with special reference to the implications for aggregate demand.

At this stage it is perhaps just as well to mention that in these chapters you were introduced to two separate and very important subjects in economics, viz. **Public Economics** (chapter 5) and **Monetary Economics** (chapters 6 and 7). If you continue with your economic studies, you will probably study these subjects in much greater detail.

The same applies to the contents of the present chapter, a closer look at the external sector, leading eventually to a more thorough study of what is known as **International Economics**. Obviously we shall only touch upon some of the major aspects of this important discipline as our attention is still focused on the determination of demand in a macro-economic framework.

8.1 The nature and background of international trade

The question of how the **external sector** or the "rest of the world" sector, as it is also known, fits into the present analysis, has already been answered in chapter 3, and more specifically in section 3.7 of that chapter. We mentioned there that aggregate demand by the residents of any particular country is reflected in domestic spending – i.e. on the amount spent on consumption (C), investment (I) and by the government (G). But domestic expenditure does not give us the complete picture, since people outside our borders are also interested in what we have to sell. This leads to **exports** (X) which represent an **addition** to domestic expenditure and must be added to it in order to arrive at an indication of aggregate demand or aggregate expenditure. At the same time local residents are also interested in goods and services produced outside our borders, which entails **imports** (Z) and hence a **subtraction** from domestic expenditure.

Our main interest so far has been in the value of (X – Z) since this would indicate whether aggregate expenditure would be greater or smaller than domestic expenditure, which in turn would indicate whether the participation in international trade has caused domestic income, employment or inflation to increase or decrease. In this chapter we shall consider X and Z in greater detail.

Absolute and comparative advantage

Why should international trade take place? It is clear that the answer must lie in the endowment of different countries with **natural resources** (including the climate), **human** resources and the resources of **capital equipment** and **technology** which are built up over the years. In this way one can explain the grain exports from countries with large fertile areas, such as Canada, the United States and Argentina. Mineral exports come from countries like Australia and South Africa, with great mineral wealth.

These cases are of course easy enough to understand, since trade is then the result of the **absolute** advantage of one country over another as a result of the difference in natural resources. But this should not be taken to mean that natural resources – i.e. raw materials – are a prerequisite for international trade. Countries such as Japan and Switzerland certainly do not have abundant natural resources, but they have overcome this major drawback by making use of the skills of their people, their efficiency, resourcefulness and the advanced level of their technology. By the production and export of high-technology goods, they can afford to import and pay for the necessary raw materials.

Nor is international trade confined to cases where, as explained above, countries have an absolute advantage over others in terms of the production of certain goods, i.e. where a good either cannot be produced at all or can only be produced at an exorbitant cost in other countries. A famous example of this was given by Adam Smith when he wrote that it would not be impossible to grow grapes under glass in Scotland – but as this would be very expensive, the Scots would be better off importing grapes from France.

International trade can even be advantageous to a country most efficient at producing **all** goods. One would think that such a country could produce anything it needed. The advantage of trade would then lie in the fact that the country could specialise in those goods where its comparative advantage was greatest. This principle of **comparative advantage** is the reason for trade taking place even where no absolute advantage exists between countries.

Free trade versus protectionism

According to the general principle of comparative advantage, the greatest benefit for all is obtained when there is specialisation according to endowments and talents between people, regions within a country and also between **countries**. This type of specialisation can arise in a natural manner provided there is no interference with market forces; it forms the background to the policy of **free trade** or free international trade, which is regarded by most policy-makers and economists as the ideal condition.

International trade however, by definition involves two independent countries and for this reason it is very difficult to put this principle into practice. Particularly in the case of countries endeavouring to catch up economically with other countries with a higher level of industrial development, it is often argued that local industries cannot get off the ground without a certain measure of protection (the so-called "infant industries" argument), and even that free trade could ruin certain existing industries. This is the opposite of the principle of free trade and is known as **protectionism**. There is no country today which does not have some form of protection for its local industries, agriculture and mining sector.

Naturally the long-term objectives of industrial growth are related to the short-term aims of maintaining a certain level of employment, as explained in chapter 3, since an increase in imports (Z) lowers aggregate demand and hence employment, whereas a rise in exports (X) has the opposite effect. In other words, a policy of protection (including export promotion) fits in well with the aims of macro-economic policy already discussed.

8.2 South Africa's imports and exports

It is general knowledge today that South Africa's trade relations with the rest of the world are no longer based on purely economic considerations. The uncertain political factors that have given rise to threats (and the actual imposition) of sanctions and trade boycotts have seriously impaired the scope and composition of South Africa's exports and imports over the past few years. In our analysis of the role of the external sector, these abnormal circumstances should always be borne in mind.

In chapter 3 it was pointed out that South Africa's economy may be regarded, on the basis of import and export figures, as a particularly "open" economy. According to table 3.2 the imports of "goods and non-factor services" constituted almost 23 per cent of the South African GDP during the eighties.[§] This percentage would be even greater if payments for foreign

---

§   Non-factor services consist of freight, insurance, travel, etc.

factor services (cf. table 2.1), which in 1991 amounted to almost R8 182 million, were taken into account.

The composition of South Africa's exports

In the previous section we mentioned that the reason for foreign trade is to be found in the differences between countries in respect of the availability of natural, human, technological and capital resources. This statement is clearly illustrated by the composition of South Africa's imports and exports, which reflect the fact that South Africa is a country with a strong primary sector (mining and agriculture) and a growing secondary (manufacturing) sector. Table 8.1, which contains import and export data for 1985 according to a number of classes, shows this clearly.[§]

If we look first of all at exports, the table shows that by far the largest single class in the export picture falls in the category of "other". This category accounts for 50,7 per cent of the total and can be ascribed mainly to the export of gold bullion (i.e. exports of monetary and unwrought gold by the Reserve Bank) which, for strategic reasons, is placed in this unclassified category. For a period of almost six years (1974 to 1980) the import and export of certain goods (including gold, military goods and petroleum products) were not included in the official foreign trade statistics for strategic reasons. All imports and exports are included in table 8.1, although the above-mentioned products are shown as part of the unclassified category.

The importance of the mining sector is further emphasised when we consider the next three most significant export classes in table 8.1. The first of these is class 5, mineral products, which includes asbestos and particularly coal; this class constitutes 13,6 per cent of the 1985 total. After this class, in the second place (11%), we find base metals and products made of base metals. The last class which stresses the overwhelming influence of the mining sector is class 14, i.e. jewelry, precious stones and precious metals, which account for about 7 per cent of total exports. If the overwhelming importance of gold in respect of class 21 is accepted and we add to this the contributions of classes 5, 14 and 15, we may conclude that the mining sector was responsible for more than 82 per cent of South Africa's exports in 1985.

---

§ We make use of 1985 figures here because that was the last year in which the Customs and Excise Commissioner published full details of South Africa's imports and exports with regard to various countries. The data in table 8.1 therefore do not agree with the totals given in tables 8.2 and 8.3. It is unlikely that the basic structure (by class, as set out in table 8.1) will have changed significantly since 1985.

Table 8.1

Imports and exports according to class, South Africa, 1985

Classes		Imports			Exports		
		Rank-ing	R million	%	Rank-ing	R million	%
1	Live animals and prodicts		96,5	0,4		331,0	0,9
2	Vegetable products		517,8	2,3		868,9	2,4
3	Fats and oils		376,5	1,7		76,1	0,2
4	Prepared food		503,6	2,2		808,3	2,2
5	Mineral products		509,6	2,2	(1)	4 996,0	13,6
6	Chemicals	(3)	2 363,5	10,4	(5)	930,7	2,5
7	Plastic materials		841,4	3,7		153,8	0,4
8	Hides, skins and leather		67,0	0,3		272,0	0,7
9	Wood and articles of wood		109,6	0,5		106,5	0,3
10	Paper and pulp		621,0	2,7		656,9	1,8
11	Textiles		694,6	3,1	(4)	1 044,8	2,8
12	Footwear and headgear		101,7	0,5		12,3	–
13	Articles of stone, asbestos, plaster, etc.		236,7	1,0		85,3	0,2
14	Jewellery and precious stones and metals		355,0	1,6	(3)	2 607,1	7,1
15	Base metals	(4)	1 161,0	5,1	(2)	4 045,9	11,0
16	Machinery	(1)	6 474,1	28,5		529,6	1,4
17	Vehicles and parts thereof	(2)	2 404,5	10,6		361,3	1,0
18	Optical and other instruments	(5)	950,3	4,2		74,5	0,2
19	Miscellaneous manufactured articles		193,5	0,9		44,2	0,1
20	Work of art, etc.		35,1	0,1		23,0	0,1
21	Other (unclassified)		4 046,4	17,8		18 649,1	50,7
22	Household possessions of immigrants/emigrants		41,8	0,2		98,3	0,3
TOTAL			**22 701,2**	**100,0**		**36 775,8**	**100,0**

Source: Republic of South Africa, *Foreign Trade Statistics*, Calendar year 1985, Government Printer, Pretoria.

Table 8.1   *This table shows that both imports and exports are concentrated in only a few of the twenty-two classifications. The nature of the South African economy is well illustrated here, since our main exports are minerals and agricultural products, whereas imports consist mainly of secondary industry products.*

The only other classes, in the order of importance, which are of any significance, are textiles (class 11), chemical products (class 6), vegetable products (class 2) and prepared foodstuffs (class 4). In three of these classes the influence of the other primary sector in the South African economy, i.e. agriculture, is clearly reflected. Nevertheless, although much smaller, the contributions of secondary industry are not negligible and may be expected to increase with further economic development.

The composition of South Africa's imports

To quite a considerable extent the composition of our imports is, as may be expected, the mirror image of our exports. As in the case of exports, there is a strong concentration in a limited number of product categories. The two main categories here are machinery (class 16) with no less than 28,5 per cent of the reported imports, and vehicles and parts (class 17) which in 1985 amounted to R2 404,5 million, i.e. 10,6 per cent of the total. A large proportion of these two categories naturally consists of capital equipment which fits in well with the picture of a country which is expanding its production capacity. Other important categories are chemicals and base metals, which are of course used as raw materials in industry. The importance of strategic products such as arms and petroleum products can also be clearly seen from the extent of class 21, which in this case constitutes 17,8 per cent of the total.

South Africa's major trading partners

In addition to a knowledge of the composition of our imports and exports, it is important to know where our imports come from and where our exports go to. In table 8.2 the exports and imports from a number of countries are reflected. The list is not exhaustive and some countries have not been mentioned, e.g. South American countries such as Brazil and Argentina, and others such as Denmark. The countries listed produce 70,5 per cent of our total imports and receive 46,1 per cent of our exports. The reason for the exports being so small is mainly due to the fact that gold exports may not be categorised per country.

From this (incomplete) listing it is clear that South Africa has trade relations with a wide variety of countries in all parts of the world. The table also shows that our foreign trade is dominated by relations with four or five countries. South Africa's most important trading partners are West Germany, the USA, the United Kingdom and Japan in a strong fourth position. After this there is a considerable gap, and then Italy followed by France, Switzerland and the Netherlands – all at approximately the same level. This becomes even clearer in table 8.3 where imports and exports are added together to give an indication of the total volume of trade between the RSA and the countries concerned.

Table 8.2

Imports and exports according to countries, South Africa, 1990

Countries	Imports			Exports		
	Rank-ing	$ million	%	Rank-ing	$ million	%
Africa		358	2,2	(6)	1 138	4,7
United Kingdom	(3)	2 052	12,4	(3)	1 473	6,0
Belgium-Luxemburg		350	2,1		463	1,9
Netherlands		340	2,0		586	2,4
West Germany	(1)	2 834	17,1	(5)	1 179	4,8
France	(5)	668	4,0		521	2,1
Switzerland*		362	2,2		616	2,5
Italy	(6)	606	3,6	(4)	1 387	5,7
Canada		152	0,9		126	0,5
USA	(2)	2 077	12,5	(1)	1 821	7,5
Taiwan		155	0,9		202	0,8
Japan	(4)	1 613	9,7	(2)	1 639	6,7
Australia		153	0,9		122	0,5
Total of countries mentioned		*11 720*	*70,5*		*11 273*	*46,1*
GRAND TOTAL		**16 545**	**100,0**		**24 306**	**100,0**

* The ranking of exports to Switzerland is not indicated because it consists mainly of gold and precious stones.

Source: Direction of Trade Statistics, *Yearbook, 1991,* International Monetary Fund

Table 8.2   *The concentration of imports and exports according to countries is even more marked than in the previous table. Our major customers are simultaneously our major suppliers.*

In table 8.3 it can be seen that Switzerland is actually South Africa's seventh largest trading partner. This is however largely a technicality caused by the fact that South Africa transferred much of its gold and diamond trade from London to Zurich during the late seventies. Out of a total amount of R1 324 million of exports to Switzerland in 1985, 92 per cent consisted of class 14, namely jewelry, precious stones and precious metals. This is why Switzerland is not mentioned in table 8.2 in the ranking of our exports; in a certain sense this country acts as our agent in the marketing of gold and diamonds.

Obviously, the threatening attitude adopted by many countries with regard to trade boycotts and sanctions against South Africa could drastically alter the conclusions drawn above. Although the countries appearing in table 8.3 are today probably still South Africa's major trading partners, there can be no certainty as to the order of their importance as reflected in the table. New markets had to be found for many of our exports and imports over the past few years. For strategic reasons these markets are not always specified.

Table 8.3

Imports and exports of South Africa's major trading partners, 1990, in $ million

Countries	Imports (1)	Exports (2)	Total (1) + (2)
West Germany	2 834	1 179	4 013
USA	2 077	1 821	3 898
United Kingdom	2 052	1 473	3 525
Japan	1 613	1 639	3 252
Italy	606	1 387	1 993
France	668	521	1 189
Switzerland	362	616	978
Netherlands	340	586	926

Source: Direction of Trade Statistics, *Yearbook, 1991*, International Monetary Fund.

Table 8.3 *If imports are added to exports we can determine who our major trading partners are.*

8.3 The balance of payments

For reasons of economic management – and, as we shall see in the last section of this chapter, for reasons of survival – it is important to be able to judge a country's trading position in relation to the rest of the world. This is done by setting out a country's transactions with other countries in an account called the **balance of payments**. Such an account consists of two parts. The first part is called the **current account** of the balance of payments. This account records the current purchases and sales of goods and services to the rest of the world.

The second part of the balance of payments is called the **capital account**. This part records the financial or capital transactions, including the borrowing and lending of funds. Although the current and capital accounts are studied separately, they form part of the same whole. The example shown in table 8.4, which presents the data of the balance of payments for South Africa in the 1980's, contains a current as well as a capital account.

Two important items on this account were dealt with in the previous section, viz. **merchandise exports** and **merchandise imports**. In principle the totals in tables 8.1 and 8.2 should be the same as the corresponding totals

Table 8.4

Balance of payments, annual figures for selected years (R million)

DO NOT NEED TO KNOW CALCULATIONS

	1981	1984	1985	1986	1987	1989	1990	199
Merchandise exports, f.o.b.[1]	9 579	12 768	19 977	24 336	25 827	39 085	42 385	45 9
Net gold exports[2]	8 340	11 684	15 460	16 719	17 792	19 228	18 070	19 6
Service receipts	3 084	4 552	5 957	6 365	6 584	9 754	10 840	11 5
less Merchandise imports, f.o.b.[1]	18 111	21 519	23 165	25 636	28 773	44 322	44 100	48 1
less Payments for services	7 351	10 141	13 183	15 735	15 398	20 857	21 712	21 7
Total goods and services (net receipts +)	− 4 459	−2 656	5 046	6 049	6 032	2 888	5 483	7 2
Transfers (net receipts +)	370	54	41	65	−37	220	304	1
Balance on current account	**− 4 089**	**−2 602**	**5 087**	**6 114**	**5 995**	**3 108**	**5 787**	**7 4**
Long term capital movements	542	2 610	−522	−3 162	−1 701	−1 230	−1 945	−2 7
Public authorities	249	701	−415	−305	−532	−646	−1 160	−1
General government	146	114	−481	−41	−100	−403	−158	3
Public business enterprises	103	587	66	−264	−432	−243	−1 002	−4
Public corporations	668	1 067	817	−75	817	436	890	3
Banking sector	−84	88	−298	−103	90	−65	−277	
Non-bank private sector	−291	754	−626	−2 679	−2 076	−955	−1 398	−2 9
Basic balance	**−3 547**	**8**	**4 565**	**2 952**	**4 294**	**1 878**	**3 842**	**4 7**
Short term capital movements not related to reserves[3]	419	−1 374	−7 799	−1 910	−1 150	−3 115	−929	−3 3
Public authorities	−74	2	75	−71	8	42	20	−
Public corporations	−241	−17	−157	−224	−40	97	−51	−1
Non-bank private sector[4]	734	−1 359	−7 717	−1 615	−1 118	−3 254	−898	−3 1
Change in net gold and other foreign reserves owing to balance of payments transactions	**−3 128**	**−1 366**	**−3 234**	**1 042**	**3 144**	**−1 237**	**2 913**	**1 3**
Change in liabilities related to reserves[3]	2 123	477	1 998	−2 195	−1 259	2 626	−2 034	1 6
SDR allocations and valuation adjustments	543	1 244	1 802	989	330	−1 190	−520	−4
Change in gross gold and other foreign reserves	**−1 548**	**355**	**566**	**−164**	**2 215**	**199**	**359**	**2 5**

Source: South African Reserve Bank: *Quarterly Bulletin,* March 1992.

1 Published customs figures adjusted for balance of payments purposes.
2 Net foreign sales of gold plus changes in gold holdings of the Reserve Bank and other banking institutions.
3 Liabilities related to foreign reserves include all foreign short-term liabilities of the Reserve Bank and other banking institutions and short-terms foreign loans to the Central Government by foreign banks and authorities.
4 Including unrecorded transactions on the current as well as the capital account.

Table 8.4 *This table presents a summary of South Africa's trade and financial transactions with other countries. It includes the current as well as the capital account of the balance of payments.*

for merchandise exports (plus gold production) and merchandise imports in table 8.4. The differences that do occur are to be found in certain balance of payments adjustments.

Many years ago, when international economic relations first came to be studied in countries such as Britain and France, there was a tendency to concentrate on the import and export of **merchandise**, also known as the import and export of **visibles**. The balance between the two was called the **trade balance**. This expression is still used when comparing the import and export of merchandise. Today, however, we are aware of the fact that **services** (or invisible imports and exports) are equally important. We shall return to this.

Net gold exports

One of the items in the current account is peculiar to the presentation of statistics in the South African balance of payments, viz. **net gold exports**. An important reason for the item appearing here, is the fact that South Africa is the greatest gold producing country in the Western world and that gold is our most important export.

But this is not an adequate reason, since there are other countries where one product is far and away the most important export – in fact, in our own case coal and diamonds have a strong claim to this position – nevertheless these products are not individually mentioned in the balance of payments. However, gold is a special kind of product. Under the Bretton Woods Agreement, which was concluded at the end of the Second World War, the value of all (Western) currencies was expressed in terms of the American dollar. The price of **gold**, expressed in dollar, was $35 per fine ounce; this price was fixed in 1933 and after 1945 remained in force. Via the dollar, the exchange rate of any one currency could be calculated against another, and so the price of gold could be expressed in terms of other currencies. The result of this was that any amount of gold could be sold at the internationally agreed price.

There was, in other words, a guaranteed market at a fixed price for any amount of gold produced. Gold could, therefore, as soon as it was produced and delivered to the Reserve Bank, immediately be counted as part of the gold and foreign exchange reserves; and this was the case, even though the gold had not yet actually been sold and exported. You will therefore note (cf. footnote 2 at the bottom of table 8.4) that the item "net gold exports" includes all changes in the **gold assets** of the Reserve Bank and other banking institutions. This item in fact represents the total **gold production** of South Africa. Earlier on this item in the balance of payments was actually called "net gold production".

The unchanging gold price meant, of course, that there was no increase in price to keep abreast of the rise in costs. For example, in the sixties the gold price (in rand) stayed at more or less R25, although the general price level rose by about 25 per cent. If one took this comparison further back, the difference between the value of gold and the purchasing power of the rand would be even greater.

The gold price – a historical review

Although we cannot here enter into great detail, it is important to bring the main aspects of the development of the gold price to your attention. Attempts to increase the gold price began in the late fifties. However, little notice was taken at an international level; to many people it seemed that such attempts were simply based on the understandable arguments of the gold producers. The United States, in particular, felt it would not benefit by such a rise. Its reasons were partly economical but also partly political. A rise in the price of gold would help two countries not very popular in the USA, viz. South Africa and the Soviet Union (also a large gold producer). Furthermore, the Americans felt that a rise in the dollar price of gold would in fact be the same as a devaluation of the dollar (cf. section 8.5), and would therefore contribute to inflation. In any case, the Americans felt that the dollar was just as good as gold since it was backed by the strongest economy in the world. The latter viewpoint was, of course, quite correct, provided that America did not spend too much outside its own borders.

However, one indication that matters were not quite so simple, was the fact that in many countries trade in unwrought gold as well as the possession of gold were forbidden by law. The traditional demand for gold in the East still existed and this gold was traded on the so-called free market. To begin with, the central banks of the ten major countries who were members of the International Monetary Fund, were committed to keeping the free-market price of gold as close as possible to the official price. They did this by selling, when necessary, a sufficient quantity of gold on the free market. The thinking behind this policy was obviously that a too high free-market price for gold was an indication of the desirability of a rise in the official gold price.

During the sixties, however, this policy led to a drop in the monetary gold reserves, i.e. to a decline in the amount of gold held jointly by various Western central banks and especially by the USA. By the end of the sixties the situation had become untenable. It was decided that central banks would in future sell no more gold on the free market so that the existing monetary gold reserves could be maintained. The official or monetary market was therefore severed from the free market and this was called the two-tier system – the free-market price being allowed to find its own level.

The **two-tier** system did not solve the basic problem of the situation, viz.

the ever-increasing liabilities of the USA towards the rest of the world. The isolation of monetary from other gold stocks did not mean that gold could not move within the system, i.e. from one central bank to another and more specifically from the American Federal Reserve system to European and Japanese banks; in fact, between 1953 and 1968 the USA lost about half of its gold stock.

In August 1971 the American government decided to stop selling gold to other central banks, which led to a complete change in the international monetary system. The USA also tried to "demonetise" gold, i.e. to abolish its role as a reserve asset. This meant that the restrictions on the possession of gold had to be removed, which considerably increased the size of the market for gold, particularly in the USA itself. The gold price was now set to rise, especially in view of the fact that inflation had reached proportions unprecedented in peacetime. It in fact increased by a factor of ten; in January 1980 the price reached the level of $800 dollars for the first time, although it subsequently declined again.

From the above one could conclude that since 1974 gold has been regarded as an "ordinary" product, yet it is still treated separately in the South African balance of payments. The result of the enormous rise in the gold price was that the value of net gold exports (or production) rose from only R837 million in 1970 to R10 141 million in 1980, and this in spite of the fact that the physical production of gold fell by about 30 per cent over the same period. The value of net gold exports declined immediately after 1980 (R8 340 million in 1981) and only moved to beyond the R10 000 million mark in 1984. The considerable increase experienced since 1984 is not however related to increases in the gold price, but merely reflect the deterioration in the relative value of the South African rand against the dollar.[§]

Receipts and payments for services

We now come to two important items in the current account which we mentioned in passing earlier on, viz. invisible imports and exports. These are recorded in table 8.4 as "payments for services" (invisible imports) and "service receipts" (invisible exports). Although these items, which consist of factor plus non-factor services, are much smaller than merchandise or visible **exports**, they are by no means insignificant, invisible exports amounting to R11 572 million in 1991 and invisible imports to R21 741 million. In South Africa the payments for services generally exceed the receipts.

---

§   The significance of this will become clearer when exchange rates are discussed in section 8.5.

The balance on current account

If we add all receipts (for visible exports, including net gold exports, and for services, including net transfers) and subtract all payments, as in table 8.4, we arrive at a figure called the "balance on current account". This is a very important concept, especially with a view to economic policy, because it indicates whether or not a country has been living within its **current means.**

The table shows that South Africa did very well during the last six years of the period covered in the table. The negative balances on the current account for 1981 and 1984 were converted into a positive balance of R5 000 million in 1985. This dramatic "recovery" lasted until 1991. What is not very clear from the table however, is the fact that South Africa was actually forced by circumstances to maintain such credit balances on its current account. These circumstances were the excessive foreign debt incurred by South Africa during the years when the gold price was high, which led in 1985 to a dramatic deterioration in the value of the rand and the resultant standstill agreement on the repayment of foreign debt contracted in September 1985. Exactly how all these matters are related to the balance on the current account of the balance of payments, will be explained further on.

The balance on the current account, as reflected in table 8.4, clearly emphasises the variable nature of the account. Of the eight years shown in the table, two were years in which a negative balance was reflected. Nor were the variations negligible in size. Within two years a negative balance of R2 602 million was changed into a credit balance of R6 114 million – a difference of over R8 500 million. It may well be asked how a country can afford such deficits on its current account. The answer is to be found in the capital account of the balance of payments.

The capital account

We said above that the capital account of the balance of payments records all capital transactions and loans. The capital account is divided into two sections: one part contains long-term capital movements and the other short-term capital movements.[§] The importance of this will become clear further on.

(i) Long-term capital movements and the basic balance

Long-term capital movements are further divided into (a) public authorities (including the general government and public business enterprises);

§   The amounts occurring in the account reflect the difference between inflow and outflow.

(b) public corporations (e.g. Sasol, Eskom, etc.); (c) the banking sector and (d) the non-bank private sector. What is interesting in an analysis of the long-term borrowing activities of the public sector (i.e. public authorities and corporations), is the fact that their loans were particularly high during the years when the current account showed a deficit. The public sector as a whole negotiated more than R2 500 million in long-term loans from foreign countries during the periods between 1981 and 1984 (when there was a deficit on the current account). During 1981, however, the long-term capital outflow from the non-bank private sector amounted to R291 million.

This means that a country, in this case South Africa, can actually afford to spend more than it produces, which is the same as to say that it can afford a deficit on the current account of the balance of payments. What has happened in such a case, is that the country has borrowed from abroad a sum of money to make this expenditure possible, and if it is a long-term debt, it can mean that the debt will be repaid out of the additional production this borrowing has made possible.

In analysing the last six years in the table, however, we find a completely different situation. Where the deficits on the current account were made possible by the **inflow** of long-term capital, it was the **outflow** of similar capital during the period 1985–91 which forced South Africa to maintain a surplus on the current account. The withdrawal of foreign capital (for political reasons) therefore obliged us to accept a lower potential standard of living. As we shall see further on when exchange rates are discussed (section 8.4), this surplus on the current account has been made possible by a drastic deterioration in the value of the South African monetary unit (the rand).

It is precisely to be able to judge whether a country can "afford" a certain deficit on its balance of payments that the next total on the balance of payments is shown, viz. the **"basic balance"**. Table 8.4 shows that this basic balance is calculated by setting off the balance on the current account against long-term capital movements in a particular year.

An interesting example of the outcome of this can be found in the year 1984. South Africa then had a deficit of R2 602 million on the current account of the balance of payments. There was, however, a long-term capital inflow of R2 610 million and this led to a surplus of R8 million. This was the value of the **basic balance** for 1984, calculated by adding the (positive) amount of the long-term capital balance (R2 610 million) to the negative amount (R2 602 million) of the current account.

(ii) Short-term capital movements

Although **long**-term capital movements were involved above, the fluctuations in the net amounts were really very large: from a positive amount of

R2 610 million in 1984 (inflow) to a negative amount of R3 162 million (in 1986). When short-term capital movements are analysed in table 8.4, it would appear as though the fluctuations are even greater. Short-term capital movements consist, *inter alia*, of import and export credit granted by banks here and in other countries. The political state of emergency proclaimed in South Africa on 20 July 1985 led to the withdrawal of credit to South African banks by these very foreign banks, which in turn gave rise to an outflow of short-term capital amounting to R7 799 million during 1985.

Such a tremendous outflow of capital could not be sustained and led to the standstill with regard to the repayment of certain forms of foreign debt as well as the reinstitution of exchange control over non-residents with the adoption of the **financial rand** system in September 1985.

Although the outflow of short-term capital reached a peak in 1985, the table clearly shows that the measures mentioned above by no means curbed the outflow of capital (long and short-term).

Gold and foreign reserves

Finally, we come to what may well be called, in more ways than one, the bottom line of the balance of payments, and this is the change in the gold and other foreign exchange reserves (hence foreign currency). Let us recapitulate, taking as our point of departure a deficit on the current account of the balance of payments; this is financed by the net inflow of long-term capital plus the net inflow of short-term capital. If these inflows are greater than the current deficit, we are left with an amount which can only be applied in one way: a change, in this case an increase, in foreign reserves; the **foreign reserves** being the amount in foreign currencies (US dollars, pounds sterling, etc.) and in the case of South Africa of gold, held mainly by the Reserve Bank. Deficits or surpluses on the current account of the balance of payments can – as shown in table 8.4 – be combined with deficits and surpluses on the long and short-term capital account in various ways. A large deficit on the current account may be accompanied by an increase in reserves if the inflow of capital is sufficiently large. On the other hand, a large current account surplus may be accompanied by a decrease in net reserves when, as in 1985, a great capital outflow occurs.

Gold and other foreign reserves are the most important total in the framework of the balance of payments and must be kept at a reasonable level for three reasons: (1) Foreign reserves are needed to finance transactions with foreign countries, especially as month to month payments and receipts do not necessarily coincide; (2) foreign reserves are also needed to even out undesirable fluctuations in the exchange rate; and (3) foreign reserves indicate what the maximum foreign deficit is if no further loans are forthcoming.

Our table also shows that there is a difference between "net" and "gross" foreign reserves. The meaning of this distinction can be explained on the basis of a specific example in table 8.4. As we have seen, the deficit on the current account in 1981 was as high as R4 089 million and was not sufficiently compensated for by the small inflow of long and short-term capital (R542 million and R419 million respectively). This meant that the change in **net** gold and other foreign reserves amounted to a negative total of R3 128 million. The **"change in net gold and other foreign reserves"** is the change which would have taken place if nothing further had happened or if no other steps had been taken. The situation nearly developed into a crisis and the large deficit of R3 128 million would have eliminated almost entirely the total amount held in foreign reserves at the end of 1981, viz. R3 705 million. Naturally, this would have placed the country in an awkward position.

This led to special steps by the authorities, particularly in obtaining credit in foreign currencies from the International Monetary Fund, overseas central banks and other foreign banks. In 1981 an amount of R2 123 million was borrowed for this purpose; these are the "liabilities related to reserves". Together with the allocation of Special Drawing Rights (SDRs) from the IMF and valuation adjustments in foreign exchange holdings (–R542 million), this created a much more favourable picture as far as **gross** foreign exchange holdings were concerned. These reserves are called "gross" because the abovementioned credits have to be repaid as soon as the balance of payments position improves.

To show once more how different combinations are possible in the composition of the balance of payments, we can take a final look at the situation in 1985 as a whole. First of all, there was a surplus on current account, viz. an amount of R5 087 million; an outflow of long-term capital amounting to R522 million led to a **basic balance** of R4 565 million. An outflow of short-term capital however led to a decline in the (net) gold reserves of R3 234 million. But an amount of R1 998 million was borrowed by the monetary authorities from central banks abroad and this, together with SDR allocations and valuation adjustments (к1 802 million), led to an increase of R566 million in gross reserves.

The considerable fluctuations occurring under the item "SDR withdrawals and valuation adjustments" arise mainly from changes in the gold price. Since April 1978 gold reserves have been valued at 90 per cent of "the last ten London fixing prices during the month". For this reason there was for example a considerable downward valuation adjustment in 1981 when the gold price fell. Before we look at the way the condition of a country's balance of payments affects the determination of the income level (or GDP), we must first establish how rates of exchange came into existence.

8.4   The rate of exchange

Foreign trade involves payment in foreign currencies such as pounds sterling (£), German marks (DM), American dollars ($), Japanese yen (¥), etc. South African **importers** have to pay in these currencies for the goods they **buy** and are therefore obliged to exchange South African rands for these currencies; in other words, there is a **demand** on the part of South African importers for DM, USA dollars, etc. On the other hand, importers in other countries, such as Germany and the UK, have to pay in rands for South African exports and must therefore offer DM, pounds sterling, etc. in exchange for rands; in this way South African exports lead to a **supply** of foreign currency. The rate at which currencies are exchanged is known as the **rate of exchange**. The rate of exchange therefore represents a ratio or proportion, but it is also a **price** which, as we shall see in this section, can be analysed and explained on the basis of a supply and demand diagram.

If you look at the exchange rate as a price it is not a difficult concept to understand, but because it represents the price of one monetary unit in terms of another monetary unit it can sometimes be confusing. One should therefore always be alert when dealing with it. For example, it is always necessary to establish from which point of view the exchange rate should be regarded in a particular situation. An increase in the value or price of one currency (also known as **appreciation**) automatically implies a decrease (**depreciation**) in the price of another currency.

The quoting of exchange rates

Because exchange rates actually represent a ratio, the price of one currency in terms of another can always be quoted in two ways. These two ways are known as **direct** and **indirect** quoting. Most countries use the direct method, whereby the exchange rate is expressed in terms of the local currency. This in other words shows how much of the local monetary unit (rand in the case of South Africa) can be exchanged for one unit of a foreign monetary unit. With the indirect method, on the other hand, the exchange rate is expressed as a certain amount of the foreign currency. In South Africa's case we would therefore be able to say how much of the foreign currency would be equal to one rand. The difference between the two methods of quoting can be illustrated by means of table 8.5 where the value of the South African rand is indicated according to both methods.

Table 8.5

The value of the South African rand in terms of certain selected foreign currencies (Date: 30/3/92)

Foreign currencies	Direct quotation: one foreign currency is equal to:	Indirect quotation. R1 is equal to
	(rand)	(foreign currencies)
USA ($)	2,8780	0,3474
UK (£)	4,9919	0,2003
Germany (DM)	1,7473	0,5723
France (FF)	0,5151	1,9411
Japan (¥)	0,0215	46,3343
Switzerland (SF)	1,9160	0,5219
Italy (lire)	0,0023	431,6539

Source: *Business Day*, 31 March 1992, p.17.

Table 8.5 *The value of the rand can be indicated by two different methods. The direct method of quotation indicates the number of rands that can be exchanged for one foreign monetary unit. The indirect method, on the other hand, indicates how much of a foreign currency can be exchanged for one South African rand.*

The table shows, for example, that according to the indirect method of quotation, on 30 March 1992, one could exchange one South African rand for 0,3474 American dollars; 0,2003 pounds sterling; 46,3 Japanese yen and 431,65 Italian lire. Similarly, one could, by the direct method of quotation, establish that one pound sterling (£) had the same value as R4,9919; and that one American dollar ($) could be bought for R2,8780. Note that the two columns in table 8.5 contain exactly the same information, since one column is simply the inverse (reciprocal) of the other. By taking the rand/dollar exchange rate as an example, we can see that $\frac{1}{0,3474} = 2,8780$ or that $\frac{1}{2,8780} = 0,3474$.

The indirect method of quotation is, for example, useful to a South African tourist who can thereby immediately ascertain how much of a foreign currency he can obtain for his rand. If, however, the exchange rate is regarded as a price, it is more logical to quote the price directly in terms of the South African monetary unit (i.e. by the direct method of quotation). Direct quotation is also the method used by the Reserve Bank for indicating exchange rates in the *Quarterly Bulletin*.

The authorised currency dealers in South Africa, including all the major banks, do not however quote the different currencies according to both methods. It is customary at present to quote American dollars and pounds sterling according to the direct method, whereas all the other currencies (such as the German mark, the Japanese yen, the French franc, etc.) are quoted by the indirect method. What happens in practice, is that the currency dealers in South Africa quote only one rate, i.e. the rand/dollar exchange rate, and that all other exchange rates are derived from this. Such a procedure is possible only because all currencies of any importance are quoted in terms of dollars.

For many years only pounds sterling were indicated by direct quotation in South Africa but since March 1988 the American dollar has also been quoted in this way. In order to avoid any further confusion, we shall use only the direct method of quotation in the rest of this chapter.

In table 8.6 certain exchange rates, as published by the Reserve Bank, are shown for a number of years. In the last column the direct rates which appeared in table 8.5 are also given. The figures show clearly that a marked change in exchange rates occurred between 1978 and 1992. With the exception of the Italian lira, all the monetary units have become considerably more expensive in terms of the South African rand; this means that the other monetary units have **appreciated** in terms of the rand. Whereas, up to and including 1978, one could exchange less than one rand for an American dollar, one has to pay more than R2,80 for the same unit in 1991. This **depreciation** of the South African rand is even clearer when it is compared with the German mark and the Japanese yen, which have increased in value fourfold and fivefold respectively. This significant depreciation of the rand is particularly alarming if we remember that all our major trading partners are included in table 8.6.

Such a depreciation of the monetary unit of course implies that **imports** become more **expensive** for local buyers and simultaneously that **exports** become **cheaper** for foreign buyers of our products.

The question now is how this price, or foreign exchange rate, can be explained and analysed. We shall do this with the aid of figure 8.1. This diagram represents a supply and demand system. We shall endeavour to ascertain how the exchange rate between the American dollar and the South African rand comes into being. The amount in dollars is measured on the horizontal axis, while the price of dollars in South African rands is measured on the vertical axis. Note that this is the direct method of quotation. In the figure this is indicated as R/$ (i.e. rands per dollar) since the prices on this axis indicate how much in rand can be exchanged for one dollar.

Table 8.6

Selected exchange rates, SA rand per unit of foreign currency, 1978–1992

Foreign currency	Average for				
	1978	1983	1985	1989	30/3/92
USA ($)	0,8696	1,1141	2,2278	2,6222	2,8780
UK (£)	1,6703	1,6891	2,9118	4,2931	4,9919
Germany (DM)	0,4342	0,4368	0,7708	1,3976	1,7473
France (FF)	0,1934	0,1467	0,2525	0,4113	0,5151
Japan (¥)	0,0042	0,0047	0,0095	0,0190	0,0215
Italy (L)	0,0010	0,0007	0,0012	0,0019	0,0023

Source: South African Reserve Bank: *Quarterly Bulletin,* (several issues). The last column: *Business Day,* 31 March 1992.

Table 8.6 *Over the past few years the South African rand has depreciated in terms of most other countries' monetary units. The deterioration in the value of the rand has been particularly noticeable since 1985.*

The demand for American dollars

Let us first analyse South Africa's demand for American dollars. This is obviously determined by the price and the quantity of products that South Africans wish to import from America. Since South Africans have to pay for these products in dollars, the price of these products will mainly be determined by the exchange rate between the two currencies. We therefore assume that the price of products remains constant in America for the time being. The higher the exchange rate on the vertical axis, the more expensive do American products become for South Africans and the less they can afford to import from the USA. The demand for dollars (D$) therefore has a normal slope in figure 8.1 from top left to bottom right. Any **depreciation** of the rand in terms of the dollar (i.e. a **rise** on the vertical axis from the current R2,50 to say R4,00) will give rise to a decrease in the amount of dollars demanded up to point A on the demand curve (D$). Tractors, computers and other American products simply become too expensive to import at this exchange rate, and imports decline. Similarly, an **appreciation** of the rand in terms of the dollar (i.e. a **drop** in the exchange rate on the vertical axis) would lead to an increase in the amount of dollars demanded (cf. for example an exchange rate of R1 = $1 at point F on the demand curve).

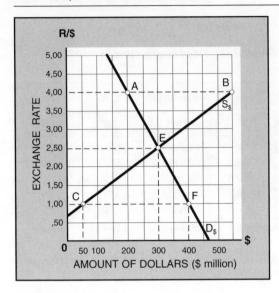

Fig. 8.1 The demand and supply of foreign currency

S$ represents the supply of US dollars and D$ the demand. The exchange rate tends towards a level of R2,50, which is determined by intersection E. Note that excess demand CF represents a deficit on the South African balance of payments and AB a surplus.

The supply of American dollars

The demand curve for dollars is a straightforward concept because it ties the demand for goods directly to the exchange rate. Its counterpart, the supply curve of the dollar, is less easy to understand because the supply curve is actually also based on a demand phenomenon: the American demand for (in our case) South African goods.

The background to the **supply** of dollars (on the South African foreign exchange market) is therefore the **demand** of Americans for South African products. Obviously, this supply curve will have a positive trend from bottom left to top right in figure 8.1. The lower the exchange rate on the vertical axis, the more expensive it is for Americans to buy our products. (Once more we assume that the price of South African products is given.) If, for example, a state of parity (one dollar for one rand) existed between the dollar and the rand on the currency market, the supply of dollars in figure 8.1 would be only $50 million because the demand for our exports would be limited (cf. point C in the diagram). However, should the position of the rand deteriorate (depreciate) to an exchange rate of R4,00, South African products would become so cheap to Americans that the supply of dollars would increase to point B in the diagram.

The determination of the exchange rate

As in any other supply and demand diagram, equilibrium is reached at the intersection of the curves. In figure 8.1 the exchange rate would therefore be determined by point E, i.e. at R2,50 per dollar. Suppose, however, that the exchange rate is equal to R1,00, with the same S$ and D$. The amount of dollars demanded for South African imports is then $400 million, whereas the amount of dollars supplied on the market is only $50 million. In other words, the imports exceed the exports by CF (excess demand), and therefore importers cannot obtain the necessary dollars to pay for their imports. CF is in fact part of the deficit on the South African balance of payments; in order to supplement the shortfall in dollars, importers will force up the price of dollars until equilibrium is finally reached at E, i.e. at an exchange rate of R2,50. From this it can be concluded that the South African rand at R1,00 per dollar, is **overvalued** and that the dollar is **undervalued**. The diagram also shows how the problem of under and overvaluation *in principle* resolves itself when left to the free-market forces. In this example the appreciation of the dollar is accompanied by a decline in South African imports (from $400 million to $300 million) and an increase in exports (from $50 million to $300 million).

In the same way one can take an exchange rate of R4,00 per dollar as one's point of departure. In such a case the dollar would be **overvalued** and the South African rand **undervalued**. South African exports would exceed imports and a surplus on the balance of payments would therefore be created. More dollars would be for sale against the available rands, so that the price of the rand in terms of dollars would rise and, as shown above, equilibrium would be reached at R2,50 per dollar.

In the example above we used the dollar to show how an exchange rate between two countries will be established according to market forces. We chose the dollar because it is in fact the only exchange rate that is quoted by currency dealers in South Africa. As we have said, the rates against other monetary units are derived from those currencies' exchange rates with the dollar. Currency dealers do not, for example, quote independently against the German mark in South Africa. If it is known that

$1 = R2,51
and $1 = DM1,8273

South African currency dealers will (taking into account certain costs and margins) be prepared to quote ± R1,3736 against the DM. The same calculation may be made in respect of other currencies.

Fixed versus floating exchange rates

A further point which should be borne in mind, is the fact that market forces of supply and demand were never allowed to determine exchange rates fully anywhere in the world. We saw that the supply and demand of foreign currency, based on the demand for mutual imports and exports, would in principle lead to an **equilibrium rate of exchange** which would ensure that neither a surplus nor a deficit on the balance of payments can occur. The implication is, of course, that all exchange rates are allowed to go up or down as the market dictates.

Such free and frequently fluctuating exchange rates (as reflected in table 8.6) are however a relatively recent phenomenon. Between 1946 and 1971 the Bretton Woods system of **fixed** exchange rates was in use in most countries. According to this system, exchange rates were only adjusted by exception. When this system was abandoned in the early seventies as a result of the USA's tremendous balance of payments deficit, the world entered an extremely unstable period. One of the main reasons the world is still trying to establish a satisfactory exchange rate system, is the disruption caused by **international capital movements**. Capital movements can be extremely unstable and, as we saw in section 8.3, can fluctuate considerably from year to year. An outflow of capital is the same as the purchase of foreign assets or it can also be described as the **import** of foreign securities. Such an **outflow** of capital must therefore be associated with the **demand** for foreign currency; nevertheless, it is not so much dependent on the exchange rate as on the difference between foreign and domestic rates of interest. The higher the foreign interest rates, the more foreign securities will be bought, the more capital will leave the country and the greater the demand for foreign currency will be.

An increase in foreign interest rates will, in other words, in a diagram such as figure 8.2, cause the demand curve for foreign currency to shift to the right (from $D_{\$1}$ to $D_{\$2}$). In a system of floating exchange rates this would lead to a depreciation of the rand from R2,50 to R3,00. It would however cause the price of imported goods to rise, which would also affect the domestic price level even though it would now be easier to export goods – it would however also tend to cause a rise in prices. This would have been fine if the outflow of capital were a permanent phenomenon which necessitated a basic change in the whole foreign trade pattern. But this part of the demand for foreign currency, which in the nature of things is based on comparative interest rates, may not be a permanent phenomenon. As soon as the flow of capital is reversed, all these price adjustments have to be undone. The disruption and uncertainty caused to importers and exporters by these continual exchange rate adjustments cannot be overemphasized. It is precisely to counteract the effect of such events that the central bank or the monetary authorities consider it necessary to keep foreign exchange reserves and to enter into the kind of foreign loans that we described in section 8.3. In this example an increase in the exchange rate could be avoided by providing F_1F_2 (cf. fig. 8.2) in dollars from foreign reserves. In this way an exchange rate of R2,50 could be maintained.

It is for these reasons that the central banks, even in the seventies, when

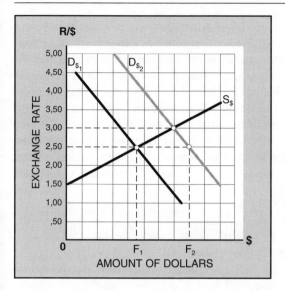

Fig. 8.2 A shift in demand as a result of a capital outflow

Capital movements also influence the exchange rate. Any outflow of capital is accompanied by a demand shift from $D_{\$1}$ to $D_{\$2}$. If no intervention takes place, the rand will depreciate from R2,50 to R3,00 per dollar.

the system of fixed exchange rates broke down, continued to monitor exchange rates carefully so that any fluctuations that might occur would not become excessive. A further point to note here, is that in most countries (with the exception of the Western industrial nations) the free outflow of capital is not allowed. This is also the case in South Africa, where exchange control will probably never be entirely abolished.

A dual exchange rate system in South Africa

The declared official approach in South Africa[§] has been an exchange rate policy of **managed floating**. This means that the exchange rate of the rand will essentially be determined by the free action of market forces without any exchange control over non-residents and with only limited control applying to residents. Apart from this, the Reserve Bank is supposed to intervene in the foreign exchange in a stabilising way only to "smooth out" excessive exchange rate fluctuations when considered necessary in the interest of the country. (Cf for example fig. 8.2). Unfortunately, this ideal of "managed floating" was only in force for a short while when the financial rand was temporarily suspended.

Although it was known under various names,[§§] there has always, since

§ As set out in the final report of the Commission of Inquiry into the Monetary System and Monetary Policy in South Africa (RP70/1984), Government Printer, Pretoria (the so-called De Kock Report), p.A51.

§§ The names under which control was exercised were the **blocked rand, securities rand** and the present **financial rand**.

1961 (with the exception of a period of approximately 30 months between February 1983 and September 1985) been some or other form of official control over the repatriation of the assets of non-residents. Permanent residents of South Africa were always subject to some form of exchange control during this period. Exchange control over non-residents is at present exercised by means of the financial rand system. The financial rand system was first instituted on 24 January 1979; on 7 February 1983 it was suspended, and on 2 September 1985 it was reinstated. Since this date, which was preceded by the state of emergency in South Africa, a **dual** exchange rate has once again existed for the rand. The two exchange rates currently exist in respect of:

(i)   the **commercial rand** – i.e. the "ordinary" exchange rate of the rand as described in tables 8.5 and 8.6. As we have seen, this is determined by the interaction of normal import and export activities which are reflected in the current account of the balance of payments, as well as borrowing activities on the capital account of the balance of payments.

(ii)   the **financial rand** which is made available for the buying and selling of owners' interest in South African assets by non-residents. The **financial rand rate** is determined by the demand for and supply of South African assets by non-residents. An appreciation of the financial rand is an indication of greater foreign confidence in South Africa since it reflects an increase in the demand for South African assets by foreigners. In the same way a depreciating financial rand indicates a decline in foreign confidence.

The basic reason for instituting a financial rand, was the protection of the commercial rand against fluctuations in capital movements occurring on foreign initiative. Many of these capital flows were politically inspired and it was felt that a separate exchange rate should be created for foreign investors moving their capital into or out of the country. Should a sudden withdrawal of capital occur, it would lead to a depreciation of the financial rand without disrupting the normal import and export activities (via the commercial rand).

The financial rand system would also provide a mechanism which would make it more attractive for foreigners to invest in South Africa. Since the financial rand is normally available at a considerable discount (as against the commercial rand), foreigners can obtain South African assets much more cheaply. The return on these investments is therefore much higher than usual. On 30 March 1992 the financial rand was quoted at R3,54, which reflected a discount of almost 23 per cent against the commercial rand on that date. This discount is sometimes taken as an indication of the risk attached by foreign investors to South African investments.

Such a dual exchange rate system requires proper control by the monetary authorities to prevent the system from being exploited. With the large gap that has formed between the value of the commercial rand and the financial rand during the past few years, the temptation to undertake illegal transactions has become very great. It is obvious that large "profits" may be made if foreign exchange can be illegally obtained via the commercial rand rate and then exchanged for ordinary rands at the financial rand rate.

In spite of these disadvantages, it is unlikely that South Africa will be in a position to do away with the dual exchange rate system for the foreseeable future. If the financial rand system were to be suspended (and no further direct exchange control measures were to be instituted regarding the repatriation of foreign assets in South Africa), the value of the commercial rand would in all probability fall lower than its current level.

8.5 The balance of payments and economic activity

We should like to conclude this chapter by once again linking up with the macro-economic model used throughout the book. To do this, we must determine how the balance of payments can be incorporated into such a model. In South Africa the statement is often made that the balance of payments places a **limit** on economic growth. To understand this statement fully, we must devote some attention to the following two facts:

(i)   the balance of payments as a whole must always balance;
(ii) South Africa, as a developing country, is dependent on foreign capital for economic growth.

Both these statements hold significant implications for the way in which the balance of payments will affect the rest of the economy. As regards the first statement, the expression **"balance** of payments" already indicates that a balance is supposed. As we have seen, the balance of payments consists of two accounts, viz. the **current** and the **capital** account. Together these two accounts must therefore be in equilibrium, or, to put it differently, there must be no outstanding balance on the account as a whole. This condition can be summarised as follows:

$$B = B_c + B_k$$
$$= 0$$

where B = balance of payments
B_c = balance on current account
B_k = balance on capital account

But we also know that

$B_c = (X - Z)$ (X and Z represent exports and imports respectively and in this case include net factor services and transfers)

Hence the condition means that

$(X - Z) + B_k = 0$
or that
$(X - Z) = -B_k$

The implications are obvious. If South Africa has a surplus on the current account of the balance of payments (i.e. $[X - Z] > 0$), a corresponding outflow of capital will take place. Or, if there is a deficit on the current account (i.e. $[X - Z] < 0$), an inflow of capital takes place. In this case B_k is positive. An analysis of the trend of the current account of the balance of payments in South Africa shows that during times of rapid economic growth, there is normally a deficit on this account. The practical interpretation of this relation is simple. South Africa is extremely dependent on the importation of capital goods (e.g. machinery, transport equipment, etc.) for rapid economic growth.

You will recall that in chapter 3 we simply assumed that exports and imports were independent of the income level. The values of X and Z were, you will remember, regarded as **autonomous**. In the analysis above we saw, however, that there appears to be a positive relation between imports and the income level (or the GDP). If we accept that this is so, and further assume that exports still take place independently of the income level – i.e. that factors outside the borders of South Africa determine how much is going to be imported from us – we can establish at what income level equilibrium will be reached on the current account of the balance of payments. It is that income level which causes Z to be exactly equal to autonomous exports, X.

This income level, where X = Z, is represented in figure 8.3 by Y_b.[§] Left of the Y_b line a surplus will occur on the current account of the balance of payments, and right of the line there will be a deficit on the account. Let us further suppose that the economy is in equilibrium at an income level of Y_e, which is considerably below the full employment level (Y_f). In other

§   It would be more realistic to assume that this income level can vary at different price levels. In other words, that in the diagram it is not a vertical line representing equilibrium on the current account. In all probability such a line would have a negative slope since a low domestic price level (relative to other countries) promotes exports and discourages imports. For our purposes we assume, however, that the value of Y_b is fixed.

words we now have three income levels (Y_e, Y_b and Y_f) to contend with and which should always be borne in mind when economic policy is formulated.

The situation in figure 8.3 is rather similar to that prevailing in South Africa during the second half of the eighties when we accumulated a surplus on the current account. The obvious solution to the unemployment which clearly exists in the economy would be to follow an expansionary fiscal and/or monetary policy in order to increase aggregate demand to such an extent that we can move closer to the full employment level of income. In the diagram this could be represented by a shift from AD_1 to AD_2 to reach an income level of Y_1. Under normal circumstances such an income level would be quite feasible even though a deficit would now arise on the current account (remember that we are now to the right of the Y_b line). This deficit is of course compensated for by a capital inflow on the capital account. This is exactly how developing countries succeed in making economic progress.

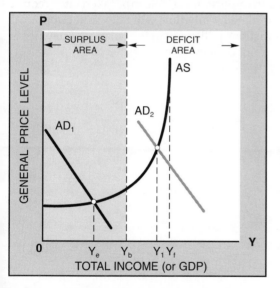

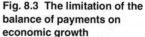

Fig. 8.3 The limitation of the balance of payments on economic growth

When formulating economic policy, careful consideration should be given to the income levels that are associated with supply and demand equilibrium (Y_e), balance of payments equilibrium (Y_b) and full employment (Y_f).

However, the state of emergency proclaimed in South Africa in 1985 and the accompanying withdrawal of foreign capital have placed the country in a position which is contrary to that of a normal developing country. Mainly as a result of political considerations, our foreign debt position overnight deteriorated to such an extent that we were obliged to remain left of the Y_b line. In other words, we were forced to maintain a considerable surplus on the current account in order to provide for the capital outflow which had become a *fait accompli*. The standstill agreement with regard to our foreign debt did provide a measure of relief but did not essentially alter the basic dilemma in which the South African economy finds itself.

The other policy measures taken to allow the adjustments to be made as smoothly as possible, were mainly related to exchange rate adjustments. For example, the exchange rate was allowed to depreciate dramatically over a number of years. Such a depreciation was aimed at shifting the Y_b line to the right in order to keep the surplus on the current account as large as possible. This policy was sharply criticized by economists who believed that the value of the rand should not have been allowed to fall to such low levels. The upheaval this caused for importers and its inflationary effect on the domestic price level should, according to these critics, have been avoided at all costs. As an alternative, they suggested that the rand be supported at a higher level by the Reserve Bank and that greater physical control over imports be exercised.

From the above discussion of the South African situation during the eighties it is clear that the balance of payments placed a serious limitation on economic growth and was an important variable to be taken into account when economic policy is formulated. Only time will tell whether political reform and the rejection of sanctions will result in the balance of payments becoming a less serious constraint during the nineties.

Selected references:

Baumol & Blinder: 36, 37.
Dernburg: 15, 16.
Dornbusch & Fischer: 5.
Evans-Pritchard: 14.
Froyen: 17.
Gordon: 19.
Mohr et.al.: 6, 22-24.
Morley: 21.
Shapiro: 7.

9 Inflation

In the introductory chapter we referred to the twin evils of unemployment and inflation. Although not always specifically emphasized, a large section of this book has concentrated on how these two evils can – as far as possible – be avoided. In the three chapters (chapters 5, 6 and 7) on the role of fiscal and monetary policy, we looked at the fine balance that must be maintained in order to steer the economy between these evils. In the previous chapter we noted the decisive effect that the external sector can have on both unemployment and inflation.

Given this framework, a chapter on inflation may seem a little out of place, especially since, apart from a short, general description in chapter 1, we have not devoted an entire chapter to inflation's counterpart, unemployment. It would be fair to say that much of the present chapter is meant to explain this apparent paradox. One of the reasons is that there are no winners in a period of unemployment. Everyone runs the risk of losing his or her job or of suffering a cut in salary. Even those who receive a fixed income from investments and who could expect to benefit by falling prices, face the possibility that bankruptcy may wipe out their assets. In a period of inflation the picture is quite different. In general the losses of one group are counterbalanced by the **gains** of the other. It is far more difficult than generally supposed to decide which predominates, losses or gains. This is the problem we will now consider.

9.1 Definition and measurement of inflation[§]

Although we have referred to the concept of inflation several times, we have not yet formulated a proper definition of it. It is a term that has formed part of the vocabulary of the man in the street for some decades now. It is usually "inflation" that is to blame for the rapidly rising prices of goods sold in the shops! In spite of the fact that everyone knows that inflation is related to rising prices, it remains one of those economic concepts that causes great confusion because it is incorrectly or inaccurately defined.

§ This section is based mainly on Mohr et al. (1988, pp.55–55) and Dornbusch and Fischer, adapted for South Africa by Mohr and Rogers (1987, pp.287–294.)

Inflation may be defined as **a continual and considerable rise in the general price level**. By taking one or other price index (usually the CPI) as representative of the general price level, the inflation rate can be calculated.

We wish to comment on this definition:

(i)   This definition is preferred to other definitions because it is **neutral** and does not attempt to define inflation in terms of specific causes. We often see inflation described in the press as a situation of "too much money chasing too few goods" or read that inflation can be associated with "an excessive increase in the money supply". Such causal definitions that highlight only one of many causes often result in the proposal of inappropriate policies for fighting inflation.

(ii) Another interesting characteristic of this definition is that it describes inflation as a **process**. We are certainly not dealing with a non-recurrent phenomenon. Unless prices increase continually and constantly, we cannot speak of inflation.

(iii) Although the meaning of the word "considerable" has probably changed over the years, it remains a significant component of the definition. In terms of this definition, inflation is not associated with negligible increases of 1 to 2 per cent in the general price level.

(iv) Finally we bring to your attention that inflation refers only to an increase in the **general** price level. An increase in the prices of individual goods and services (for example, meat prices) does not necessarily represent inflation.

In chapter 2 we discussed the three different price indices (the CPI, the PPI and the GDP deflator) which may be used as indicators of changes in the general price level. The pattern of all three indices points to the presence of inflation in the South African economy. Only in the period before 1940 were there short periods in which prices did not rise continually and considerably. We now turn to the question of how we determine the extent of inflation.

Our comments on the measurement of inflation are limited to the CPI, since this is the index most commonly used as a basis for determining the inflation rate. However, this does not mean that the CPI is the best criterion in all circumstances. Each index has its advantages and disadvantages, which were briefly discussed in chapter 2. Although our discussion is limited to the CPI, there are a few points of a technical nature which we have to consider in order to prevent any confusion about the precise extent of inflation. We use the data on the CPI in table 9.1 to illustrate the problems associated with determining the rate of inflation.

A variety of rates of inflation can be calculated on the basis of the data in table 9.1. However, the one important point to bear in mind is that the rate of inflation should always be expressed as an **annual rate**. This means that although we may be interested in the rate of inflation over a specific period of six months or two years, it must always first be converted to an annual rate. Since inflation has been described as a prolonged process in terms of our definition above, it does not make much sense to calculate an inflation rate over a period of less than one year.

Table 9.1

Consumer prices in South Africa. Index: 1990=100
(Seasonally adjusted)

Month	1990	1991	Quarterly average (1991)
January	94,2	107,7	
February	94,6	109,2	
March	96,5	109,8	108,9
April	97,1	111,1	
May	98,2	112,9	
June	99,3	114,2	112,7
July	100,0	115,8	
August	101,3	117,2	
September	102,8	118,6	117,2
October	103,5	120,9	
November	105,8	122,1	
December	106,7	123,8	122,2
Average for year	**100,0**	**115,3**	

Source: South African Reserve Bank: *Quarterly Bulletin,* March 1992.

The following inflation rates can be calculated on the basis of the data in table 9.1:

(i) *Month on same month during previous year*
    The most commonly accepted indicator of inflation in South Africa is obtained by comparing the index in a particular month with that of the corresponding month in a previous year. In this way the inflation rate in December 1991 can be calculated as 16,02 per cent. The following formula is used for this calculation:

$$[(123,8/106,7) - 1] \times 100 = 16,02\%$$

This is an extremely popular method of measuring inflation. It extends over 12 months (representing an annual rate) and usually indicates what has happened to prices in the most recent "year". Because the indices for corresponding months are compared, any possible seasonal effect is automatically eliminated.[§] However, the rates calculated using this method are subject to considerable fluctuations. An unexpected increase in the petrol price or in general sales tax, for example, may suddenly raise or lower the inflation rate in a particular month.

(ii) *Month on previous month at an annual rate*
Using an index in which the seasonal effect is eliminated (such as the data in table 9.1), this method provides relatively reliable information about the most recent inflationary trends. This method allows us to use the two most recent months to calculate the rate of inflation. In December 1991 such a calculation would have given us an inflation rate of 18,05 per cent. The formula is slightly more complicated than the previous one because the rate has to be converted to an annual one. This is calculated as follows:

$$[(123,8/122,1)^{12} - 1] \times 100 = 18,05\%$$

As is to be expected, this rate is subject to considerable fluctuations and varies greatly from month to month.

(iii) *Quarterly average on previous quarterly average at an annual rate*
This method is not often used. The inflation rate is based on quarterly figures calculated by means of monthly figures. Such quarterly averages are given as examples in the last column of table 9.1. The inflation rate of the fourth quarter of 1991 compared with the previous quarter can be calculated with the aid of the following formula:

$$[(122,2/117,2)^{4} - 1] \times 100 = 18,19\%$$

§   The figures in Table 9.1 were, however, compiled in such a way that the seasonal effect is already eliminated.

(iv) *Annual average on annual average*

This method appears to produce the most acceptable measure of inflation. It is calculated by comparing the average of a 12-month period with that of the previous 12 months. In this way 24 index figures are used in calculating the inflation rate. Any short-term fluctuations in the index figures of specific months are eliminated by this method. The calculation has the added advantage of being simple, because it is not necessary to convert to an annual rate. Using this method, the inflation rate for the calendar year 1991 would produce the following result:

$$[(115,3/100,0) - 1] \times 100 = 15,3\%$$

Note that this method does not limit us to comparing calendar years. Any 12-month average (for example, from June to May) may be compared with the previous 12-month average in order to determine the rate of inflation.

From our discussion it is obvious that no single rate of inflation can be calculated on a specific date. We have seen that each of the four methods produces a different answer, despite the fact that each of the formulae measures the rate of inflation at the end of 1991.

9.2 The effects of inflation

In chapter 4 we saw that although at first glance unemployment appeared to be a simple concept, its measurement is anything but simple because it is necessary to distinguish between frictional and structural unemployment and also between these and cyclical unemployment.

We have also seen that there are difficulties in measuring inflation. In addition to there being various indices used to measure changes in the general price level, there are also different methods of calculation to be considered when determining the rate of inflation. Today the CPI appears to be accepted as the best measure of inflation because it clearly indicates the effect of inflation on the purchasing power of consumers (the largest single group within the population).

This change in the purchasing power of money brings us to one of the most significant consequences of inflation, namely the **distribution effect**. We look now at some instances where inflation influences the distribution of income and wealth.

The distribution effect

The first significant redistribution of wealth which we wish to consider, is that between debtors and creditors. The basic rule applying here, is that inflation **prejudices creditors (savers)** and **benefits debtors (borrowers)**. It is a very important rule to remember, because many of the other consequences of inflation derive from it. It is not hard to find an explanation for this rule, since it is associated with the effect inflation has on the purchasing power (or value) of all assets for which value is fixed in nominal terms.

This effect is best explained using a simple example. Suppose that a person, D, borrows an amount of R10 000 from another person, C, (or from a bank) in January 1990 on the understanding that the principal amount of R10 000 is repayable in full at the end of 1991 and that interest at 10 per cent (that is, an amount of R1 000) is payable annually. Table 9.1 shows that the general price level in South Africa, measured in terms of the consumer price index (CPI), rose from 94,2 in January 1990 to 123,8 in 1991. The purchasing power, or real value, of the R10 000 therefore fell to R10 000 $\times \frac{94,2}{123,8}$ = R7 609 on the date of repayment in 1991.

Creditor C therefore receives, in real terms, only about two-thirds of the money he loaned to debtor D three years previously. This indicates a clear redistribution of wealth from C to D or from creditor to debtor. But the creditor is also prejudiced in another way. The contract stipulated that he would receive R1 000 per annum for the period of the loan. However, this amount, like the principal sum, also decreases in **real value**. This shows how income, too, is redistributed in favour of D. Seen from another angle – if we compare the annual inflation rate with the interest rate – the debtor may, in fact, pay a negative interest rate. The inflation rate over the two years was 14,6 per cent[§] – thus a 10 per cent interest rate would mean that the creditor paid (14,6 – 10) = 4,6 per cent interest to the **debtor!**

This redistribution of wealth naturally applies to all assets of which the nominal value is fixed, for example, money, government securities, bonds, insurance contracts (policies) and some pensions.

It is obvious that people are not easily classified as creditors, debtors, landowners or receivers of a fixed nominal income (such as people drawing certain pensions). There are many people who are both debtors and creditors. In addition to all of us owning money and therefore being nominal **creditors**, many of us have homes financed by bonds, the nominal value of which is fixed. In the latter instance we are also **debtors** who benefit from inflation because the real value of our loans continually decreases. Those who borrow money to purchase expensive consumer goods such as motor

§ $[(123,8/94,2)^{0,5} - 1] \times 100 = 14,6\%$

cars (the prices of which doubled in three years) also benefit from inflation because their real debt is reduced by inflation.

As a result of all these inconsistencies, the impact of inflation is extremely uncertain. This makes it difficult to evaluate its effect on the economy as a whole. In addition, creditors and debtors are also found outside the private sector. Redistribution also occurs between the private sector and the government.

The redistribution mechanism in this instance works in exactly the same way as described above. Here the private sector are the holders of financial assets in the form of government securities, treasury bills and so forth and the government is the debtor. There can therefore be no doubt that the government benefits from inflation.

There is another way in which the government can be "enriched" at the cost of the private sector. This has to do with the taxation system in force in most Western countries. As explained in chapter 5, personal income tax is progressive, which means that the taxation rate (average and marginal) increases with the income level. (See table 5.4.) The higher the income bracket, the greater the percentage income tax to be paid. During periods of inflation it may therefore happen that taxpayers' average and marginal taxation rates rise whereas their real income remains constant. This phenomenon, which is known as "bracket creeping", causes a definite redistribution of income to the state. It is interesting to note that the combination of inflation and progressive income tax has the same effect as an increase in the tax rate. This increased income from taxation is called the **fiscal dividend**.

Whether one considers this redistribution in favour of the government "good" or "bad" will depend on whether or not one trusts the government. Some people believe the government to be a necessary evil and feel that its influence and expenditure should be kept to a minimum; others hold the opposite point of view. Those of the opinion that the government "belongs" to all of us might find it quite acceptable that greater purchasing power should be channelled in the direction of the government. But this would have a detrimental effect on the market system, which would in turn damage economic efficiency.

Economic effects

This brings us to the economic effects of inflation and, more specifically, its effect on economic growth. As we will explain in greater detail in the next chapter, economic growth is usually measured by the percentage increase in the real GDP. Economic growth is generally considered desirable and the question is whether inflation tends to increase or decrease the percentage increase in the real GDP.

For a long time it was believed that inflation would result in economic chaos or, at the very least, a lack of economic growth. The reason for this belief appears to be that for many years inflation occurred only during or after wars or other economic upheavals. Peacetime inflation was a virtually unknown phenomenon until after the Second World War. Then for a period of nearly 25 years, that is, until the end of the sixties, there was a systematic increase in the general price level of between 2 and 4 per cent in most developed countries and also South Africa – this is referred to as **creeping inflation**. Contrary to expectations, this inflation was accompanied by steady and significant **growth** in the real GDP, implying that inflation encouraged growth. It was for this reason that inflation was seen to pose no real danger – those who had lost as a result of inflation could be compensated from the additional return from a higher growth rate.

At this stage it was also possible to find a causal relationship between inflation and growth: steadily rising prices are associated with a steady increase in demand, which carries relatively little risk. Entrepreneurs were therefore encouraged to borrow, to invest and to expand their operations – which is the essence of the growth process.

The uncertain and unpredictable nature of inflation was never more obvious than at the time when everyone began to think that it was not such a dangerous phenomenon after all. At the end of the sixties and certainly in the early seventies inflation was increasingly associated with the opposite point of view, namely that inflation (as believed in earlier years) results in a lower growth rate.

In the seventies and eighties there was a drop in the rate of economic growth which was accompanied by inflation in South Africa and other countries. As we saw in table 1.1 (chapter 1), the inflation rate during this period went into **double figures**. As the table clearly shows, this combination of poor economic growth and high inflation rates was particularly noticeable during the eighties. The optimism of entrepreneurs and investors turned into pessimism. More and more effort was made to protect assets against inflation. As mentioned previously, greater significance was attached to real assets in order to protect the purchasing power of people's money to some extent. Money was invested in paintings and other works of art, collector's items such as postage stamps and, of course, gold, land and fixed property. Added to this was a distortion in the investment process and long-term investment in buildings (remember the negative real interest rates) tended to replace investment in factories and so forth.

However, it must be emphasized that the combination of poor economic growth and high inflation rates does not necessarily point to any causal relationship between the two phenomena. There are economists who argue that the combination of the two evils during the seventies and eighties was merely coincidental. In other words, the one did not give rise to the other.

According to them, sufficient reasons can be found to explain why there was both high inflation and poor economic growth during this period.

Another point to be mentioned under the economic effects of inflation is that a decrease in the growth rate and thus an increase in unemployment may be caused by an **anti-inflationary policy**. This is probably the most unpleasant aspect of inflation for the government because it continues to benefit from inflation (in the ways discussed above). But once inflation goes into double figures, it can no longer be ignored. Whereas a 2 per cent rate of inflation has barely any effect, a rate of 10 per cent or more cannot be ignored. The population becomes anxious about their income and savings and this forces the government to introduce anti-inflationary measures, which unfortunately may mean that one evil is exchanged for another or traded off against the other.

Yet another point to be considered, is the **balance of payments**. Because of continually changing prices, inflation encourages imports but discourages exports. Countries that depend on foreign trade for economic growth may find themselves in a vicious circle if their inflation rate is constantly higher than that of their larger trading partners. South Africa has been experiencing this particular problem for the past few years. It has resulted in repeated depreciations of the rand, giving rise to renewed inflationary pressure.

Social and political effects

Our study would not be complete without a reference to the social and political consequences of inflation, which may influence the economy indirectly. A rise of 10 to 15 per cent in the general price level means that most prices are rising, but it does not mean that all prices are rising at the same rate or that price hikes are the same in all shops or supermarkets. Since the ordinary consumer purchases between one hundred and two hundred different articles on a regular basis, it becomes more and more difficult for him to keep up with their relative values and the household budgeting process becomes all the more complicated. The constant struggle against the assault of increasingly expensive foodstuffs may lead to *a feeling of uncertainty and even despair*.

Because many prices in South Africa are administered (that is, they are established at the discretion of some or other body), constant announcements of price increases may have an extremely unfavourable influence on a community. An example of this is the social and political unrest caused by increases in rents and bus fares.

The general conclusion is that an inflation rate of 10 per cent or more is felt by all, although it does not necessarily affect everyone, and that all find it disturbing. The resultant upheaval prejudices economic growth and necessitates government action. Before looking at the latter, we must first establish the causes of inflation.

9.3   The causes of inflation: demand pull and cost push

Having discussed the most significant effects of inflation, we return to certain comments made at the end of chapter 4 to find the cause of inflation. After all, we need to know the causes if we are to fight inflation. We look at two phenomena in particular: **demand pull inflation** and **cost push inflation**.

Increases in real demand and demand pull inflation

What exactly happened between 1945 and 1970 that made inflation such an intractable problem? The answer was indicated in chapter 1 and also chapter 5. As mentioned, the 1930s depression caused so much unemployment and misery that it left a permanent scar; it also engendered in the post-war generation the feeling that a repetition was to be avoided at all costs. A large section of this book concentrates on the fact that fiscal measures (chapter 5) and monetary policy (chapter 7) make it possible to maintain demand at a level compatible with full employment. Thus in the well-known example in figure 9.1 it would be possible to increase the GDP from Y_1 to Y_f; this can be achieved by increasing demand from AD_1 to AD_2. As we have already pointed out, the possibility of maintaining the GDP at the full employment level was borne out by practical example during and after World War II.

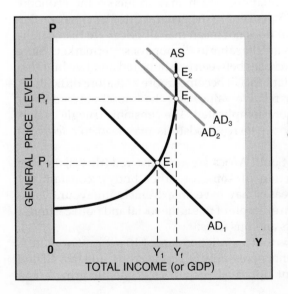

Fig. 9.1 Maintaining full employment

By increasing aggregate demand, full employment can be achieved and maintained. However, the decrease in unemployment is accompanied by an increase in the price level from P_1 to P_f and therefore in inflation. This is a clear example of the trade-off principle.

The problem of unemployment was, in fact, a minor one in the period 1945 to 1970, but we know that it was at a cost and this is borne out by the diagram. At income levels close to full employment, an increase in Y can be achieved only if a rise in prices – in other words, a measure of inflation – is accepted. But throughout the quarter-century it seemed that the price of inflation was well worth paying (despite the warnings of more conservative economists).

As a result of the war and the general mood of the times, many people and also the authorities came to believe that the government should take upon itself many more tasks than before. It was to take responsibility for certain branches of education, health services, housing and social security, as we have mentioned before. The government could, of course, meet its responsibilities only by increasing government spending, which inevitably led to a general increase in the aggregate demand curves – an increase in spending is seldom wholly offset by an increase in taxes.

This helped to keep demand at a high level. On the other hand, if full employment is achieved with aggregate demand equal to AD_2 (in fig. 9.1), a further increase in demand to AD_3 would lead to **pure inflation**. Pure inflation is an increase in the price level without an increase in production, as indicated by the movement of E_f to E_2.

Apart from this rise in demand brought about by the government's increased role (see also chapter 5), spending on defence and space research in various countries, especially the United States, was exceptionally high throughout the period 1945 to 1970. Whether such spending was designed to maintain high employment levels or whether it was for the reasons discussed above, the fact remains that inflation was caused by a high and rising **demand**. Inflation caused by shifts in demand as from AD_1 to AD_2 to AD_3 is therefore termed **demand pull** inflation. The price level is, as it were, "pulled up" by the increase in demand.

It is generally considered important to point out that demand pull inflation may be caused either by **real factors** (factors playing a role on the goods and services market) or **monetary factors**. The process described above is demand pull inflation caused by real factors.

Demand pull inflation may be caused by monetary factors alone. As explained in chapters 6 and 7, an increase in the money supply lowers the interest rate. It raises investment and probably consumer spending because of the extension of credit. In figure 9.1 it would be shown by a change in aggregate demand from AD_1 to AD_2.

According to monetarist theory, the principal cause of inflation is large increases in the money supply; real factors play a secondary role. In terms of this theory, price rises continue only if there is a corresponding increase in the money supply. For the sake of simplicity, we do not pursue this line of argument.

Inflation and expectations

We have already mentioned that for almost a quarter of a century (1945–1970) inflation had no serious consequences. We also know that prices do not all change at the same rate or according to a definite pattern. It is therefore quite possible that the ordinary man will not notice an inflation rate of 2 to 3 per cent. Price changes over a number of years may be ascribable to changes in quality. Other price changes may not be noticed at all and yet others may be forgotten in time.

In other words, prices are probably perceived as constant when the inflation rate is low. But when prices rise year in and year out and the rate of increase rises from 2 to 5 to 10 per cent, reality as we perceive it, changes, and price **rises** rather than price **stability** become the expected norm. Expectations that prices will rise are especially significant when it comes to the fixing of wages.

Expectations and wages

The participants in the economic process will obviously make every effort to protect themselves against decreases in their real income owing to inflation.

With regard to wage earners, it is well known that (i) a significant proportion of wages are fixed in negotiations between employers and trade unions, (ii) a large portion of the South African labour force is employed by the government, and (iii) wages fixed by the government and in negotiations with trade unions serve as examples to each other and also in those instances where formal negotiation is less frequent. In this type of wage setting environment employees will attempt to maintain at least the real value of their wages. They do so by compensating for losses in a new contract. If further price rises are expected, they may also try to discount any future loss in purchasing power by negotiating an additional wage increase.

When price rises are expected in all quarters, it is quite likely that employers will offer only token resistance to their employees' demands. This has serious consequences because it means that every unit of output in the economy is produced and offered for sale at a higher price. In a diagram such as that in figure 9.2 – which is very similar to figures 4.11 and 5.7 – it means that there is a upward shift to the left of the total supply curve from AS_1 to AS_2.

The nature of cost push inflation

If the economy in question was in equilibrium at Y_f and a price level of P_f, this shift in the AS curve would result in an increase in the price level from P_f to P_1. Clearly there is no change in demand; the cause of and background to this phenomenon are to be found on the supply side and this is why we speak of **cost push** or **supply** inflation. The process described above is also sometimes referred to as **wage push** inflation to distinguish it from **profit push** inflation (in both instances costs are presumed to push price upwards). Profit push inflation is the result of producers overcompensating for inflation on the same principle adopted in the case of wages.

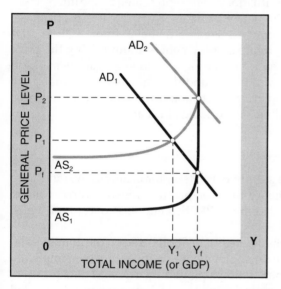

Fig. 9.2 Cost push inflation

An upwards shift in the supply curve causes Y to fall (resulting in unemployment) and prices to rise. A return to full employment can be achieved only at an even higher price level.

An important aspect of cost push inflation is that it may derive from outside the domestic economy. This is sometimes referred to as **supply shocks**. In the early seventies there were two types of supply shock. The first was the result of poor coffee and grain crops, causing food prices to rise considerably. The second was the formation of the OPEC cartel and the enormous oil price increases it introduced. This also led to an upward shift in aggregate supply which, as illustrated in figure 9.2, resulted in inflation (price hikes) and stagnation (unemployment), the twin evils of the seventies. To avoid unemployment by raising demand – as shown by the AD_2 curves – would only aggravate inflation.

It should be noted in passing that the greater the role of foreign trade in a country, the greater the possibility of **imported inflation**. In other words, if imports amount to as much as 20 per cent of the GDP, as in South Africa, changes in foreign price levels necessarily affect domestic price levels; again this occurs through the mechanism illustrated in figure 9.2. Smaller countries may find it extremely difficult and even impossible to control their own inflation rates if inflation is rampant elsewhere (unless it can be counteracted by a change in the exchange rate).

9.4   The Phillips curve

At the beginning of this book we explained that the study of macro-economics originated in the 1930s depression, during which the greatest problem was general and persistent unemployment. If you page back to figure 4.10, you will see that such a situation can be represented by the intersection of AD_1 and AS_3 in its completely horizontal (perfectly elastic) phase. Successful demand management increases demand from AD_1 to AD_2 increasing the GDP and therefore employment **without raising the price level significantly**. Not even a further increase in aggregate demand to AD_3, for instance, would raise prices unduly. The result was that price changes were largely ignored in macro-economics for many years; the focus was mainly on "total spending" as explained in chapter 3.

Background to the Phillips curve

The **form** of the aggregate supply curve (see, for example, AS_3 in figure 4.10) is concurrent with a theory based on practical research carried out by A.W. Phillips in 1957. This led to the **Phillips curve**, a concept for which Phillips became famous.

Phillips's hypothesis – that there is a relation between the annual inflation rate and the percentage unemployment – has been accepted implicitly throughout most of this book. Phillips plotted the relevant data for more than one hundred years, mainly for the United Kingdom and the United States, on a diagram. This exercise gave rise to a curve like P_1 in figure 9.3. In this diagram the percentage of unemployed workers is measured on the horizontal axis and the inflation rate is indicated on the vertical axis. Phillips found that the statistical relation between inflation and unemployment could be illustrated in such a diagram by a curve running downwards from left to right. Lower unemployment levels are, in other words, associated with a higher rate of increase in the general price level. More specifically, in figure 9.3 this would mean that at an unemployment level of 2 per cent, for example, inflation would be approximately 4 per cent. The inflation rate can be reduced to nil only if unemployment (u) is allowed to increase to the 5 per cent level. As the diagram shows, high rates of unemployment may be associated with possible deflation (a decrease in the general price level).

In the terms used in this book, this means that changes in aggregate demand occur mainly in the normal area of the aggregate supply curve, because it is in this area that an increase in employment (that is, a decrease

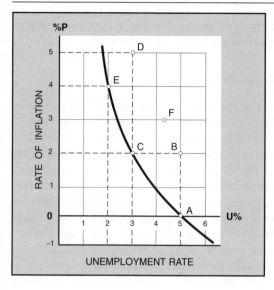

Fig. 9.3 The Phillips curve

The Phillips curve relates the unemployment rate (u) to the inflation rate (p). The seventies saw new combinations of p and u which did not appear on the existing Phillips curves for different countries. This indicated that the Phillips curve itself had shifted.

in unemployment) leads to a rise in price ("inflation"). If we interpret the vertical axis of the aggregate supply curve as the **inflation rate** rather than the price level (which is quite acceptable), the AS curve becomes the exact counterpart of the Phillips curve.

The trade-off principle

Because the Phillips curve was based on numerous observations and was valid for so long, it came to be regarded as a clear indication that **unemployment** and **inflation** could be **traded off** against each other. In other words, a lower inflation rate could be achieved by trading it off against, or exchanging it for, greater unemployment. You will remember that this is exactly the case with demand management in the normal area of AS. The trade-off principle – "higher employment at the cost of some inflation" – was important for a number of countries when establishing practical economic goals.

The Phillips curve was initially a statistical device with little or no theoretical background. Unfortunately, and for reasons similar to those discussed in the previous section, the whole basis of the curve collapsed to the extent that many concluded that the trade-off between inflation and unemployment was no longer possible and that the Phillips curve had lost its significance. Because the Phillips curve was based on statistical facts, this type of warning was heard at the end of the sixties and throughout the seventies when combinations of unemployment and inflation, differing completely from the existing Phillips curves, occurred. Examples are B and D in figure 9.3. The basic pattern seemed to have disappeared.

The disappearance of the trade-off principle

The basic pattern reflected by the Phillips curve in figure 9.3, for example, is an unemployment rate of 3 per cent at an inflation rate of 2 per cent. A decrease in unemployment (or an **increase** in employment) to 2 per cent brought about by an increase in demand could be achieved only at an increased inflation rate of 4 per cent. However, empirical observation showed that unemployment did not decrease as expected. On the contrary, it was found that an unemployment rate of 3 per cent was now associated with an inflation rate of 5 per cent, for instance (see point D in the figure). Empirical research also produced other points (F and B, for example) which did not lie on the original Phillips curve. Not surprisingly, it was declared in the late sixties that the trade-off principle according to the Phillips curve had disappeared. Later it was realized that it was the Phillips curve itself which had shifted.

The explanation for this change is to be found in the shift of AS_1 to AS_2 in figure 9.2. In figure 9.3 this would produce a new Phillips curve including points D, F and B, but on this curve trade-off is still possible. This trade-off process would, however, entail a different set of figures.

9.5 Economic policy and inflation

A large section of this book has dealt with economic policy measures introduced to combat demand pull inflation. We have looked at fiscal and monetary policy as instruments of demand management designed to neutralize excessive demand. In this chapter we do not consider these conventional stabilization measures for fighting inflation – the emphasis is on policy actions addressing the more complex problem of cost push inflation.

Incomes policy

It has become clear from the previous section that there is no easy answer to the policy dilemma of cost push or supply inflation. It was obvious to many economists that demand management alone would not solve the problem. Since demand management leads to greater unemployment or higher inflation under such circumstances (see fig. 9.1), other solutions had to be sought. The causes of cost push inflation are to be found on the supply side – it therefore makes sense that policies to counter this type of inflation should come from the same side. Measures have to be found that will either shift the supply curves to the right or at least prevent them from shifting further to the left. Inflation has to be reduced without prejudicing economic growth. This is exactly what an incomes policy attempts to do.

An incomes policy implies some form of direct government intervention in the determination of wages and prices. The action taken by the authorities may vary from the formulation of **guidelines** on the determination of wages and prices to **compulsory control measures**. For any incomes policy to be successful, it has to appear equitable to all parties involved.

In principle this amounts to an agreement (between the state, employees and employers) on how national income is to be distributed. This usually entails a call to workers to limit their demands for nominal wage adjustments to the average productivity increase in the economy. If prices can then be kept constant, such an agreement ensures that the relative share of wages and profits in the economy also remains constant. This principle is perhaps best illustrated by means of the numeric example in table 9.2.[§]

Table 9.2

Example of the operation of an incomes policy

	Year 1	Year 2	Percentage change
Labour productivity (index)	1,0	1,1	10
Employment (numbers)	100	100	0
Real National Income (rand)	100	110	10
Remuneration of employees (rand)	80	88	10
Profit (rand)	20	22	10
Nominal wage (rand)	0,80	0,88	10
Unit cost of labour (rand)	0,80	0,80	0
Price level (rand)	1,0	1,0	0
Real wage (rand)	0,80	0,88	10

In the table a fictitious economy is analysed for two consecutive years. Assume that labour productivity increased by 10 per cent from Year 1 to Year 2. The incomes policy being applied stipulates that wages may be increased only in accordance with increases in productivity. If we accept that the number of workers remains constant, this means that the national income also increases by only 10 per cent. We assume that the national income is divided between wages and profits in the ratio of 80 to 20 per cent. Since wages may increase by only 10 per cent, the relative share of labour and profit remains constant over the two years provided prices do not also rise. **Increases in the wage rate equal to the increases in produc-**

§   The example is based on a similar example in Dernburg (1985, p.419).

tivity mean that the relative share of workers (remuneration of labour) and employers (profit) remains the same if prices do not change. The unit cost of labour is calculated by dividing money wages by labour productivity. These variables both increase by 10 per cent, which means that the unit cost of labour does not change.

If everything works out as presented in the table (that is, the share of the different market participants remains constant), there is no reason for price hikes and the fight against inflation is won. The simple economy represented in the table is an indication of how difficult it is in practice to apply an "equitable" incomes policy.

Although it is possible to calculate the per capita increase in the real GDP for the labour force and to use this as an indication of the average increase in productivity, there are necessarily industries in which the increase in productivity is far larger. Hi-tech industries, which are not labour intensive, fall into this category. Other industries, especially the personal services industry, may show no increase in productivity. An equitable, negotiated distribution of the increase in production is not quite so simple in such circumstances. The incomes policy means that both employees and employers cannot act as stipulated by micro-economic principles. How is a rapidly growing industry to enlarge its labour force if it cannot offer higher wages? How does a firm, which is fully prepared to co-operate on incomes policy, react if one or more of the other undertakings in the industry do not give their co-operation?

Largely as a result of this type of problem, most of the bigger wage and price control programmes in the USA (1971–1974), the United Kingdom (1972–1974) and Canada (1975–1978) did not last very long. Except for short periods, such attempts were never very successful in any market-oriented economy.

Comprehensive, enforceable wage and price control has never been introduced in South Africa. The possible negative effect on economic growth and labour relations has meant that policy makers have always shied away from such a policy. In 1975 a tentative effort was made to introduce an incomes policy in South Africa when representatives of the authorities and various private sector bodies signed the **Anti-Inflation Manifesto of 1975**. It was a voluntary agreement in terms of which the different parties undertook to absorb 30 per cent of all increases in the CPI. This meant that only 70 per cent of any increase in the CPI would be taken into account when fixing wages and prices. The experiment continued until March 1977, but its success remains doubtful. In the final analysis, the market forces of supply and demand were simply too strong.

This failure does not mean that the authorities should give up completely on a wage and price policy. It is a fact that the governments of the world, including that of South Africa, have a very important role to play in fixing wages and prices in modern society. The South African government, for example, is the single largest employer in the country and indirectly determines more than a third of all wages and prices. It is obvious that wages and salaries established in the public sector will influence those in the private sector.

In South Africa a large number of prices are fixed directly or indirectly by the government: post and railway tariffs; the price of electricity, steel and several agricultural products via the control boards. Seen from this angle, the government has to adhere to the same principles, albeit on a smaller scale, as stipulated by an incomes policy. Prices and wages that are controlled by the government should be closely and effectively monitored.

Other supply-side policy actions

A discussion of anti-inflation policy, launched from the supply side, would not be complete without mention of the role played by **tax concessions** in the early eighties, especially in the USA. In terms of this "supply-side recipe"[§] applied at the beginning of the Reagan administration, a stringent monetary policy was to be combined with tax concessions to counter the twin evils of inflation and unemployment. This combination of fiscal and monetary policy was effective in the short term but did not succeed in sustaining economic growth in the long run.

The decrease in taxation rates was meant to encourage people to save more so that more funds would be available for investment and the promotion of economic growth. Increased saving would keep interest rates low which, in turn, would stimulate further investment and growth. In this way the total supply curve is shifted to the right (see the analysis made in chapter 5 with the aid of fig. 5.7). The restrictive monetary policy was in the meantime to keep the inflation rate under control.

As mentioned, this policy was initially successful. Unfortunately both measures began to put pressure on interest rates. On the one hand there was the restrictive monetary policy which, predictably, caused interest rates to rise. On the other, private saving increased at the expense of an increased **budgetary deficit**, which also resulted in higher interest rates. All this had a negative effect on investment and expectations of economic growth were never realized. Although inflation was to a certain extent brought under control, it was at the expense of greater unemployment.

Compensatory measures

In this chapter we have seen that during the seventies it became more and

§ Known in the literature as "Reaganomics".

more difficult to fight inflation. Despite varied efforts, many developing countries, including South Africa, have since 1974 seldom, if ever, succeeded in keeping the inflation rate below the double digit mark. In many instances this occurred in spite of serious economic collapses and unemployment and in spite of attempts to relieve the pressure of inflation by means of incomes policy.

The many disappointments in the fight against inflation have resulted in various institutional measures, all of which were designed to eliminate as far as possible the negative effects of inflation. The background to these measures is the belief that if it is not possible to stop inflation, one can at least attempt to reduce its consequences. The most important compensatory measures introduced have to do with **indexation**. This means that certain prices, wages and pensions are linked to price indices (for example, the CPI) to eliminate the undesirable effects of inflation.

In countries like Brazil and Israel with a long history of high inflation rates, the governments have had to apply indexation more formally. When the inflation rate rises to 100 per cent or more, they have no alternative but to introduce indexation in all spheres of the economy. We have indexation in South Africa, but it is on a more informal basis. We refer here to periodic adjustments to civil servants' salaries and social pensions. Formal and informal indexation help communities to cope with inflation. But at the same time this impedes the fight against inflation, since the result is less reason to take effective steps against it.

Selected references:

Baumol & Blinder: 16, 17.
Dernburg: 13.
Dornbusch & Fischer: 8.
Evans-Pritchard: 12, 13.
Gordon: 8, 9, 11.
Mohr et.al.: 54.
Morley: 8, 9, 10.
Shapiro: 21, 22, 23, 24.

10 Economic growth

For many years macro-economics was concerned almost exclusively with the problem of maintaining demand at a level consistent with full employment of the country's productive resources.

However, as we explained in the previous chapter, maintenance of demand is no longer the only problem to be solved; the **control** of demand has become just as important. But even before this change, people had begun to consider the possibility of raising living standards in not only the "rich" but also the "poor" countries of the world. This led to the study of **economic growth**, which is our topic of discussion in this chapter.

10.1 The meaning of economic growth

For want of a better criterion, economic growth is usually defined as the annual rate of increase in real gross domestic product (GDP, preferred in South Africa) or the rate of increase in the real gross national product (GNP, used in many other countries).

Qualifications concerning economic growth

The reason for defining economic growth in terms of data expressed in **constant prices** (real values), is not hard to find. In chapter 2 we pointed out that an appreciable difference may exist between the change in the GDP at **current** prices and the GDP at **constant** prices. As we have seen, the former has risen far more quickly than the latter.

This is naturally emphasized when the rate of inflation goes into double figures, as happened in many countries in the seventies and eighties – as borne out by figure 2.2 (see section 2.4 of chapter 2). Consider also the following example: between 1990 and 1991 South Africa's GDP at current prices rose from R263 812 million to R296 667 million, an increase of 12,45 per cent. But in real terms the change was from R263 812 million to R262 307 million, which means a decrease in growth. Although an indication of the change in the GDP at current prices is indispensable in many instances, growth is considered a **real** phenomenon. No economic growth is possible if the change in the GDP or the GNP is simply the result of price rises.

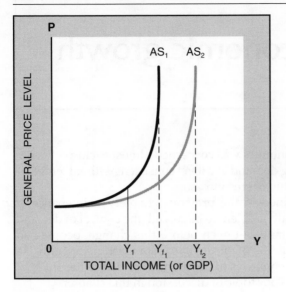

Fig. 10.1 Growth in capacity output

Economic growth may be repre-sented by a shift to the right of the agrgregate supply curve. Note that a change in the GDP from Y_1 to Y_{f1} on AS_1 is not growth in the real sense.

There is another instance in which it is assumed that there will be no growth: when the economy recovers after a period of slack or depression (with production below full capacity) and the GDP increases as a result of improved capacity utilization – in other words, when the economy moves from unemployment to full employment. Such circumstances are repre-sented in figure 10.1 by means of two examples of the now familiar aggregate supply curve. An increase in the real GDP from Y_1 to Y_{f1} on the aggregate supply curve AS_1 is not actually growth, because there has been no change in the production potential. It was to this that we referred in the previous paragraph. However, there is economic growth if the full employ-ment level of the GDP increases from Y_{f1} to Y_{f2}, for example, in which case the whole AS curve shifts from AS_1 to AS_2. Economic growth (in terms of this interpretation) can therefore be defined as an increase in the real potential (full employment) income. Naturally, growth comes into its own only if this potential is utilised to the full.

There is yet a third qualification in respect of economic growth. Growth always implies improvement – improvement of the economic lot or living standards of those who form part of the economy in question. From this we deduce that there must be an increase in the (potential) GDP **per capita** (per head of the population) before we can talk of economic growth. If this is to be our criterion, the South African economy has performed exceptionally poorly in the last few years.

With the exception of the fact that the GDP has to be measured in real terms, it is difficult to eliminate the other qualifications in respect of the definition and description of growth. It is extremely difficult to determine

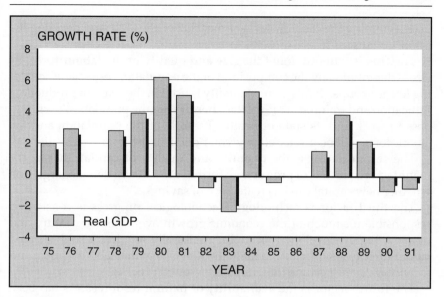

Sources: South African Reserve Bank: *Quarterly Bulletin,* March 1992.
South African Reserve Bank Occasional Paper, No. 5, September 1991.

Fig. 10.2 Annual rates of growth in the real GDP of South Africa
The growth performance of the South African economy was quite erratic between 1975 and 1991.

the real **potential** GDP from year to year, especially in South Africa where capacity (like full employment) is not easily measured. If we look at figure 10.2, for example, it is difficult to judge whether the economy returned to full or partially full capacity in 1984 after negative growth in the previous two years. Population figures can likewise be compared with GDP data only over relatively long periods. As a result the annual changes in the real GDP, shown in figure 10.2, are accepted in practice as a good indication of growth. The figure shows that there were considerable fluctuations in the annual growth rates and confirms what has been said before, namely that from an economic point of view the years after 1975 were difficult ones. Because population growth is more than 2 per cent per year, the GDP per capita apparently rose over the period 1970 to 1980, which made it possible to raise the living standard of the population as a whole. It is, however, less certain what occurred in the eighties.

Four factors in the growth process

There are four groups of factors which are generally held to be instrumental in determining the capacity level of the GDP or the GNP and deciding the opportunities for future growth.

The **first** is without doubt the **size and quality of the labour force**. Its size is determined by the composition of the population, especially according to age groups. In this context quality is used in the sense of production. Education and training are important here, as are the population's willingness to work and its state of health. The role of the population and the labour force will be discussed in greater detail in the following section.

The **second** factor is the **quantity and quality of capital**, that is, the manufactured means of production; further growth will depend largely on whether new capital can be created out of savings.

The **third** factor is **technology**. Technological progress is considered responsible for much of the economic growth over the past century and more. A highly developed technology naturally requires a sophisticated labour force to install, run and maintain it. It is clear that labour, capital and technology have become integral to the growth process.

The **fourth** factor is the **availability of natural resources**. As has been shown in the case of Australia, Canada, South Africa and other countries rich in natural resources, this factor is a great advantage in economic development. But as is evidenced by countries such as Switzerland, Japan and nowadays Taiwan, Singapore and Hong Kong, raw materials may also be imported profitably provided the knowledge and means are available locally to process them further.

Per capita GDP in different countries

The appearance of several new independent countries on the world scene after 1945 – most of them part of the **Third World** – gave impetus to the study of economic growth. In many of these countries people lived in conditions differing vastly from those in most of the economically established countries. Table 10.1 gives some idea of the differences in economic activity in various countries.

An analysis of the average per capita GDP for 1989 shows variations from more than $19 000 in countries such as the United States, Sweden, Japan and Germany to less than $500 in Ethiopia, Tanzania, Nigeria and Kenya.

When making such international comparisons, we should remember that whatever the figures used, they produce only an approximate indication of differences in economic prosperity. As is obvious from table 10.1, we use the dollar as the common currency for measuring production in the different countries. The current exchange rates in the year in question are used for the conversion to dollar values.

Table 10.1

GDP, population and per capita GDP for various countries, average for mid-1989

Country	GDP ($ millions)	Population (million)	Per capita GDP $
Australia	281 940	16,8	16 782
Brazil	319 150	147,3	2 166
Germany (West)	1 189 100	62,0	19 179
Egypt	31 580	51,0	619
Ethiopia	5 420	49,5	110
France	955 790	56,2	17 006
Israel	46 030	4,5	10 229
Italy	865 720	57,5	15 056
Japan	2 818 520	123,1	22 896
Canada	488 590	26,2	18 648
Kenya	7 130	23,5	303
Korea	211 880	42,4	4 997
Netherlands	221 680	14,8	1 498
Nigeria	28 920	113,8	254
South Africa	80 370	35,0	2 296
Sweden	166 520	8,5	19 590
Tanzania	2 540	23,8	107
United Kingdom	717 870	57,2	12 550
United States	5 156 440	248,8	20 725

Source: *World Development Report*, 1991.

Table 10.1 *Direct comparisons of the GDP of different countries have many shortcomings. Nevertheless, the differences both in the absolute size of the GDP and in the per capita GDP are so large that they are a reasonable indication of the orders of magnitude involved.*

Although this may at first appear to be a most suitable method, this type of conversion casts doubt on the reliability of the comparisons. The reason is that the exchange rate is not necessarily an accurate reflection of the actual purchasing power of the two currencies. The fact that $1 can be exchanged for approximately R2,87 on the foreign exchange market does not mean that a person in South Africa can buy the same quantity (or basket) of goods with R2,87 as a person in the United States can buy with $1. Furthermore, it is clear that in an era of volatile exchange rates such as the world is experiencing at present, sudden exchange rate adjustments may cause considerable fluctuations in the dollar value of the different countries' domestic product.

Despite all these difficulties underlying international comparisons, the considerable differences reflected by table 10.1 point to a fundamental problem. This problem is confirmed if we consider criteria such as number of hospital beds, number of telephones or kilometres of tarred road. Adopting a reasonably unbiased view, we can say that the economic backlog in Third World countries is the major problem area in the world today.

Growth versus development

The vast difference between the level of economic activity in economically established countries and in developing countries (also known as LDCs or **less developed countries**) has led to a difference in terminology. **Economic growth** describes the process of increases in the GDP in developed countries. In these countries the basic pattern of production has been established and any growth is, almost literally, growth in what already exists, that is, factors such as capital, technology and labour.

The expression used in the case of LDCs is **economic development**. Economic development, too, is a process which results in an increase in the real potential production (per capita). But whereas economic growth describes a gradual increase in the means of production, economic development implies a fundamental change in the community as a whole and in its economic system, that is, it affects how and where people live and work. Of particular significance is the physical displacement from rural to urban areas, but also adjustments, often radical, in cultural patterns, a valiant and necessary attempt to train workers, a totally different approach to health services, transport and so forth. This is, in principle, the difference between development and growth. Naturally there are instances where the two processes overlap and the difference is merely one of degree, but the difference cannot be denied.

10.2 Population and the labour force

In the section on the per capita GDP we referred in passing to the importance of the size of the population. Countries like Brazil and India have achieved relatively high levels of total GDP, but their per capita GDPs are low because of the enormous number of people living there. In fact, the problem of population plays a significant role in the analysis of economic growth and development. However, population is not always the root of the problem. The point is, of course, that the people have to be fed, but at the same time they are the only source of productive labour. At times the emphasis has been on the latter point of view, but attention has been focused mainly on the former.

Adam Smith's optimism

One of those who regarded population as the basis of **production** rather than **consumption** was **Adam Smith** (1723–1790), who published his famous work *An Inquiry into the Nature and Causes of the Wealth of Nations* in 1776. Smith is generally regarded as the father of economics. One aspect of the economy analyzed and emphasized by Smith, was the phenomenon of the division of labour. Production may be increased by dividing the production process into several different operations and having people specialize. The extent to which this type of specialization can be implemented, depends on the size of the market. In other words, the more people, the larger the market, which results in greater specialization and therefore higher productivity and increased total production.

Smith is therefore considered an optimist, because he had confidence in the possibilities of economic growth and development. This can be expressed somewhat more modernly and more formally in terms of a **production function**. A production function indicates the relation between production or GDP (called Y) and employment (N). As is to be expected, Y increases with N – this is borne out by figure 10.3. Note, however, that Q_1 rises at an increasing rate (it becomes steeper as N increases). If Y/N is an indication of productivity (since it represents output per unit of labour), then we can say that productivity at A_2 is greater than at A_1 because $\frac{A_2B_2}{OA_2} > \frac{A_1B_1}{OA_1}$ (that is, the slope of OB_2 is greater than that of OB_1). This is apparently the type of increase that Smith had in mind. Of course, no further growth is possible if natural resources are exhausted, but Smith did not consider this a serious threat.

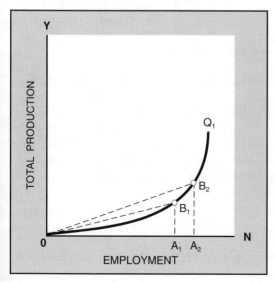

Fig. 10.3 Example of a production function (1)

In this production function output rises at an increasing rate. This is the type of production function that Adam Smith had in mind.

The pessimism of David Ricardo

The next major author in the **classical school** was **David Ricardo** (1772–1823). He was considerably more pessimistic about long-term economic prospects than Adam Smith. Ricardo was particularly concerned about the **law of diminishing returns**, in terms of which production may increase but only at a decreasing rate until a maximum is reached. In figure 10.4 we have an example of the operation of this law. Although the Q_2 curve rises as N increases, it does so at an increasingly slower rate (the slope decreases); average production (per capita or per unit of labour) also decreases, as shown by the fact that $\frac{A_2B_2}{OA_2} < \frac{A_1B_1}{OA_1}$, which is the same as saying that the slope of OB_2 is smaller than that of OB_1. Y reaches a maximum at B_3.

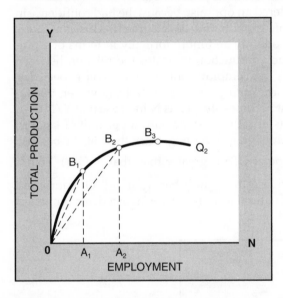

Fig. 10.4 Example of a production function (2)

According to this production function, output increases at a falling rate and reaches a definite maximum at B3. Ricardo may have thought of production in this way.

There is, of course, another possibility – as figure 10.5 shows, the two production functions may combine, as it were. The production function Q_3 shows an increasing slope and therefore also increasing average productivity to B_1. Then the Ricardian idea of decreasing productivity comes into play until maximum production is reached again at a point such as B_3. No matter which of the latter two production functions is used, the outlook is pessimistic since there are definite restrictions on the possibility of economic growth.

Malthus and population

Ricardo's pessimistic outlook was reinforced by the work of **Thomas R.**

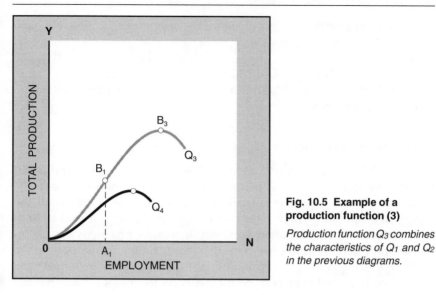

Fig. 10.5 Example of a production function (3)

Production function Q₃ combines the characteristics of Q₁ and Q₂ in the previous diagrams.

Malthus (1766–1834). Malthus added his **law of population** to the law of diminishing returns.

Malthus argued as follows: according to his observations, the production of food increases according to an **arithmetic series** or, in other words, in a sequence of 1, 2, 3, 4, 5, 6, 7 and so forth. But according to natural laws, the population increases according to a **geometric series** such as 1, 2, 4, 8, 16, 32, 64 (note that each time we have seven terms and begin with the same base). Population figures will therefore always catch up with the production of food (or consumer goods in today's terminology). This means that the average amount of food available per capita would continue to decrease until a mere subsistence level was reached. Even slightly subnormal harvests would result in starvation, thereby reinforcing Ricardo's pessimism. Economic growth, especially if defined as an increase in the per capita GDP, would be totally out of the question.

Optimism vindicated?

Nothing came of these dire prophecies. Economic growth and development, even if measured as per capita output, became a feature of the economies of First World (Western) and Second World (Eastern bloc) countries. Continuous growth lasted virtually from the Napoleonic wars of the nineteenth century onwards; in the twentieth century it was interrupted, but not halted, by two devastating wars and a severe depression. It is therefore not surprising that Malthus and his theories were disregarded for more than a century. It is only since the seventies that his ideas have once again become prominent.

Why, for more than a century, did Malthus's theories not apply in the (now) economically established countries of the world? The reason is to be found on both sides of the Malthusian equation – the change in production, and that in population.

The increase in production

Looking first at the production process, we can say that the **Industrial Revolution** saw innovations being applied at an increasing rate in the economic process. These eventually had a favourable effect on all the factors of economic growth referred to above: (i) unprecedented technological developments resulted in vastly increased productivity; (ii) increased production led to greater savings, even among the working class, and thus to adequate capital formation; (iii) alternative raw materials were discovered (e.g. coal for wood, oil for coal) and technology made natural resources more accessible, thereby increasing their availability; and (iv) increased production meant that there were more funds available for training labour. For many years a growing population was considered a favourable factor since it gave rise to both a **market** for consumer goods and a **labour force** to produce increasing output.

Formally this meant that people no longer worked according to the same type of production function; on the contrary, the old production functions were replaced time and again by functions at a much higher level and by maxima occurring at higher levels of employment. This is obvious if we compare Q_3 with Q_4 in figure 10.5. Practical examples are to be found in agriculture, where comparisons are possible because products are very similar to those of the past. Even in the quarter-century after the Second World War, innovations in electronics (computers, televisions, telephones) meant that national economies grew faster than ever before.

Food production did, in fact, keep pace and increased faster than any arithmetic series would suggest – other than Malthus claimed, not only the population **shows exponential growth**.

The change in population

But even this enormous growth in the GDP would have had to yield to continued exponential growth in the population. Having said, in effect, that Malthus completely underestimated the possibilities of growth in the GDP, we must now ask ourselves what happened on the other side of the equation (that is, the population).

This can be explained with the aid of figure 10.6, where we measure the

birth or death rate per 1 000 of a population along the vertical axis. The
dotted line represents the death rate and the unbroken line, the birth rate;
it is obvious that any change in the population will be determined by the
difference between these two lines.

For hundreds and even thousands of years the human birth rate was
only slightly higher than the death rate. The population consequently grew
very slowly and starvation and misery was the lot of the majority of people.
This may be referred to as stage I of the growth in population. This stage,
which was a long-term phenomenon, endured well into the seventeenth
and eighteenth centuries.

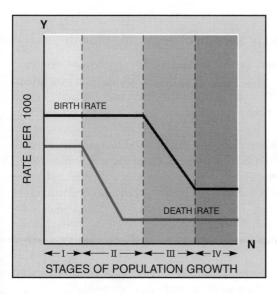

**Fig. 10.6 Four stages of
population growth**

*In stage II there is a decrease in
the death rate, resulting in a considerable increase in the population. In stage III the birth rate
begins to fall until in stage IV
there are only slightly more births
than deaths, which is similar to
the position in stage I.*

During the eighteenth century and at the beginning of the nineteenth
century, when Malthus made his calculations, Europe and the American
colonies in particular (which became the USA in 1776) moved into stage II.
This stage is characterized by a sharp decrease in the death rate – the result
of adequate food supplies – with an equally sharp increase in the percentage growth rate of the population. Malthus did not recognize this as a
"stage II" (implying a subsequent "stage III") for a very simply reason.
Populations had previously also entered stage II as a result of innovations
in food production, but once this growth was complete, the death rate had
reestablished itself (basically because of starvation) and there had been a
return to stage I.

But after Malthus's time, in the nineteenth and twentieth centuries, this
return to stage I did not occur. A new phenomenon made its appearance:
possibly as the result of a higher average income, increasing urbanization

and improved education, there was a significant decrease in the birth rate. This is presented as stage III in the diagram. The rate of increase in the population became smaller and smaller until in stage IV the change in population was comparable to that in stage I. There can be no doubt that this decrease in population saved the day for developed countries.

To conclude: improved technology and increased capital formation – which Malthus had underestimated – and the eventual deceleration in the rate of increase in population – which Malthus could not have foreseen – resulted in Malthusian pessimism being replaced by a generally optimistic feeling about growth prospects. This optimism has been less obvious since the seventies.

10.3   The desirability and prospects of economic growth

For many years there was a general optimism about the process of economic growth. As we have mentioned, the facts had proved that the pessimism of classical economists like Ricardo and Malthus was unfounded. Even in the countries which had lost the Second World War, growth was nothing short of spectacular.

Economic growth in both the West and the East led to a steady increase in living standards. The redistribution of wealth and income, which many considered an important objective in itself, was more easily effected (even if the rich were deprived of some of their wealth, they still had sufficient funds) and also less necessary (economic growth had raised the living standards of the impoverished). In other words, economic growth was not only extremely desirable, but the prospects of further growth appeared highly favourable.

We now have to turn our attention to the following questions: **Firstly**, what does growth **cost**, or what are its **disadvantages**. **Secondly**, how much longer can the process continue?

The cost of economic growth

One of the points sometimes raised today about economic growth, is whether or not it was worthwhile. If a high standard of living is supposed to make one better off, one should also be happier than before, but this does not seem to be the case. There are several drawbacks to life in the modern world. One hears about the tensions of modern existence and the deterioration in our quality of life. It is therefore argued that if happiness and contentment are to be the yardsticks for measuring the advantages of growth, we might as well have spared ourselves the trouble.

This argument is highly subjective and cannot be substantiated. Nostalgia for "the good old days" is really nothing new. But other disadvantages associated with economic growth can be measured far more objectively. Some of these are found on the consumer side and others on the production side of the economic circuit.

Economic growth is usually associated with urbanization, because the modern means of production are in the towns and the cities. This leads to overcrowding in cities, which may cause people to move out of the central urban areas. Urban sprawl and a shortage of open space results; this necessitates an expensive road network linking the suburbs with the metropolitan area. Private cars mean that the inhabitants can live far from their places of employment – and when the roads are not busy, they can reach home in a reasonably short time. But peak-hour congestion nullifies all that has been achieved. Congestion and overcrowding are also common in recreation areas and noise and litter is everywhere. The beauty of nature has been destroyed and it is no wonder that stress is on the increase, that the modern way of life is loathsome to many and that psychiatrists earn a fortune.

The problem of externalities

The cause of most of the detrimental effects of economic growth lies in what are known in economics as **external effects** or **externalities**. Such effects have an impact on other participants in the economic process. Driving a car, for instance, is advantageous to the driver and passengers, but their presence on the road affects the convenience, speed and safety of all other road users in the vicinity. When too many other drivers are on the road – and the possibility arises that the traffic may come to a standstill – it may be pointless to go out in one's car. Such external effects may continue in a vicious circle. In many of the more prosperous suburbs of South African cities, traffic is so heavy (at certain times) that it is dangerous for children to ride their bicycles to school. They are therefore driven to school, which means that the danger is greater and that even fewer cyclists take to the road.

The external effects of consumption are unpleasant rather than dangerous, and perhaps less serious. External effects are also felt in the production process and here their impact may be greater. In production, external effects take the form of cost elements not borne by the producer. In the majority of cases the disposal of waste products is involved.

The problem of waste products, known as **pollution**, was not very serious when the world's population was low and production was on a small scale. But with the growth of population and production (at an exponential rate) the problem of **solid** waste products has increased, although it has not yet taken on insurmountable physical proportions. **Liquid** and **gaseous** wastes, not to speak of radioactive materials, represent a far greater danger to the world. These problems, for which no obvious solution has yet emerged and which are regarded as the permanent cost of economic growth, have led economists to ask whether the advantages of economic growth have not been overestimated.

The new pessimism – the Club of Rome

Thus optimism began to give way to pessimism, since not only was the cost of economic growth considerable but there was also a definite return to Ricardo's and Malthus's thinking on the **prospects** of such growth. As has been explained, an improvement in technology, which is accompanied by an increase in labour productivity, results in growth, that is, an increase in potential output without additional physical resources being used. This is termed **disembodied** growth, in other words, growth based on factors that are "invisible" or "intangible". This growth does not produce waste products and is the converse of **embodied** growth, which is based on the utilization of additional natural resources, equipment and labour. Embodied growth means that goods are used and then discarded. The problem of pollution did not (initially) deteriorate because of disembodied growth or, to put it differently, because of technological improvements. And the optimism about economic growth was based largely on the possibilities presented by disembodied growth.

In the early seventies a considerable amount of work was done on the description and analysis of economic growth. The established national economies had experienced another twenty-five years of growth (1945-1970); it was, in fact, exponential growth – production had doubled and trebled in even fewer years. It was inevitable that exponential growth would be analysed in greater detail.

Such an analysis was made by the **Club of Rome**, a group of independent experts who ran a computer simulation based on current data. They produced a theory also known as the **doomsday model**, holding that we are heading for economic ruin.

The report of the Club of Rome on the limits to growth, caused a sensation in 1972. The criticism against it was that its assumptions were the same as its conclusions, namely that exponential growth had to end at some time. The report was also based on the assumption that disembodied growth **could not** increase at an exponential rate. Another point of criticism was that it did not take into account the operation of the price system. The scarcity of certain resources might, because of their prices, lead to the use of alternative resources and thus prolong the life of the former.

The zero growth rate

At the time of writing, it seemed that most of the warnings from the Club of Rome had been forgotten – despite, and perhaps also as a result of, the

1973 oil crisis. We say **despite** because the oil crisis was a clear sign of the exhaustibility of one of the world's most important natural resources; after all, this was one of the major concerns of the report. We can also say **as a result of** because the crisis was a significant factor in the development of inflation. It led to the recession of 1974–76 and later, and the twin economic evils of recession and inflation began to claim more and more attention. Even the fear of pollution faded into the background. As a result of inflation, the effect of the price system on oil consumption was minimal for a long time, especially in the United States. It was not until 1980, seven years after the first serious warnings – and partly as a result of Japanese competition – that the American automobile industry began considering fuel-efficient vehicles. The price system also focused attention on coal, North Sea oil, solar energy and so forth.

Under the influence of all these considerations, a new concept made its appearance – the possibility of **zero economic growth** (ZEG). Rather than encourage economic growth, it should be controlled in order to avert a catastrophe as foreseen by the Club of Rome. Such a situation would, naturally, have to be accompanied by ZPG, that is, **zero population growth**. For the world as a whole ZPG is certainly still some time off, although it has virtually been achieved in the established economies.

10.4 The desirability and prospects of economic development

In our discussion of the doomsday model in the previous section, we deliberately glossed over the greatest problem in respect of exponential growth, namely population. Perhaps Malthus was not so unrealistic when he put forward his idea of exponential population growth. For example, the population of the world is increasing annually by two per cent. This is very close to the growth rate in South Africa and it means that population figures double every 35 years. If the population of South Africa (including the TBVC countries) was approximately 35 million in 1986, then the number of people will increase to 140 million in the next 70 years. In another 105 years (approximately the year 2160) the population of South Africa will be 1 120 million – more than that of China today. It seems logical to expect that somewhere along the line something drastic will have to happen, for example, an enormous increase in production or, more likely, a decrease in the birth rate. The problem facing the world as a whole is exactly the same: a quadrupling of world population within the next 70 years unless something is done.

The population explosion

If we look at the world as a whole – at "spaceship earth" as it were – the danger of exponential growth in the population (also referred to as the **population explosion**) is that it is occurring in the countries that can least afford it – in the less developed countries (LDCs). The reason for this, and for it giving rise to problems, was suggested in the previous section. The established economies moved into stage II of population growth (a decrease in the death rate) because the people were more prosperous and better fed.

However, stage II in the LDCs is principally the result of improved health services, inoculation against diseases and so forth. The already fragile economies of these countries are thus overburdened with people. Any increase in potential production is simply swallowed up by an even more rapid increase in population. In such instances the pursuit of zero population growth is justifiable – and, as mentioned above, it will one day have to come about in one form or another.

Unfortunately the pursuit of ZPG may have certain political disadvantages. Many of the LDCs are small countries and, as held by mercantilism many years ago, political power depends on the size of the population. Only countries with very large populations like China and India can afford to adopt a ZPG policy without prejudicing their international status. Since these two countries represent approximately half the world's population between them, any success on their part is extremely significant. But in India in particular such efforts may be at odds with very powerful cultural forces – in 1977 they led to the downfall of Indira Gandhi's government. Success is thus not easily attained.

Nonetheless, it remains difficult to achieve zero population growth in the short term. Populations grow from the bottom up, that is, from young to old. Once a population begins increasing, it will gain momentum over a number of years because as young people reach marriageable age, the population as a whole becomes more fertile and the birth rate increases once again. Any population that is becoming younger also creates another long-term problem as there are more people to feed than there are to participate in production.

The desirability of economic development in the LDCs

Whereas zero population growth is highly desirable in the LDCs, the same cannot be said of its counterpart, zero economic growth. As explained at the beginning of this chapter, there are vast differences in the per capita GDP (and thus in average economic activity) of the LDCs and the economically established countries of the world. Although ZEG is justifiable in the latter, the position of the LDCs is so different that economic growth must be considered imperative.

Economic growth, or economic development as it has come to be called, is therefore considered not only highly desirable but also feasible. Initially this optimism was based partly on the successes achieved in the reconstruction of Germany and Japan and, in fact, of all the belligerents of the time. One of the ways in which this was achieved is illustrated in figure 10.7.

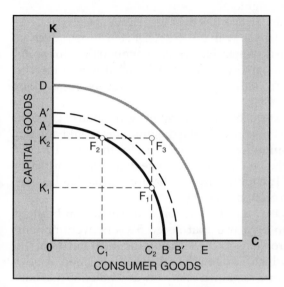

Fig. 10.7 The importance of foreign aid

Foreign aid amounting to F_1F_3, used for investment, allows a consumption level of OC_2 and also a higher rate of growth. Compare DE with A'B', for example.

The curves represented in figure 10.7 are **transformation curves**. As our starting point we take two such transformation curves, AB and DE, which show what combination of capital goods (K) and consumer goods (C) can be produced in a certain economy when all production factors, that is, labour and capital, are employed in the production process. The curves are therefore also called **production possibilities curves**. Each curve shows that a whole number of choices are possible between quantities of C and K. The shape of the curves illustrates the operation of the law of diminishing returns. In other words, the more one is already producing of one type of good, the more one has to sacrifice of the other good to be able to produce an additional unit of the first type of good. Economic growth is indicated by a shift from AB to DE, which means that greater quantities of C and K can be produced (on DE) than previously (on AB). We use this type of diagram to show that we have to do with the concept of trade-off in the economic growth process. In this instance, inflation is not traded off against unemployment as in the previous chapter, but the trade-off now entails a choice between **consumption** and **investment**.

In figure 10.7, AB is assumed to represent the production possibilities curve of an economy at a given time. F_1 and F_2 are two of many combinations of consumption and investment. At F_1 consumption is equal to OC_2, whereas the production of capital goods is represented by OK_1. The choice at F_2 results in the production of OC_1 consumer goods and (in comparison with F_1) a larger quantity of investment goods OK_2. The more that is invested, the higher the potential production and the further the transformation curve will shift to the right.

In a less developed country with a low average GDP, consumption has to be relatively high in comparison with the total GDP. On its own, such an economy could probably do no better than the combination F_1 with capital formation equal to OK_1. The growth in potential output would then be represented by the relatively modest increase of the production possibilities frontier to $A'B'$.

However, a consumption level of OC_2 and capital formation of OK_2 can be achieved if **foreign aid** is obtained. In the diagram this would amount to K_1K_2, for instance. Consumption and investment for the period would be represented by F_3 and the new production potential would shift even further to DE, for example. It is for this reason that foreign aid has become such an important factor in economic policy.

In time it became clear that the devastation and exhaustion brought about in Europe and Japan by a war that lasted 5 years, were nothing compared to the type of problems in the less developed countries of the world. Even in Germany, which suffered the greatest destruction of cities and factories, the infrastructure remained relatively unscathed so that only repair and maintenance were required. Here we refer to the road network, the railways and the telephone, electricity and water supply systems. Although the death toll was extremely high, more than enough teachers, doctors, engineers, skilled workers and farmers survived the war to set things in motion again. The problem was therefore essentially to stimulate economic growth in an established economy where the basic organization remained intact. In these circumstances the injection of foreign capital and aid was especially beneficial.

In the LDCs, however, it is the existing system that has to be adapted and changed to meet modern demands and it is for this reason that their problem is referred to as one of **economic development** rather than of reconstruction and growth. The result is general frustration in the LDCs and the rest of the world because far too little is achieved. Some claim that less than nothing has been achieved in the sense that the gap between developed and undeveloped countries, or between North and South, has become increasingly larger over the past fifteen years.

Prospects of economic development

The results of development policies have therefore been discouraging and the prospects are not much better. Why is this so? Firstly there is the problem of population growth, and we have said enough about this not to have to repeat ourselves.

Apart from this, the LDCs show a shortage of everything needed for development. Even carefully conceived plans are difficult to implement, especially if they depend on foreign aid. And there have been rumours that a significant portion of such aid goes into the pockets of local leaders.

It is possible to list (as we did in section 10.1) the different factors necessary for economic growth and development and in each instance we would find that the LDCs had a problem. Training is very often inadequate and the local population lack the required skills. But the emphasis may be too much on literary and academic skills rather than skills necessary to modernize the economy. In this way funds are misapplied.

Although modern technology and know-how may be imported by multinational companies, for example, this does not necessarily mean that a larger number of the local population will find employment. Technology developed in the established countries is usually labour saving but it is **labour** rather than **capital** that the LDCs have in abundance. Basic private services such as banking may be either lacking or inefficient. The same is true of social capital or the infrastructure. Apart from those countries fortunate enough to have subterranean oil, many of the LDCs do not have the basic raw materials on which to base a development effort. But even if they did, their prices might be subject to such fluctuations on foreign markets that their efforts would be frustrated.

The prospects of economic development are therefore very discouraging. However, economic conditions in these countries are such that there is no choice but to aid them in their development efforts. And twenty years' experience must surely make it possible to avoid the more obvious mistakes made in the past. There are, after all, some countries, particularly in the Far East (e.g. South Korea and Taiwan), where development has been successful. Some reason for hope about the future of LDCs does therefore exist, especially if a solution can be found for the consequences of the oil crisis, which hit these countries very hard. But as we said at the beginning, development remains our most serious problem. Only a satisfactory solution to this problem will ensure the world of a relatively peaceful future.

Selected references:

Baumol & Blinder: 39.
Dernburg: 14.
Evans-Pritchard: 15, 16.
Gordon: 18.

Mohr et.al.: 66, 94.
Morley: 19.
Shapiro: 20.

INDEX